P res. Con

CW00432165

My Ever Best Friend

To Ann

Thank you for your support
in this venture.

Every blessing,

Charles Cane

February 2011

My Ever Best Friend

CHARLES CANE

© Charles Cane 2010

Published by Courtney Publishers

All Rights Reserved. No part of this book may be reproduced, adapted, stored in a retrieval system or transmitted by any means, electronic, mechanical, photocopying, or otherwise without the prior written permission of the author.

ISBN 978-0-9567201-0-8

Prepared and printed by:

York Publishing Services Ltd
64 Hallfield Road
Layerthorpe
York YO31 7ZQ
Tel: 01904 431213

Website: www.yps-publishing.co.uk

Contents

Acknowledgements

I invite you to read what has literally taken me a lifetime to complete and, without the help of two people, my narrative would have remained a jumble of disjointed notes and, more importantly, the purpose for my birth may never have been achieved. To the fore is the enduring love of my wife Sandra which never faltered throughout many years of living with my parallel life. I am very conscious that my scant array of words, despite a legion of good intent, does little to stress the fact that I could not have progressed without her love and support.

Fragmented sights and events from my parallel or previous life began at an early age. They were vividly real and I resisted several attempts to dismiss them as illusions; in fact they steadfastly refused to be ignored and effectively aroused, within me, a keen sense of curiosity albeit tainted with deep trepidation of the unknown. What was all this about and why was it happening to me? I could not escape from it yet who, other than my wife, would ever believe that my claims were genuine?

For decades I lived within this impasse until I discovered the services of Andrew Hillsdon DHP, DPLT, DSCT, MNCH and FPLTA of the Past Life Therapists Association, who helped me to find the door to an age when my story began. Within its threshold I became the immediate beneficiary of detailed yet breathtaking revelations that enabled me to complete the narrative I set before you. Additionally I was given insight into my real identity, and what my quest was all about. I am grateful to Andrew Hillsdon and I firmly recommend his talents to anyone who has shared, or desires to resolve, experiences that are similar to my own. Readers will note that from time to time I refer to Andrew Hillsdon, in my narrative, under the title of 'my mentor.'

Introduction

It is my intention to share with you all that I have learned about my previous life, as Charles Ganton, in the 18th to early 19th centuries. It began in 1752 within a comfortable and happy family in colonial India and England, until threatening storm clouds broke when my wife was murdered in 1781.

For a long period my mind was unhinged and, but for the love and care of family and friends, death by my own hands was a favourable option. In due course I recovered my mental stability and moved on to become prominent in the East India Company until death released me in 1811. I did not remarry and my love for my wife remained as strong as it was on that tragic day when she died.

Thus the soul that was Charles Ganton returned to the spirit world wherein, or so it would appear, it was not reunited with the soul of his wife. My reason behind this conclusion evolved from two very important inferences that became evident as my narrative progressed. Foremost is the fact that her soul became trapped or fragmented in this life, meaning that Charles was not reunited with her in the spirit world. Secondly, and through divine intentions beyond my understanding, his soul was reincarnated, within my body, for the exclusive purpose of finding and releasing the earthbound soul of his wife.

Through the guidance of my mentor I have amassed a wealth of information about my past life which, if recorded in the form of a reference work in support of reincarnation, may simply fall into an abyss of deep and contentious debate. Were this to be the case I am very aware that many aspects of human behaviour, in terms of laughter and sadness so prevalent in this work, may become secondary or even lost in a cloud of philosophical dialogue.

In my determination to avoid such literary pitfalls I decided to present my narrative to you in the form of a pseudo novel, in which all that I witnessed is in date order and will, hopefully, make for easy yet informative reading. It is necessary for me to add that my work, although in novel form, is a serious study of past life regression and is, of course, totally devoid of fiction or guess work.

Nevertheless I am aware that sufficient material is available to launch a work of creative writing covering such themes as cultural romance, a love story that defied society's expectations, a murder mystery with several suspects, exploits of the East India Trading Company and life in 18th century England and India; whilst not forgetting a small taste of 18th century naval history.

At all times I would urge you to remember that the words you will read, and the sights I will describe, are not of my creating but come from my liaison with Charles Ganton. Obviously my written claim of co-authorship, with a man who died almost 200 years ago, demands urgent explanation and it is my intention, to the best of my ability, to add substance to my assertions within the pages I now present to you.

In order that you may know me better I will briefly introduce myself and go on to share with you certain fragmented recollections from what I now know to be my past life. I was born in 1931 from working class parents and attended a local council school, which I left at the age of 14, and began work as a sawmill labourer. Six months later I became a general duty worker in a laboratory which inspired me to study part time, and eventually qualify as an industrial chemist; from which I retired in 1994. Since then I have been fully involved in other paid work and, at the age of 79, I still enjoy an active week mainly helping victims of our society. Yet even at the height of my professional career be it in a laboratory in England, or a conference room abroad, I never lost the 'feeling' that I was someone else; albeit I could not begin to define what it was all about.

The advent of my past life began rather suddenly when I sensed that an anonymous 'someone' had, without warning, become a major part of my life; and there was nothing I could do about it. Have you ever had the feeling that someone was walking alongside you yet remained tantalisingly outside your range of vision? This was my experience when, at the age of 14, I first became aware that someone was walking with me and, at times, it felt as if that 'someone' was holding onto my left arm and depended upon me.

I retained these sensations within my mind and, as an active 14 year old boy, gave priority to such pressing matters as climbing on the roof of street air raid shelters or fishing from the banks of a local drain. Nevertheless as the day progressed, and I found myself wandering home, I would again become aware that I was not alone and I began to look forward to walking with my silent and invisible companion, in whose presence I felt happy and secure.

As time moved along I became conscious that my friend was slowly materialising into the form of a young woman with dark brown skin and black hair that hung either in tresses or ringlets down to her shoulders. It was clear even to my tender years that she was not of this country, and it must be remembered that in those days white skinned people were the norm; other than the occasional coloured seafarer seen around dockland areas. I was amazed because she resembled no one I had ever met, seen or read about either in school books or through the media; such as the media was in that wartime age of closed cinemas and colourless newspapers.

Whilst still a youth a series of mental recollections began to appear, and were retained in my mind awaiting further explanation. These included:

1. Falling autumn leaves within a woodland scene rich in trees and bushes and, on occasion, gale force winds would batter the woodland with a severity that promoted fear and disturbed dreams.

   It must be remembered that I was born and raised in an industrial area, containing several factories and a labyrinth of narrow streets and terraced houses. Woodland scenes were a far cry from this region of urban smog and depressing buildings.

2. Occasionally on the radio I would hear prolonged peals of church bells that caused me to comment either inwardly, or to anyone who happened to be with me, "They remind me of some past event."

   In my youth local church bells never amounted to a classical peal but, upon very special occasions, a cracked and solitary parish church bell would toll for whatever reason. Also during the period 1939 to 1945 all bells were prohibited other than to proclaim enemy invasion of this country.

3. As a boy I enjoyed the retained memory of what I later discovered to be the sound of metallic wind chimes which, in reality, I did not meet until many years later.

In modern terms several of my retained memories were comparable to mental 'power point' images that tarried for a few moments, and then disappeared. Included in these visitations were:

4. Women in long and ornate dresses reminiscent of England in the 18th century.

5. A tall well built man of friendly disposition who suddenly fell face down and remained still.

6. A large detached house with three steps leading to a pillared and covered porch, with double entrance doors, giving access to the reception hall.

7. Handing tankards of porter to two apron clad servants in a stable tack room.

8. Sitting inside a very hot stage coach when a chicken fluttered through the open window and sat on the window sill, within seconds it flew away.

These fragmented memories were allowed to mature and my policy was never to rush matters in case imagination took over and ruined fledgling truth as it made its slow entry into my life. It was gratifying to later note that these isolated events did appear, within context, in the narrative I am to place before you.

My major preoccupation was with the dark haired girl, by my side, and through what seemed to be thought transfer I learned, again over many years, that her name was

Moneysa and that she was born in India, of Indian parents. I have reproduced her name as above mainly because I only twice saw it in written form; ever assuming that the spelling was correct. As a point of interest I checked a published list of traditional Indian names for girls that included Monisha (meaning intellectual) from which Moneysa could be a derivative, although in phonetic terms it appealed to my ears as 'Moneeshah.'

Since the year 1945 she has always been with me and I began to feel that I was her only contact with a 'something' that meant everything to her. At times she appeared distant yet was never far away. As I became older the bond between us grew stronger until she became an integral part of my life not, I stress, as a pretend wife or mental lover, but as someone whose life overlapped mine and vice-versa. From this developing union I began to appreciate the real meaning of the expression 'soul mate,' yet I was unable to discover who Moneysa was, and why she played such an important part in my life. I had almost resigned myself to the fact that this mystery and I would rest in the grave together until, in 2005, all was resolved.

During the year mentioned I began to study regression analysis and, with the help of my mentor, I broke into what was my past life. The flood gates of retained memory were thrown open and I was overwhelmed with a vast amount of detail describing what I, as Charles Ganton, did over 200 years ago which I have preserved in my narrative.

In a work of this nature it is essential that imagination, fuelled by a desire to tell a good story, is never allowed to become part of the written process. It will be appreciated that my entire narration is set in India and England, during the 18th and early 19th century, thus giving me hours of interesting research from which I have been able to verify, and subsequently record my findings, as an addendum to the main theme of my account. Fortunately my career as an industrial chemist has helped with this mental discipline.

Having gained access into my previous life I can now view and hear whatever is before me **but only when Charles Ganton is present within that scene**. When he departs then I go with him. Charles, for obvious reasons, kept strictly to his central theme and had little or no time for peripheral detail which, in my view, is necessary to give breadth to my narration. Fortunately I was able to observe situations, and hear and learn of family records, which I have included in support of Charles's account.

However, there are times when I am drawn into Charles Ganton and feel his every emotion, as a living part of him, yet I am unable to influence what he says or does. At such times Charles Ganton takes over the narrative which, in general, means those are special events dear to his memory and essential to his story.

Hence it is very important that you remember the following system of presentation:

In order that you may know whose words you are reading I have devised the following change of font scheme illustrated below:

1. *When I, Charles Cane, become the narrator then my words appear in Italics*

2. When Charles Ganton takes over the narration his words are in Roman font.

Then there is the matter of dialect within the words I hear spoken which I have ignored and reproduced as better known expressions. For example words such as 'takest' ' trembleth' 'knoweth' were not unusual and, in a village setting I heard children shouting "that yan owr there…."I want yan av those." Frequently 'int' was used instead of 'in the' together with 'ont' rather than 'on the.'

The above annotations are the basic stage set for my narrative and, thus in place, we can open the curtain upon my previous life, and its impact upon the present time, through the legacy left for us by Charles Ganton.

CHAPTER ONE

The legacy left by Charles Ganton

Charles Ganton was warmly clad in an ankle length coat, drawn in at the waist, with fur collar and matching wide lapels, yet his consumptive state rendered him unduly warm, despite a late Autumn chill, as the year 1811 drew to its close. Although the passage of time and the onset of illness were evident upon his now pale and drawn face, and his former fair and wavy hair was enriched with timely grey, he still radiated a strong sense of purpose which, in essence, is what this narrative is all about.

"Keep well wrapped up and do not over-stress yourself," were the words of well meant concern from my dear loyal friend Elizabeth who, despite all that she had suffered, firmly believed that my return from India would restore peace and happiness to the three of us.

As we left Ganton Hall together she made light of the fact that only yesterday a specialist doctor had confirmed that my illness was terminal, and there was nothing that he or the medical profession could do to extend my life beyond the next few days. With rising optimism Elizabeth continued with, "I did not believe all that the consultant said because, for once, I know more than he does. It is a truth, unknown to him, that fresh northern air is your best medicine," she declared, "It is a fact that your cough has steadily eased since you came home."

Her words of hope, so frequently contradicted by fact, meant little to me as we approached the entrance to a wooded paradise that Moneysa and I called 'our secret little forest.' It looked overgrown but, in character and retained memory, nothing had changed and without effort I could picture my wife waiting to welcome me. My unexpected greeting of, "Hello Monnie, your aging husband has come home," was accepted by Elizabeth, who knew what this reunion meant to me.

She also knew that for Moneysa and me this woodland had, for a while, been our only sanctuary against a rising tide of acrimony that, although isolated, was intent upon our destruction. It was impossible for this developing force of evil to ever forgive us for brushing aside the demands of convention as our cherished love blossomed into marriage, which lasted for only seven wonderful days, before this malefic force of ill will found and murdered my beloved wife within this leafy domain.

"Tormentor of my soul know that I will ever hate you for what you did," was my muttered curse upon my antagonist only to be followed in louder terms with, "You may laugh at a dying man grieving for his lost wife but, be assured, the power of our love will soon crush your serpent skull."

"Are you alright, Charles?" cried a startled Elizabeth as she gripped my arm, both alarmed at my outburst and the bout of coughing that had developed in its wake.

"Yes thanks," I eventually replied as we continued our slow walk aware that no one had set foot in this woodland place for thirty years; which was a fact that filled Elizabeth's mind as much as it did mine.

"See Charles, I have had men remove fencing from what was the entrance path at the foot of the slope; but do be very careful for it looks like a wilderness, the branches have spread so far they have almost obliterated the old path. It worries me Charles, please let John and myself come with you."

"No thank you Elizabeth because this is a journey that I must make on my own albeit I am thirty years too late."

"I do not know what you mean but I will wait, hope and pray that you will come back to me very soon, then we can start our lives all over again ….just you and I, Charles ….." were words that faded in my ears as, now alone, I began my slow ascent through the rich undergrowth.

The sudden re-appearance of a long absent human being went by unnoticed as, with great intent, nature entered the restless stage of its annual cycle. Oblivious to my presence gusts of cold wind reminded the trees and bushes that it was autumn as it sought and stirred, within its eddying embrace, nomad leaves until they became golden mounds of refuge for creatures fearing the chill to come. I paused to admire the architectural ability of the wind at work whilst giving my own life force, cum breathing power, time to recover.

Soon the terrain levelled off and from the positioning of well remembered trees and rhododendron bushes I began to trace what was our original path, despite a new crop of fallen autumn leaves. As I trod that familiar woodland footpath my mind resounded with recollections of those far off days with such questions like "Do you remember this Charles? Or do you remember that?……" as evergreen memories became words that fell from my lips while I walked and talked alone in my world of distant dreams.

Suddenly inspired I called out aloud, "Yes, I do remember the time when Moneysa and I walked hand in hand through the ancestors of these fallen leaves. We were very happy and the conversation was of no consequence until suddenly I sensed 'mischief in the air.'

Monnie had slipped her hand out of mine, and tarried to study the bark of a nearby tree whilst I walked slowly ahead.

Without warning I was engulfed in an avalanche of fallen leaves as repeated armfuls were thrown upon me from behind." Quickly I retaliated until, with arms around each other, we fell happily into a large pile of leaves, out of breath, and agreed a truce from hostilities.

We lay there in peace as I carefully removed fragmented leaves from her hair whilst making plans about how we would spend the day. Moneysa agreed with my suggestion that we went to the village and talked to those involved with the parish end of year party; but on condition that we rest awhile after our battle with the fallen leaves.

For some time we lay side by side with our hands locked together in restful silence as we watched the leaves falling and squirrels racing through the trees, with birds urgently flying around for no reason other than their love of flying.

Raising herself up on to her elbow Moneysa looked down on me, smiled and declared how happy she was, "In truth Charles, my idea of heaven is to spend eternity here with you," she whispered, as her slim forefinger gently smoothed my eyebrows causing my eyes to close in appreciation.

Through my bliss I opened one eye in acknowledgment on hearing my name and, "After our marriage in India can we live in the same house that you were born in and where I first met you and your family?"

When I lifted my hand to caress her shoulder length tresses I found myself, momentarily, without words as the vision of her dark brown eyes held mine in a deep yet unspoken bond of love.

Overcoming an initial stammer I replied, "Of course we can," and a wide smile lit up her face when I added, "Then there will be many years of total happiness with lots of little Chamon's running around the house."

Her eyes filled with tears as she ran her hand through my hair and whispered, "Thank you Charles and please let us always love each other like this and never allow anything to keep us apart."

"Nothing will ever separate us, Monnie … that I promise …."

Then words were no more and became mere spectators to the depth of our emotion as slowly our lips met and we gradually submerged into our bed of leaves and the comfort of our oneness.

Without warning, reality intervened and dismissed this treasured memory as a bout of painful coughing racked my body. I felt tears running down my face induced perhaps as the product of consumptive pain, or the memory of happiness now lost … I know not and it is too hurtful for me to dwell upon the difference.

"Keep going Charles, you must never give in," was the self induced battle cry that I shared with the trees around me followed by, "If only ….. If only real life was like a traditional romantic novel."

I picked up a handful of leaves and let them slip slowly through my fingers as I visualised, in story book fashion, a sudden gentle glow lighting up the way ahead and then, as my imagination gained momentum, I saw Moneysa walking towards me in her blue wedding gown inviting me to come home.

Instantly I was young again and with our hands clasped together, we walked happily away into the beckoning glow of eternity as the ethereal music faded away.

Watching the last leaf fall from my hand I murmured, "No Charles, those are silly dreams that can never be. Remember what Cymol said about the fate awaiting his sister both in this life and the next. Have you forgotten the enemies you made, and all the deep disappointment that your actions and attitudes brought into the lives of others, not least those of your good friend Elizabeth and her parents?"

Through pain I am able to smile that an out of place word as 'forgotten' should form part of any indictment against me because such an attitude is totally absurd. How could I ever forget the hurt of separation that dominates me or deliberately close my eyes to the daily presence of Moneysa in my fading life.

Despite Elizabeth's optimism I know that the doctor was correct and, for the first time, I have been forced to accept that my life is fast drawing to its close; yet what a fool I have been to keep to myself the outcome of the séance, held shortly before I left India, when I learned about the fate that had befallen my wife.

I now know that the suddenness of Moneysa's death, which occurred at the peak of her happiness and long before her appointed time, has left her trapped in this woodland of memories; and I am the sole legatee of the whereabouts of the one I love above all others. Whilst I am alive she is able to reach out and walk with me, wherever I am, but when I leave this life Moneysa will be a lost soul within this leafy prison.

So much is clear, from my Indian sessions with Jarita, that only I, in spirit form, can liberate the soul of Moneysa and thus enable her to return to the spirit world. I accept that my soul will return in another's body but how do I draw that person, whoever he or she is, to this very place where Moneysa died?

Momentarily, I was distracted as a withered leaf fluttered down upon my shoulder and rested awhile, before sliding down my coat to its forest floor grave.

Was this a sign to me?

Suddenly I seized on to the thought that the very trees, rocks and natural fabric of this woodland may well retain and care for the spirit of Moneysa and my dying words as both await rebirth?

Whereas falling leaves symbolise death reborn as buds in the warmth of spring, could not words spoken from the depth of my heart rest in this place until reborn, in the life of one who has been drawn to this place, because of the presence of my reincarnated soul in his or her earthly body?

I could feel my heart rapidly beating with excitement, perhaps to the detriment of my failing health, but it was of no consequence. It was suddenly very clear to me that, without fail, I must commit my story to this woodland scene that it may, in the fullness of time, be transmitted into the life of that future stranger who will be host to my restless soul.

I know that I am doing the right thing for appearing before me is a now moss covered mound which I know to be 'Monnie's rock', where she sat to remove her tight shoes and duly forgot them, when latent feelings became living emotions as I carried her to the house......and then ....." I paused, wiped my eyes, **and realised that I must tell of all that happened in a constructive and time related manner, for ease of future narration.**

Hence sitting upon 'Monnie's rock' and in the fullness of faith I began my verbal account, in this woodland of recollections, in trust that my spirit endowed words will linger like falling leaves until reborn within another's care........."

..... which 137 years later awoke the reincarnated soul of Charles Ganton within me, when in the year 1948, aged 17, I first walked in woodland known as Silver Hill, near Keswick in what is now Cumbria.

It is very important that you do not think of me as Charles Ganton reborn.

I am just another soul (or spirit), striving for fulfilment following my previous life, during which something happened to interrupt my forward journey. I know that I have a special mission before me yet I remember nothing about my former life as Charles Ganton.

When I first entered Silver Hill I immediately felt the sensation of having been there before but dismissed the matter in favour of enjoying the scenery, and listening to the birds, as I progressed happily along a woodland trail. I paid little attention to occasional branches that hung across my path until the leaves of a particular rhododendron bush swept against my face.

Instantly an overwhelming feeling of deep yet personal sorrow filled my mind and I could not take another step. It was as if cries for help were rising from the very spot upon which I stood, yet all I was aware of was the sound and sight of nature at work around me.

Finally I left Silver Hill confused and concerned, yet aware something had happened that I would not forget; in fact, for me, life would never be the same again.

Since 1948 I have often returned to those woods during the day, and once in the depth of night, ever seeking the source of that which was calling, nay appealing to me for help.

Sadly my understanding of the spirit world was insufficient for me to intervene, until my mentor helped me pass through that final door. Awaiting within its portals were those same words left by Charles Ganton, almost 200 years ago, that *were progressively revealed to me in the form of a story that was mind boggling in detail, and heart rending in its climax, from which I now know where my soul friend can be both found and liberated.*

It is clear that Charles Ganton dictated this account for one reason only and, following the liberation of his wife, it would have no further part to play in his plan. Although his soul is within me I still think like Charles Cane who cannot allow a testimony such as this, and the remarkable way in which it was revealed to me, to drift away like a forgotten dream. Therefore I will now recount all that I learned about the Ganton story in the hope that it will be of the same spiritual help to others, as it was to me, when it taught me that birth is not the beginning and death is not the end of our timeless journey.

So let us follow the legacy of words, left by Charles Ganton, to where it all began in 18th century India.

CHAPTER TWO

Early family life in India

In the year 1751 Edward Ganton, following an earlier appointment with the West India Company received a commission, from the East India Company, to manage one of their leading trade areas in a fast developing part of India. It was an exciting appointment for Edward in that it followed his 1748 marriage to Molly (maiden name unknown) and the birth of their first son, John, in 1750.

Trade interest began in India, during the 17th century, in the form of settlements mainly in Bombay, Madras and Calcutta to meet a worldwide demand for cheap washable lightweight cotton and silk fabrics for dresses and furnishings produced by Indian weavers. These trading posts rapidly grew into major commercial townships, under British jurisdiction, in the form of the East India Company.

Within the turmoil of Indian towns and dusty villages, awash with human and animal life, Edward Ganton prospered as a kind yet astute business man who was respected by all stratas of society. His enhanced income ensured high living standards for the entire family which, by the year 1752, had increased to two sons with the birth of Charles Ganton.

They lived in a residential area that followed the English class separation system. In the centre was a modest hospital with two resident doctors and their assistants who, at times, where hard pushed to deal with the many Indian derived illnesses that played havoc with English East India Company employees and their families. Also in this region was a general school and rooms for private tutorial classes enjoyed by the children of senior managers who, from their own funds, imported higher grade teachers from England. However at most times of the year heat and humidity meant that these buildings were not used and classes would be held in shaded zones in the adjacent grassed areas.

The all important shopping facilities were located within the same area as an Anglican church bordered by a garden, cemetery and grassland that was used for weddings, parties and similar events. English women rarely ventured into nearby towns and villages except when escorted by their husband or within a family group. Even on those occasions they carried a small fire-arm, often within their muff, as a deterrent against Mughal agents who, according to long standing rumour, were set to abduct white women into high class harems.

Surrounding this township, built in the shape of a horseshoe, were wooded hills that gave a sense of peace and natural beauty to the location which, sadly, was often threatened with the danger of flooding as water cascaded down the hills in the wet season. With this hazard in mind all buildings other than the stone church, which was set upon a mound, were wood constructed and accessed by steps leading up to verandas set some 4 to 5 feet above the ground level. The Ganton house and two smaller staff houses were situated at the base of the horseshoe affording a stunning view of the hillside rich in trees and large bushes overhanging the garden boundary fence.

Having thus introduced the stage upon which we will begin our journey let us open our eyes to our first scene, in India, during the summer of 1766 as Charles and John complete their lessons for the day. Before we advance too far it is good that you should know that John Ganton was consistently referred to as 'Brother John' as a token reflection of his deep interest in Christianity from early boyhood days.

"Did all that make sense to you?" I remarked to Brother John as we left our corpulent tutor, awash with perspiration, at his desk beneath copious bushes and shady trees. "Initially yes, but it was an effort to concentrate as the temperature increased." I nodded my agreement as I furiously dislodged all manner of flying creatures from my moist forehead whilst making rapid progress into the relative cool of our house; courtesy of two Indian boys slowly wafting large palm leaves.

"Don't forget our family gathering this evening," remarked Brother John as he stretched out on a cane reclining chair holding a glass of tepid lime water. Shading my eyes against the sun I asked John to remind me what it was all about. "Surely you remember that father has engaged a new head staff manager cum butler who, together with his wife and children, will be presented to us over tea and niceties. I hope he turns out better than the last one we had who was a man of instant promises without a hint of action."

Anticipating my needs one of the palm leaf wavers presented me with a bowl of chilled water, straight from a nearby fast running stream, in which I gratefully swilled my face, head and neck whilst muttering, "Married and with a family eh, that should steady him down. How many children are involved?" John stared into space and replied,

"Two I think – a boy and a girl. He comes with great recommendations from former district senior manager George Tingle following his retirement to England. I suppose it is a sort of gift to father who has taken over his job responsibilities. However, I do know that his name is Drebar and that father has already decreed that he and his family will move out of that sun scorched dust heap called a village and live in one of the staff houses. According to father Drebar is noted for his loyalty and ability, and is astute enough to recognise that progress is through the use of the English language, which he speaks fluently, and daily teaches English to his children as a matter of priority."

"I envy your wide knowledge of day to day matters John," I slowly murmured as, with hat over my face, I was fast sinking into my afternoon siesta. "Or it could be that I have a nosey disposition," he remarked, with a laugh, as he sank into his chair.

Dinner was over and a warm yet refreshing tropical breeze brought some relief to the Ganton family, as they relaxed upon the wide veranda lit by oil lamps suspended from the guttering and candelabra flickering on the tables. Edward Ganton and his wife Molly sat together on a deeply cushioned cane bench and, despite the heat of the day, Molly was never without a woollen shawl wrapped around her shoulders. Her health was slowly deteriorating which was reflected in her pale and drawn face framed by a dark grey bonnet.

Edward Ganton adored his wife and, to please him, she invariable had her hair set in the style of bunched ringlets that reached down to her shoulders. He frequently lavished attention upon his wife as if he knew that their time together was slipping away. He loved giving her pleasant surprises, one of which was to leave a series of written instructions for her, in the form of a treasure trail, which led to various parts of the house. At the end of the trail, usually beneath a cushion or bed pillow, was a small box containing a brooch or other item of jewellery together with a hand written note declaring, 'My dearest Molly. Thank you for marrying me and I love you.'

Of late their laughter had been curtailed by prolonged and painful bouts of coughing that Molly dismissed as an 'Indian cough' but was, in fact, the advancing stages of consumption that would soon claim her life.

The command, "Books away boys," broke into my studies as father required our undivided attention in the matter of meeting our new head servant and his family who, at a respectful distance from the house, awaited father's invitation to introduce themselves to their new employers.

Precisely at the time set for him a small man dressed in white trousers and three quarter length white coat appeared before the Ganton family and bowed low before them. His facial hair was close trimmed and his open and honest face expressed an inner depth of care and sincerity mingled with a twinkle of humour born from a good nature. This description does not originate from speculation but, rather, from my later knowledge of the loyal and consistent support this man would give to the Ganton family.

My father went over and shook the hand of our new arrival and, standing alongside him, announced, "This gentleman is our new butler and head servant and Drebar is his name."

Both John and I went over and exchanged firm handshakes whilst mother, begging pardon for not standing up, greeted him with a smile and wave of her hand. Drebar, speaking perfect English, thanked father for employing him and promised never to falter in his promise to provide us with consistent and loyal service. Following this he asked leave to introduce his family, who in Muslim custom, stood in a line barely visible in the shadow of the house.

We were first introduced to his wife Lajila who smiled shyly and curtsied before us. As father directed her to a chair Drebar explained that his wife was an excellent cook, had a natural ability for sewing and all manner of craftwork, she could understand orders and that her spoken English was improving.

The next to appear was a young man dressed not unlike his father but with a traditional Muslim prayer hat upon his head. With pride Drebar invited us to meet his son Cymol who, at the age of 9, had a natural ability for gardening and took great pride in his work. He, with self conscious dignity, greeted us with a bow and Brother John waved him to a seat alongside his.

Suddenly I was aware that, without invitation, a little girl had appeared on the veranda completely at ease with herself as confirmed by a wide smile upon her face. Taken by surprise and smiling benevolently, Drebar took her hand and invited us to meet his daughter, Moneysa, who was five years old. It was then I noticed that in her other hand she clutched, by its neck, what appeared to be a stuffed woollen creature that had a body and head not unlike that of a chicken but with a singularly long neck.

Pointing at the creature I asked Moneysa, "What is that in your hand?" Gripping its neck even tighter she, with a smile, said something that sounded like 'Ergar.' I held out my hand and asked her, "May I hold Ergar?" With a mischievous grin Moneysa thrust the creature behind her back and replied, "No... Monnie's."

Her father explained that Moneysa, who was often referred to as Monnie, was very clever and was quickly learning how to speak the English language that was so important to her future. He went on to tell us that this was the moment she had been working hard for in that, with our permission, she would now like to address us in English. With that her father stepped to one side and Moneysa held centre stage with a manner and confidence in advance of her years. Her long and gently waved black hair was almost upon her shoulders, and stood out in contrast to her white three quarter length cotton dress, which was all very ordinary until she suddenly looked directly at me. For those few seconds I felt that I already knew her which in reality was crazy; surely she was just another young village girl? Her face did not display classical beauty mainly because her high cheek bones and full mouth were prominent features; yet I was drawn to her dark brown eyes, shining white teeth and infectious smile that had immediate impact for good upon all who held her attention.

Suddenly she faced her audience, dropped Ergar upon the floor, and slowly began her address preceded by a deep and wavering curtsey.

"Hello ….. My name am Moneysa."

Here she paused and smiled as we, in turn, were held captive by her natural charm and her lovely accent, which had almost a musical quality to it. Drebar, looking anxious, whispered to his daughter for her to carry on, which distracted her sufficiently for me, out of devilment, to pick up Ergar and place the creature upon my knee.

"Thank you for us coming here ……. I like here ….. and you are my friends"

A further less deep curtsey signalled the end of her address which prompted a spontaneous applause, whilst her father beamed proudly, and Moneysa basked in her new found popularity. Together we watched with interest as Moneysa looked away from us in search of her beloved

Ergar which, eventually, she saw lying upon my knee. Quickly she ran forward and snatching it by its neck gave me a look of mock censure. She turned and slowly walked away seemingly deep in thought, then, without warning, she rushed back to me thrusting the creature into my hands, and looking me full in the face, slowly announced, "You have Ergar …you Monnie's ever best friend ….. You be my friend? …what your name please?"

Much moved by this I sat alongside her on the step of the veranda and we smiled at each other as I replied, "Thank you, Moneysa, for giving me Ergar. My name is Charles and we will always be very best friends."

I still think back upon that happy little group who first met together on that warm Indian evening as I, at the age of 14, sat there with a little 5 year old Indian girl radiant in her new friendship.

"In truth instant friendship is the surest bond of all and may its presence grow within each of us this night and through many years to come," were the words from my father, followed by a sincere "Amen" from Brother John, and a hand to mouth giggle from a wide eyed Moneysa.

That evening Drebar and his daughter gave us much cause for laughter and happy conversation and father, true to his word, decreed that they would leave their village first thing in the morning and occupy the larger of the two staff houses, which the Drebar family had already viewed and declared to be fit for a Mughal emperor and his family.

Much later I lay awake listening to the traditional night chorus of creature melodies that, often as not, were soothing and therapeutic to minds seeking refuge from retained pressures of the day. However on this occasion I was immune to their restorative powers because of the unusual nature of my concerns which, surprisingly, were centred on household servant issues. I was aware that we needed a household staff for many reasons, not least of which was their attention to my needs, for which I expressed my gratitude to them as they sank into the background of my life. Yesterday evening was so very different, so much so that sleep became secondary to my need to discover what was it about Drebar, and his family, which elevated them above the status of hired additions to the household? By definition they were servants, but to think of them in that context made me want to immediately apologise, unreservedly, for my gross disrespect.

Those early morning hours were sole witnesses to my belief that there was something special about the Drebar family; so much so that I could feel my life changing for reasons that belonged to the future, whereas today had its special needs.

Within the short duration of the Indian dawn I had, with father's prior permission, saddled up my horse and was on my way to the nearby village that was already wide awake with traders preparing for their journey to the market. It was a tight knit community in which there were no strangers and my request, "Where can I find Drebar and his family?" was swiftly answered and, following an enthusiastic welcome, I began helping them load their belongings into a horse drawn cart which father had provided.

Moneysa, kneeling in the dust, sadly offered seed and said "goodbye" to her two hens doomed to remain in the village, in exchange for a neighbour's home embroidered wall drapes "fit for a staff house" according to a proud Lajila. However Moneysa soon regained her humour when marauding monkeys, curious to know what was happening, crept into the vacated house and were promptly ambushed, teased, and chased away by a jubilant brother and sister.

Soon all their possessions were packed on to the cart and we were ready to set off. I declared that I would ride behind the wagon to collect anything that may fall off during the journey and, wanting to help, Moneysa asked if she could ride with me. Drebar agreed and passed his daughter up so that she sat on the saddle, in front of me, yet enclosed within my outstretched arms as I held the reins. In this position she felt both safe and highly delighted at her first ride upon the back of a horse, so much so that she reached into her small bag of special possessions and withdrew a grape. Smiling at me, whilst searching for the correct words, she slowly announced, "For my ever best friend." Much moved by this spontaneous act I accepted and ate the grape as she carefully watched for my reaction. "Like it?" she asked. My smile and nod of gratitude was enough to light up her face and, having exhausted her range of spoken English, she happily continued in her native tongue.

With that the convoy moved off and began the journey to their new home along a series of ruts and holes which was proudly termed to be 'the main road from the village.' Moneysa was ecstatic as she waved farewell to the villagers pausing only to shout words, presumably of encouragement, to Cymol who was perched on the very top of the cargo. Drebar had decided to walk with and lead the horse around the potholes, while his wife looked anxiously at the stack of assorted furnishings swaying behind her. Eventually we arrived at their new house and, with the assistance of the household staff, Drebar and his family were soon unloaded and installed in what he claimed was 'his haven of rest.'

Hereafter followed what was a period of routine family and household affairs during which I had occasional glimpses of Charles and John at their studies and felt the happiness that Drebar had brought into the Ganton household. He was truly a man of many talents not least of which was his ability to do or say the right thing, at the right time.

His daughter Moneysa was also an ardent scholar and father had included her in a class designed for younger European and Indian students, particularly when the latter had high learning abilities, and the overall project was funded by Ganton senior using tutors employed by the East India Company. Sadly the normal village tradition would have meant that Moneysa would not have received any education other than learning how to look after the needs of a future husband; but Drebar had convinced Edward Ganton of her high inborn ability which, if not developed, would be a tragic loss to the Company and some future husband of better standing.

Edward was not slow to agree with Drebar because he saw first hand the ability of this young Indian girl who was rapidly becoming a family member. Between working hard at their studies they played and fooled around together as a happy and contented family unit. I saw several scenes of great fun – like the time when Charles decorated an old coat sleeve to look like the body of a snake which he then pushed his arm into. Over his hand was a glove like unto the head of a snake, with a gaping mouth operated by his thumb and fingers. Much to everyone's delight he chased a screaming Moneysa around the lawn who thoroughly enjoyed every moment of her pretend terror.

Assorted musical turns would follow in which Moneysa and Cymol would teach Charles and John how to play the Indian Sitar, but the highlight was when Drebar entertained all present with conjuring tricks and juggling acts followed by his specialty in the form of a traditional sleight of hand trick called 'cups and balls.' Drebar would set up five small cups on a table and place a nut beneath one of them followed by rapid interchange of cups and the invitation to select the cup that hid the nut. Needless to add no one ever succeeded.

Throughout all this entertainment Molly Ganton sat on the veranda alongside her husband and Lajila enjoying, what Edward Ganton would later refer to as 'the happiest times of their family life in India.'

CHAPTER THREE

Period 1770 – 1771

I was not further drawn into the affairs of the Ganton family until I became aware of a marriage celebration in 1770. I have no idea whose wedding it was but I am certain of the date because I heard a voice, which may have been Brother John, remarking how grown up Moneysa now looked although only 9 years old.

Then I saw Charles, now at the age of 18, looking much a man of fashion in tight fitting grey breeches with an open necked white shirt, with vertical ruffles running parallel to the buttons and fastening holes. The area between his knees and buckled black shoes was encased in grey coloured, tight fitting gaiters all of which, together with his almost blonde wavy hair, gave him a 'presence' which by his constant 'fiddling' with the back of his hair suggested that he worked hard to both cultivate and preserve.

There were many people present, of Indian and European nationalities, but my attention was focused on those I knew, namely the Ganton family and close contacts. In conversation I heard that Molly was confined to her bed but had insisted that the family should attend on her behalf. Drebar was in the centre of a crowd, always at the side of Ganton senior, and was highly successful in promoting laughter from his vast library of anecdotes. His wife and son did not appear to be present. Then I saw Brother John and Moneysa who would readily have passed for a young teenager rather than a 9 year old.

Pausing to compare her with European children who were present, and of the same age, led me to conclude that Indian children bodily develop at a faster rate than European youngsters. Moneysa had dressed according to the fashion demands of this occasion and looked resplendent in her dark blue sari wrapped and pleated around her waist, over an underskirt and short sleeved top (choli), and draped over her shoulder. She wore a loose fitting pale blue head veil (Odhani) which complimented her black hair resting upon her shoulders.

A stranger to India would be forgiven for thinking they may have stumbled upon a fancy dress gala held upon a typical English village green on a summer's day; that was until the full impact of scorching heat and high humidity drove home the fact that this was a tropical climate that did little to improve the health of many Europeans employed by the East India Company.

Dotted around were large umbrella style sun shades beneath which many, mainly Europeans, sought refuge from direct sunlight upon their unconditioned skin. Above laughter and voices music could be plainly heard and, as I moved closer, I saw a number of Indian men playing an instrument composed of two strings (Sarod). There was a Punch and Judy show, acrobats, a sword swallower, fire breathers and a stocky Indian man, with a white band around his forehead, in charge of a dancing bear. Shaded tables were set out complete with a wide choice of food and the many helpers were busily discouraging flies from taking their places at the tables.

With that the scene began to fade leaving me a little bemused as to the purpose of my presence within it? At no time was I part of Charles Ganton and the entire episode left me with the feeling that it was merely a 'passing- of- time scenario' en-route to more serious events to follow?

Then I became aware that the year had moved on to 1771; yet the heat and humidity was unchanged meaning that the dry season (November to June) had come and gone in favour of the humid and high rainfall season, which had burst upon the scene before me. Torrential rain did little to cool the oppressive heat which was evident in the figure of Charles Ganton, standing upon the veranda with shirt unbuttoned to his waist, as he stared at the storm before him.

"Blast this weather for adding to my mother's pain," I muttered to rain bent trees and water raging over what had been our lawn. Was that a voice above the storm? Yes, there it was again only this time with greater urgency, "Charles please come quickly." I rushed into the bedroom where my mother lay on her bed, with father and Brother John in attendance and the ever faithful Drebar standing behind with his hand upon father's shoulder.

Suddenly the East India Company doctor leaned forward to mop perspiration away from her face and, looking at my father, he slowly shook his head. Her breath was now a series of short gasps, with an increasing time delay between intakes, until one final deep breath slowly faded away leaving the silence of death in our midst.

The voice of anguish from my father rose above the storm raging around the house … "NO … NO ….MY DARLING MOLLY …. PLEASE DO NOT LEAVE ME." In tears we held on to him as in a lowered voice he slowly pleaded, "Please Lord …not now Lord ….. I love her as no man has loved before."

There are few words to describe the emotional atmosphere, within that room of death, as John and I stood at the foot of the bed, shocked into a state of tearful silence. Father had part recovered his composure and now knelt at the side of the bed holding Molly's hand whilst muttering words I could not hear.

I longed for something to say that would comfort him but, instead, drew reassurance from John as he quietly began to recite the 23rd psalm. Father nodded in agreement with the words, "Yea, though I walk through the valley of the shadow of death, I will fear no evil: for thou art with me …" as he gazed longingly at the pale yet serene face of his wife.

"My darling Molly," he murmured as he stroked her forehead and ran his fingers through her hair. "You gave me two wonderful sons yet life denied us a daughter who would have kept your memory alive." Devoid of words I watched tears run down his face as he stared at the silent figure of his wife, whose love and encouragement had made him the success he was.

It was Drebar who broke the silence when he respectfully moved forward and slowly knelt alongside father. "I am very sorry sir, so very sorry. But from the depth of our grief I have great comfort to offer you." After a few moments of silence father turned his face towards Drebar and asked, "My friend, what is the comfort you offer me?"

Obviously what he had to say was very important because even Drebar paused in order to be sure of his words.

"Sir, since my family joined you Moneysa has always referred to you as her 'other father' as, in turn, she looks upon your sons as her brothers. That is the comfort I offer you. It is the knowledge that Moneysa yearns to be your daughter and her gift to you would be the love and loyalty that the relationship offers. Please do not be offended Mr Ganton, but I felt you should know this, particularly at this time of such deep grief."

Suddenly father threw his arms around Drebar as he whispered, "Thank you my friend, thank you for giving me the incentive to carry on living."

I was present at the funeral of Molly Ganton but was drawn into Charles only once during the entire service and committal ......

...."Do you share my thoughts John?" I whispered to my brother as we left the Station chapel and walked, in procession, to the nearby cemetery. "I know that funerals are sad events but that service was more dead that those unfortunates beneath the ground."

Without raising his head from studying the path John replied, "I agree with you. This day the Holy Spirit has been replaced with an employee, working as a Company official rather than a man of God."

The disappointment expressed by the brothers led me to research Company policy in this matter which revealed they only accepted overseas employees from the Protestant (Anglican) faith which, as in the case of this Station minister, took precedence over ministerial ability. Essentially Anglican clergy existed only for the care of the English staff and local Station missionaries. Their arrival began in the mid 18th century. However towards the end of the 18th century Company attitudes had, in part, to change in order to accommodate a new governmental decision to raise extra recruits, for the Napoleonic and American wars, which opened the way for the recruitment of Catholic soldiers from

Ireland; much to the deep disgust of conventional Company members.

CHAPTER FOUR

Arrival of the Salter family

It was early in the dry season of 1771 (November) that my attention was drawn to the arrival, from England, of family friends Derbie and Elizabeth Salter, and their daughter Elizabeth (aged 17), who, in conjunction with the untiring efforts of Drebar and Moneysa, did much to raise the depressed spirit of Edward Ganton. I was able to establish that Edward Ganton and Derbie Salter had been close friends stretching back to boyhood days and they had remained in regular written contact.

This, the first meeting between the Salter family and the Ganton brothers, led to much socializing and local visits until, much to her embarrassment, young Elizabeth Salter had to admit that despite being the cooler part of the year, the heat was making her ill and the matter was getting worse. Regular bouts of sickness, nausea and severe headaches became almost a daily event regardless of medical help. She even surrendered her English dress, and accessories, in favour of a simple sari and other light fitting Indian garments purchased with the help of Moneysa and her mother who, in a rapidly spoken native tongue, had negotiated bargains worth having. Although she rather liked the feel of her new style of dress it did not fully release her from the burden of the heat around her and her health became a matter of concern for the family and their doctor.

However this hitch was addressed by Edward Ganton who claimed a long overdue leave of absence and transported his visitors accompanied by Charles, John, Drebar, Moneysa and a number of servants to his rented property set some distance away upon high ground, within a forest clearing, with stunning views of a large lake surrounded by the lush vegetation of a tropical forest. It was located in an area of similar 'retreats' much loved by English patriots seeking respite from the heat and humidity of lower regions. The cool fresh air was declared to be ideal for the well being of young Elizabeth although Cymol and his mother remained behind declaring that it would be too cold for them.

"I consider myself fortunate in that I am able to live with the Indian weather," I remarked to Elizabeth over the breakfast table set out on the veranda. "Perhaps inheriting from my parents their comfort with the cooler English weather and being weaned and raised in the heat of India, means I am at ease within a wider ambient temperature than most."

"You are fortunate Charles," replied Elizabeth ruefully, "Despite feeling fully at ease in this beautiful sari my fair complexion is against me but, in truth, it is a small price to pay for the opportunity to meet you and your family together with your lovely Indian friends." I wondered if it was my imagination but did her blue eyes really reflect her smile as a light breeze gently moved her hair from her shoulders? "Forgive me for staring at you Elizabeth but you are unique, in that both Indian and English dress styles are shown to maximum effect when you wear them." Elizabeth shyly averted her eyes as she whispered, "Thank you kind sir."

"Morning Elizabeth, morning Charles," greeted Brother John as he and Moneysa strode along the path leading to the house. "Monnie and I have already eaten and worked up another appetite walking to the river and back in order to break ourselves in for the forest trek today. Are you both ready to start or are you planning to sit there all day?"

Before Charles could answer Moneysa crept up behind him, snatched his bunch of breakfast grapes, and fled laughing down the garden. Shouting threats Charles ran after her followed by laughter from John and Elizabeth with assorted squawks from a variety of birds they had disturbed.

Suddenly the sight of their three Indian guides, carrying packs of provisions, told the quartet that the time to enter the forest had arrived. It is worth recording that these guides were local men who made a comfortable income out of regular escort services of this nature.

After a pause for ablutions, and the application of various creams to ward off curious insects, the column set off with two Indian guides in the lead, followed by John, Elizabeth, Moneysa, Charles and then the third guide.

"You have nothing to worry about Elizabeth and you can take my word for it that tigers have not been seen in these parts for a number of years. There are too many Europeans carrying guns for their liking."

"Perhaps so John," I replied. Then quietly coming up close behind Moneysa I shouted, "But do not forget the snakes." Moneysa gave a yell and ran forward then turned and, with tear filled eyes, shouted at me, "Charles, you know that I am terrified of snakes."

"Forgive me Monnie," I replied as I stepped forward and put my arm around her and gently patted her back. With her face buried in my shoulder I assured her that she had nothing to worry about because snakes would not attack anyone who had been eating stolen grapes.

Then, much to the delight of John and Elizabeth, Moneysa quickly replied, "That means I am safe from you, Charles Ganton."

When the laughter died down Brother John, in a more serious voice, did remind us that many cobra snakes were around but we were safe if we remained on the path. After which it was unanimously agreed that talk about snakes was banned for the remainder of the day.

Happy conversations and light hearted banter made a carefree start for the four explorers but, as the gradient ahead of them increased, conversation lessened in favour of increased rates of breathing. Then around a bend in the path Elizabeth suddenly stopped, in amazement, beside a number of large bushes with deep green leaves and flowers ranging in colour from white to crimson.

"How delightful," she announced. "These are rhododendrons and they grow around our house in England."

"Quite so," remarked John, "The higher we go along this path the more rhododendrons we will see because the climate in higher altitude forests is ideal for their growth. You seem very interested in them Monnie, you must have seen them before?" "I have," she replied, "and they are my favourite flower but I never knew their name. Tell me again what you called them."

"Rhododendrons," John replied.

Moneysa made several attempts to pronounce rhododendron and eventually gave up the attempt.

"I have just made up my own name for my favourite bush. From now on I will call them 'rhodies' and think of you all when I see them."

"Thank you," replied Elizabeth, "Although they grow in

the woods around where I live in England I will now look upon them, and you, as being the 'flower of India."

As the party moved slowly on, and Moneysa remained in front of the rhododendron bushes admiring their beauty, I stood beside her and put my arm around her shoulder, "Are we friends again Moneysa – sorry if I upset you earlier on."

"You are a silly Charles," she replied as she put her arm around my waist, "I am your ever best friend and this should prove what I have just said." With that she quickly reached up and pulled my lace tied pig tail which hung below my collar. Immediately she ran laughing down the path with me in hot pursuit, closely followed by a couple of friendly monkeys who were keen to take part in the chase.

Laughter, good conversation and the simple enjoyment of being together sealed their friendship and made it a day to be remembered.

Of all the many joyous happenings one that remained firmly in my mind began with the four walkers, sitting on wide rocks, with their feet immersed in a fast flowing shallow stream that ran down the forest slope into the distant lake. It was blissful relief for their hot and dusty feet, and was the subject of many later debates as to who started the friendly mêlée that followed. Perhaps by accident or intent someone's foot splashed someone else, who immediately kicked water at another member of the group who responded accordingly. This situation quickly deteriorated until the four of them, bent double, furiously hurled handfuls of water at anyone within range.

The three porters looked on in total amazement at the saturated and frenzied quartet, whilst disturbed forest creatures added their distinctive sounds to the hullabaloo set within that mountain stream. The 'battle' ended with the four contestants sitting down in the fast flowing cool

*water and laughing until they were literally out of breath.
Eventually the still giggling party, with water trailing behind
them, continued along the path to a designated clearing that
had been set aside for parties of European adventurers to rest
and be fed.*

"One good thing about Indian weather, in the summer
season, is that wet clothes quickly dry even when worn." I
exclaimed.

"But only in India where you can get away with wearing
hardly any clothes," said Elizabeth, "At home it would take
a season for my many layers to dry even if I survived an
attack of snuffles in the process."

*Already a small camp fire was burning beneath a metal
container in which tea was brewing, and bamboo high backed
chairs were scattered around the camp area into which the
now tiring party gladly relaxed. With aprons covering their
long white trousers the three guides appeared, each carrying
a wooden platter containing an assortment of nuts, fruit and
what looked like small pancakes.*

"Thank you, that is very welcome," exclaimed Elizabeth
as she took the proffered plate. In turn both John and I
expressed our gratitude, at which they bowed before us and
began to walk away.

*As an aside I must add that forest guides and porters
were not so much concerned with the needs of the English
but, infinitely more so, with the lucrative work contract
upon which they and their families depended. With this
in mind we must not lose sight of their apparent humility
which, understandably, was designed to protect their only
form of income.*

Amazed and not a little annoyed I stood up and bellowed
after them, "Have you forgotten something?"

The head porter bowed before me and said, "What is
that, Sahib?"

Pointing to a rather dejected looking Moneysa I said, "What about some food for my friend eh?"

Looking uncomfortably at Moneysa he responded, "Please forgive me Sahib but we are Hindus and cannot serve those of Islam, but there is food left for your servant to supply herself." He wilted beneath my glare as I snapped at him, "The servant you refer to is my best friend and my equal in this life and the next."

With that I knelt alongside Moneysa and offered her my plate with the request, "Please take this Moneysa, I am sorry that you have been so badly treated by those who know no better." It grieved me even more when I saw a tear trickling down her cheek. "Monnie, it is from Charles, please take the plate."

She smiled as she took the plate but her attempt to say something was thwarted when she began to sob. Elizabeth quickly took over and sat with her arm around her whilst I turned my attention to the apprehensive porter before me.

"I do not know which of your Hindu gods made that ruling but I will have you know that the only God, of this Sahib, is a God of love who teaches that we are all one and should serve each other."

Despite my irritation I began to feel sorry for the worried and embarrassed porter so I gently added, with a smile, "Now this Sahib is a very hungry Sahib and I am wondering if you are going to stand there and watch me starve to death?"

Feeling much relieved the porter scampered away to prepare my plate as John exclaimed, "Well said Charles. In truth that was delivered with the conviction of an open air preacher and I agree with every word you said."

Kneeling down alongside Moneysa I held her hand by way of reassurance. She smiled at me and said, "Thank you," then gently kissed the back of my hand and added,

"My ever best friend." I grinned at her but quickly turned away to hide my emotions only for her next words to restore laughter within our group. I heard her call, "Charles," and as I turned round she continued, "Charles, I am sorry that I stole your grapes this morning."

With laughter and joviality restored to the group our attention settled upon a crowd of monkeys, who had become over interested in what we were eating, and had successfully defied every attempt made by the porters to drive them away. Several of them had gathered within 'grab and run' distance of our food supplies and the situation looked grim for our stomachs.

What followed has remained in the recesses of my mind as one of the funniest acts I have ever witnessed. I love my brother John but, despite our closeness, I would have to admit that he was very reserved in his nature and not given to wild antics except upon this occasion with the monkeys. Without warning Brother John squatted down upon his haunches and, uttering high pitched squeaks whilst waving his arms, he rapidly hopped towards the monkeys who, as one, retreated through the trees in great alarm and confusion never to be seen again.

It was a full ten minutes before our laughter, which had us rolling about on the ground, finally subsided and we were able to finish our meals; not without occasional giggles as we viewed the now sedate Brother John acting as if nothing had happened.

In due course we began to wander slowly home betwixt conversation, laughter, 'hide until found' and 'chase about' until Moneysa, leaning against a tree, announced that she was too tired to take another step.

"Come to Charles little sister," was my reply as I scooped her into my arms and with her arm around my neck and head upon my shoulder I walked on softly singing one of mother's favourite lullabies to her until she quickly fell into a gentle sleep. The light was beginning to fade as the Indian evening began its rapid descent prompting an entire chorus of strange sounding tropical birds to begin their evening serenade. Monnie remained in a deep sleep whereas we three trudged on, quietly reliving the happiness of the day, yet feeling too tired to even yawn.

CHAPTER FIVE

Christmas and New Year 1771 - 1772

Much to the dismay of Moneysa, and for reasons I am unclear about, she and her mother and brother had to return to the Ganton main residence as Christmas 1771 approached. I have a feeling that it was connected to a particular Muslim event in which Cymol was involved as he gained favour within the mosque hierarchy.

However the ingenious Drebar, because of his prominent post in the family circle was quick to claim exemption from whatever rules threatened his position within the Ganton household. It must be understood that Drebar and his daughter Moneysa were very alike in that they were intelligent, quick witted, loyal to their friends and were both 'luke-warm' in their practice of Muslim rules; in particular the ones that dictated how they should live.

However Moneysa because of her sex was unable to take the same stance as her father and had, albeit not without a verbal fight, to conform to requirements. Further to Moneysa's distress was being faced with having to say goodbye to the Salter family who were scheduled to leave India early in

1772 with, as it was then, little prospect of them ever meeting again. A strong bond of friendship had developed between Elizabeth and Moneysa and, when the time came to depart, they both burst into tears and flung their arms around each other until they were coaxed apart by emotional family members. It fell to Cymol to lead his rebellious sister into the waiting coach leaving a sobbing Elizabeth Salter to stand and wave until it was a dust enshrouded distant speck.

To many the sight of an emotional scene begets emotion and I am no exception to this rather blessed human attribute. Almost as a reflex action I moved toward Elizabeth who responded to my arm around her waist, by burying her face into my shoulder, as I found words to comfort her. From the corner of my eye I was aware of the two father figures giving one another 'knowing nods and smiles' and I heard Mrs. Salter remark that their daughter would find comfort in the arms of Charles.

I next became aware that Christmas Eve had arrived when the Ganton and Salter family spent their time in preparation for the day to follow. It was almost like the Sabbath day in that much time was spent in prayer and Bible study, led by Brother John, who gave a cleverly constructed homily bridging Christmas with the commitment to evangelise the message of Christian salvation. This was followed by several sung carols (?), accompanied by young Elizabeth, who gave a talented performance upon a box shaped instrument which I later identified as a clavichord. I was familiar with only one sung item which was 'Joy to the World' which I researched and found was a popular hymn in colonial America and was written in the 1730's by Isaac Watts, with music added by George Frederick Handel in the 1750's.

A substantial dinner set the stage for much conversation which retained its momentum with the help of several bottles of a vintage wine that Edward Ganton had saved for this special friendship event.

Points of conversation that remained in my mind were the future of Brother John as an ordained Church of England priest and that Derbie Salter, upon his return, would raise the topic with the diocesan bishop who was also his friend and riding companion in the local hunt.

Then, as part of table conversation, Edward Ganton apologized for the absence of holly sprigs to decorate the house since it only grew in distant parts of India, but hoped that sepia coloured leaves, which were scattered upon window ledges and tables, would suffice. He went on to explain that his late wife Molly loved 'point leaves' since they quickly faded from green to sepia which, in her view, was 'the colour that memories were formed from.'

I was intrigued to hear Edward Ganton's reference to 'point leaves' which led me into a detailed study of botanical references, particularly in India, which failed to reveal foliage by this name. Perhaps 'point leaves' were a family expression or, alternatively, I may have simply misheard what was really said?

I glanced at Elizabeth and sensed that she shared my discomfort at having eaten too much and, feeling out of our depth now that the conversation had focused upon 'predestination' we stood and asked permission to leave the table. Permission was granted and, much to my surprise, Mr. Salter winked at father whilst Mrs. Salter gently gripped her daughter's hand.

Soon we were standing upon the veranda breathing in the cool evening air, as we listened to many different sounds of night creatures and watched a myriad of fireflies adding their dots of luminescence to the scene before us.

I complimented Elizabeth upon her appearance which, I assured her, would cause nature's beauty to fear such competition even within its own domain. She smiled shyly at me whilst releasing something, behind her neck, that allowed her fair hair to fall in a series of ringlets upon her shoulders. The light cast by the many hanging oil lamps, each fitted with shades of different colours, did much to enhance her appearance and give tribute to her ankle length dress, with a tight fitting low cut bodice supported on the edge of her shoulders, leading to sleeves ending in frills just below her elbows. The waist setting was high and a velvet belt, with an ornate clasp, completed the picture. She wore a simple chain necklace that held a star with small pearls at the end of each star point which, earlier, she had referred to as her 'Christmas necklace.'

"Thank you Charles and I must say that you look rather dashing yourself," she replied. "However after a meal of that magnitude I yearn to be back in my loose fitting sari. This dress and undergarments, together with the rest of my wardrobe, are designed for women who never eat."

As we walked towards the lakeside our hands joined in an involuntary act of unity born from just being together, and sharing the beauty of the moment which became breathtaking as the moon reflected its glow upon the large lake before us. Gazing at the scene in silent awe we were captivated by a gentle harmonic tinkling sound from several metallic chimes, of differing key settings, hanging in the trees around us. "Truly a symphony of satisfaction," declared Elizabeth who was clearly moved by all she saw and heard.

Please permit me to briefly interrupt and comment upon the wind chimes which were not heard around the lake, or indeed anywhere else on the site, prior to the arrival of

Christmas Eve. Christianity was very much a minority faith within a land dominated by Hindus and increasing numbers of Muslims and Buddhists. Nevertheless English Christians were the founders of a regular wage income which may have led site managers to install the wind chimes in honour of the feast of Christmas? Alternatively the chimes may have been instrumental in an obscure Buddhist or Hindu festival? I know not but felt the need to comment not only upon their presence, but also the fact that metallic chimes formed part of my previously referred to 'island recollections'.

I do not know how long we stood there entranced by the beauty around us whilst being gently fanned by an evening breeze through the trees, which carried a sweet odour of forest blooms to the background of those haunting chimes. Truly our stage of natural wonder was complete. I suddenly returned to reality when the sound of my pocket repeater watch quietly announced that midnight had arrived.

My "Happy Christmas Elizabeth" was immediately followed with "Happy Christmas Charles" as we faced each other. I remember the love that shone upon her face as our lips, almost as a reflex action, closed together and our arms clasped each other in the first of many embraces. As I held her in my arms numerous questions raced through my mind; dominated by the knowledge that both our families yearned to be united through our marriage. Would my strong affection towards Elizabeth be sufficient to uphold us as husband and wife within the affluence of an English country manor house, or was I merely infatuated with this moment born from nature's beauty around us?

The moonlight, chimes and fragrant blooms united to hold my heart captive and, as if by ransom paid to my captor, I murmured, "I love you Elizabeth." Looking me full in the face she smiled, kissed me again and again, then replied, "And I love you Charles. In fact from the moment we first met I knew that I was in love with you and just hoped that you would find it within yourself to love me." Time passed without measure as we held one another and experienced those joyful emotions flowing from our love so recently declared within our special 'Garden of Eden.'

The spell was broken when Charles's repeater watch again intervened and announced the half hour and the couple, hand in hand, set off back towards the house.

"Later today I will ask permission of your father and mother to enter into an official courtship agreement with you Elizabeth. How do you think they will react to that?" "They will be overjoyed and willingly give their blessing to our love that will unite the Salter and Ganton families for all time," she replied as she tightly gripped my hand as we walked on.

Suddenly turmoil filled my mind over what I had allowed to happen and I felt panic within; as if I wanted to rush back through a door that had just closed behind me. Were my feelings as sincere as those flowing from Elizabeth or was I simply in love with the romance of India, so magnified in the beauty of the forest's sights and sounds that arose from my Garden of Eden before me? Had I, in fact, surrendered to the open secret of both families and agreed to a pseudo 'arranged marriage' and would life in England prove to be my prison? If I was to marry Elizabeth then, perhaps, she would agree to live in India with me; but I had the greatest doubts about that as demonstrated by the discomforts she had already experienced.

Would I never again see 'my ever best friend' who would become a distant memory lost within an arranged village marriage to a man old enough to be her father?

"Please Lord, tell me what to do" was my silent plea as I led a radiantly happy Elizabeth back to the house.

Deep in thought they both walked on seemingly unaware that the scene around them was changing. A sudden influx of clouds had obliterated the moon and a strengthening wind promoted discord from the once harmonious chimes. Then like the drawing of stage curtains dark shadows slowly covered the once idyllic scene.

Christmas Day was an unforgettable day both to the memory of the Holy Infant born, and the joy experienced by all present, as they freely gave themselves gifts of love and goodwill. After all it was Christmas Day and the large food filled table bore tribute to that glorious fact. Both families and the entire Indian staff, ranging from young stable boys to the servant manager Drebar, had a place at that table, sitting in front of name cards, which meant they were evenly dispersed between English family members.

Edward Ganton fought hard and successfully not to allow the fact that it was his first Christmas without his beloved Molly to cast a shadow over the proceedings and, ignoring protests from the table, he insisted that both he and his good friend Derbie Salter would serve the various food courses to all present.

Happiness, love, compassion and the very essence of seasonable good will was the torch that lit the day. Family friends and Indian staff ate well, played well, hunted the slipper well, and were well entertained by the inimitable Drebar as he baffled all with his traditional sleight of hand tricks to which I have previously referred. Then he introduced a range of conjuring acts that reduced the housemaid to hysteria when Drebar produced a boiled egg from behind her ear and, seemingly, went on to swallow it without visible effort or discomfort.

What next followed was, I strongly suspect, the result of prior arrangement between the respective fathers. At 5pm precisely, both families retired to what Edward Ganton called his 'Conference room' which was, in fact, the drawing room and general rest room.

I was the last to enter the room and it was no surprise that every eye was upon me. As I sat alongside Elizabeth my attention was immediately drawn to the distant sound of lakeside wind chimes, as they responded to the freshening evening breeze, complimented by the gentle swaying of beaded cord blinds as they protected the open windows against winged insects. Sadly my mental soliloquy suddenly ended, and I returned to the matter before, me when I sensed that Elizabeth was looking inquisitively at me.

Despite my reservations I had requested this meeting and was sufficiently progressive in thought to realize that senior family members were aware of the agenda; otherwise why were Mr. and Mrs. Salter blatantly smiling at each other and my father, most untypically, sitting with turned head and lips set in a silent whistle whilst nonchalantly studying nothing of significance on the nearby wall?

Those who know me better will agree that I am rarely, if ever, overcome with reluctance born from embarrassment. Thus with maximum confidence I arose and approached Mr. and Mrs. Salter who, in recognition of their role, viewed my presence with serious facial expressions. As I drew near to them I noticed muscular twitches at the corners of their mouths scarcely hiding an abundance of joy seeking to break free from conventional requirements.

Heartened by unspoken signs of support I addressed Mr. Salter with, "Sir, Christmas Eve gave me a further blessing in that, unworthy as I am, your daughter Elizabeth joined me in a spoken bond of love that we seek to share for the remainder of our lives. With respect sir, I beg that you will enable us to take our first step together by granting your approval of our courtship followed by formal engagement and marriage."

After a pause consisting of serious looks and pretend consideration the bubble of convention broke and Derbie Salter leapt to his feet, furiously shook my hand, and then threw his arms around me whilst announcing, "Charles, welcome to the Salter family as my son through law to be." Elizabeth senior and daughter fell into each other's arms amidst tears and laughter. Whereas, my father, with tears unashamedly running down his face, hugged me before handing me over to Brother John for his congratulations. When released by her mother, Elizabeth was quickly embraced both by father and Brother John who welcomed their daughter and sister to be with words of love and total acceptance.

Soon glasses of vintage port wine were clinking in proposed toasts to the future happiness of us both and the long hoped for joining of the Salter and Ganton families through marriage.

I listened and joined in the hubbub of voices until, momentarily, their voices faded as an inner command, with unwavering clarity, challenged me with, 'Are you really serious Charles or are you just being swept along?' Half aloud I murmured, "I do not bloody know …." when a passing servant, assuming that I asked for a drink, held the wine tray before me. I grabbed a glass of port, drained it in one gulp, and then quickly took another for later reference.

When the family members eventually returned to their chairs there was a period of conversation in which the logistics of the new born courtship were discussed. Clearly the mail delivery system was the only means through which Charles and Elizabeth could communicate with each other. However, Edward Ganton agreed to speed delivery times by including their correspondence with routine dispatches to and from East India headquarters in London, via fast sailing sloops of war.

Derbie Salter updated all present with rapid economic growth in England that had improved cross country postal systems with better roads and modern stagecoaches to carry mail between cities and towns.

Fortified by further glasses of port wine family confidence grew as communication problems diminished, and a tentative time framework was agreed, wherein the engagement would be formalized next Christmas (1772) at the Salter household in England. Since Brother John would be present at this celebration Derbie Salter announced his intention to arrange for him to meet his social friend, the diocesan bishop, with a view to finalising John's ordination into the Church of England.

Resulting from what was an historic occasion for my two families, reinforced with excited conversation abetted by an unending supply of wine, I was beginning to feel tired yet quickly recovered my presence when, in a loud voice, Derbie Salter invited the 'future Mrs. Charles Ganton' to play some relaxing music for us.

I was aware that Elizabeth was an accomplished musician, but had never had the opportunity to sit and listen to her prowess upon the keyboard; hence I was doubly thrilled when Elizabeth seated herself at the clavichord and began to play several short works which were both pleasing and relaxing to my ear.

In due course I was suddenly awakened from my reverie of peaceful thoughts when my mind was alerted, and instantly captivated, by a tune that arrived as a stranger to my ears yet began what was to be a lifelong resident within my mind.

"Elizabeth you never cease giving me gifts of joy and not least that beautiful melody you have just played. What is it called?"

Elizabeth stared down at the keyboard then, in a voice alive with sincerity replied, "And I will never cease trying to please my husband to be. Prior to finding your favour that tune was without a name hence, from this moment, I duly name it 'our melody' and when we are apart I will play it as a symbol of our happiness together *(this was met with gentle applause from both families)*. In truth I do not know its published name but it is a tune popular in the north of England where I live."

"Thank you Elizabeth," I replied. "Please honour me by playing again 'our melody' knowing that it harmonises perfectly with the love I hold for my wife to be."

At this stage I can reveal to you that the melody I heard played upon the clavichord, which affected Charles Ganton to the degree described, is the still loved and remembered ballad 'And believe me if all those endearing young charms which I gaze on so fondly today, were to change by tomorrow and fleet in my arms, like fairy gifts fading away ....'

As previously stressed I have never hesitated to research, where possible, new events, sights and sounds in order to confirm the authenticity of the account I have placed before you and, by doing so, eliminate any suggestion that imagination rather than fact may have set my stage.

Resulting from my initial research I was totally devastated with what I learned about the song I have described to you. Share with me my distress and disappointment when I discovered that 'Those Endearing Young Charms' was written and published by the Irish poet Thomas Moore, in 1808, almost 40 years after the recital I have thus described.

Sometime later I realised that I had been guilty of an unjustified assumption in that, at no time, did I hear words sung or spoken. All I heard was a tune that I assumed was composed at the same time as the lyrics to the song that has survived the decades to date.

*With renewed vigour I researched the origin of the **tune alone** and found that it was a 'traditional' melody generally ascribed to one Matthew Locke in 1665. **Since its publication it has been used to accompany several songs** including the rather sad ballad 'My Lodging it is in the Cold Ground' which was popular in the north of England during the 18th century, so giving credibility to the fact that Elizabeth Salter chose to play it during a family gathering.*

The next scene that appeared before me was the time when the Salter family left India and returned to England.

To me it is very singular that human friendship, when faced with temporary separation, adds to the emotional pain by prolonging the process of saying 'goodbye.' The gentle snorting of four horses attached to a waiting coach did little to coax the Salter family aboard and on to their appointment with an England bound 'India Man' waiting at the docks.

Elizabeth and I stood silently holding hands whilst remaining family members went through their emotional farewells. Finally Mrs. Salter held out her hand for Elizabeth to join them in the coach.

Turning to me, and desperately trying to hold back her tears, Elizabeth whispered, "Please do not stop loving me Charles." Overwhelmed with emotion we tightly held each other until, with a sob, Elizabeth quickly joined her parents inside the coach which gaining momentum rapidly left our sight, although our waving arms continued to pay tribute to the bearers of happiness who had left our midst.

It is apparent to me that Charles Ganton, during his woodland period of dictation, parted only with information that was relevant to events that would shape his narrative; meaning there were long time gaps from which, despite in-depth meditation on my part, nothing of any great significance was revealed.

I was aware that Charles was now working hard within his father's section in the East India Company and that Brother John had gone elsewhere to graduate prior to ordination. On two or three occasions Charles was censured by his father for long delays in replying to the many letters from his fiancée Elizabeth Salter and was unhappy with his response that he was absorbed in the work he had been given to do.

The ever faithful Drebar was still the backbone of household management and mentor and friend to Edward Ganton.

Moneysa had advanced to senior school level and, much to the disgust of her conventional Muslim brother, loved to appear in a dress that Elizabeth Salter had given to her in memory of their time together.

The year 1772 passed quickly and the time came for Charles and his family to travel to England, in order to formalize his engagement to Elizabeth Salter, and my only involvement in the entire journey came after their disembarkation in London.

CHAPTER SIX

England in 1772

"Welcome to London Charles and John," exclaimed father as we were reunited with our luggage aboard a shining new stage coach and began our journey to the north. As we threaded our way through London's congested cobble stone streets I was suddenly deafened by a spontaneous outburst of bell peals, pitched differently and following a variety of changes such that I thought my head would burst. Clapping both hands to my ears I enquired, "What on earth is all that about?" Immediately father informed me, "You are honoured Charles because those are the famous London church bells calling the faithful from their beds." Both Brother John and I agreed that London churches must be packed to capacity since no one could possibly sleep with such an onslaught upon their ears.

Perhaps these were the aforementioned bells of my 'retained memory' mentioned in my introductory section?

Although 48 hours had elapsed since Charles and his family had arrived, to an emotional welcome at the Salter residence, he still felt disorientated and confused with life in England having spent his twenty years of life exclusively upon India's soil.

It seemed to Charles that Mr. Derbie Salter recognized this fact and spent time helping him to understand what, after his marriage, would be the life style expected of him. He quickly learned that owning land was the main form of wealth in 18th century England, and that political power and influence was in the hands of wealthy landowners. The top tier of this power alliance belonged to the nobility and the second level of influence was occupied by rich gentlemen farmers, better known as 'gentry', which included the Salter family.

Ordinary people were in the basement of English society and looked upon meat as an absolute luxury. They had to be content with bread, butter, potatoes and tea as their basic diet whereas, to quote Derbie Salter," it is our duty to set an example for them to look up to."

"Do not worry about them my boy, they are the backbone of England and thrive upon your Indian tea. They work hard and, considering the size of their families, seem to play hard what," said my future father through law with a broad grin.

My society baptism continued, with no small amount of urgency, because our engagement party was now only three days away. Elizabeth and her mother and father patiently taught me the basic moves of sequence dances which, they stressed, were important both now and throughout my future social life. I did work very hard on the dance floor tasks set for me, and managed to come to terms with sequence movements such as 'back to back, cast off and cast up' whilst speculating how Moneysa would have laughed had she been party to my antics. Despite my stumbling,

Mr. Salter encouraged me with such compliments as, "You are doing fine me boy. Just relax a bit more and you will become the best lead dancer on the floor, and a master of step change dances like 'Hunt the Squirrel' and 'The Old Mill', which are far more challenging than something called the waltz that is raging through Vienna."

In hushed tones Mrs. Salter announced that waltzing relied upon the same male and female being in close contact throughout the entire dance, and that the church had banned it as a serious sexual sin. "Sounds like fun to me," whispered Elizabeth in my ear.

At this stage I must add that I have never heard of dances known as 'Hunt the Squirrel' and 'The Old Mill' but that is what Derbie Salter clearly said. In fact throughout this entire section I felt that Charles wanted it recorded, in general terms, because it traced his path towards the catastrophic climax that lay ahead. In parallel it did enable me to observe a little of 1772 life lived by the upper middle classes.

Women appeared to sport a wide range of generous wigs whereas the tendency for men was an abundance of their own hair (where applicable) together with a wig of diminished proportions. In fact I never saw Charles wearing a wig and Brother John only wore one when preaching.

Most of the men I saw wore knee length breeches and white stockings or gaiters with buckled shoes, three cornered hats were also popular. Many women particularly those present at the engagement party dance wore hooped petticoats under their dresses, and frequently fanned themselves with a range of small, ornate folding fans for a variety of reasons. One rather rotund lady cleverly used her fan to disguise a yawn whilst others relied upon it as a shield to cover instant and clandestine conversations. Pretended embarrassment was enacted with the fan held beneath flickering eyelids. I noted that fans were very active when the time came for Elizabeth Salter and Charles Ganton to formalize their marriage engagement.

The area bishop and hunting friend of Derbie Salter led the event and blessed the couple after Charles had placed a ring upon Elizabeth's finger. After several speeches a choir consisting of two men and three women sang, accompanied by a clavichord, a love song that was well received and repeated as an encore. Hearing it twice enabled me to remember some of the lines which were as follows:

Sweet are the charms of her I love...... More fragrant than the damask rose...... Soft as the down of turtle dove......Gentle as wind when Zephyr blows......Refreshing as descending rains to sun burnt climes and thirsty plains.

Since it had no great impact upon my narrative I did not bother to research the origin of the above seemingly popular love song.

As mentioned previously I was only able to be present in a room, or be a party to a conversation or other actions, when Charles Ganton was in the immediate area. If he moved away then I was drawn away with him and, on this occasion, he unwittingly introduced me to a less salubrious part of the house. To some extent I was grateful for this because, as the evening wore on, the room became hot and stuffy with an unpleasant background odour. The reason for this discomfort was made clear when following in the wake of Charles Ganton I discovered the close proximity of 'toilet rooms' for individual sexes.

The room reserved for gentlemen contained several screened commode chair toilets or, if preferred, a number of chamber pots were available within an abundance of cupboards. Also a discreet wall notice advised all interested parties that, if preferred, earth toilets were also available outside the house.

As the evening progressed and couples began to tire they drifted into designated rooms wherein the men launched into card games of which Backgammon appeared to be the favourite. Alternatively they would sit around in conversational groups with servants ensuring that wine glasses remained full.

"Come and join us Ganton" were the words of invitation from a naval officer wearing the rank epaulettes and dress uniform of a naval post captain. Shaking my hand he introduced himself by the surname of Brentwood and said he was the cousin of Derbie Salter.

I sat and nodded to three other men who made up the group. Not sure of what to say I came out with, "Thank you for your support at this landmark event in my life."

Facing me was a rather corpulent man characterised by a huge chin that ran in the form of several tiers down to his ornate waistcoat. "Welcome to the club me boy," he exclaimed followed by a resounding belch that passed without comment.

"How does all this compare with life in India?" asked another. "I was born in India so it is the only life I know and this is my first trip to England," was my now routine reply to this often asked question. "Then you have done well to land one of the most charming and eligible spinsters in the area," he said. With a meaningful smile he continued with "I have never seen native Indians so how do Indian lasses compare with our English ladies eh?"

In an attempt to introduce humour into the conversation I quickly said, "One major difference is their skin which is a deep brown colour."

This was met with silence broken only by a further belch from the corpulent man.

My repeater watch intervened and advised me of the hour, which I explained was the agreed time for me to meet with my fiancée on the terrace. "Must not keep the future Mrs. Ganton waiting," added Captain Brentwood as they stood for my departure.

Adjusting my eyes to the subdued light of late evening I saw Elizabeth emerging from one of the many open French windows that ran the length of the terrace. Quickly we met and embraced then, with my arm around her waist, we began to walk along the terrace...... only for us to dissolve into laughter when we realised what had happened.

In my attempt to press close to Elizabeth her hooped petticoat had made way for my presence by, in bell fashion, moving far away from the perpendicular thus effectively blocking the terrace to oncoming walkers. "I am thinking that your dress is designed to deter amorous young men like myself," I declared amidst further laughter. "Not for much longer according to my dressmaker who assures me that the fashion is changing. Rather than a hooped skirt I will soon wear small cushions upon my hips that will minimize dress expansion both for your gratification and my satisfaction," she replied.

Thus in a very happy frame of mind we continued our first walk together as a couple engaged to be married, and heirs to the comforts and affluence of life as accepted members of the English landowning society.

'Many would be ecstatic at the thought of such a future ahead of them so why do I not feel that way?' I silently mused only to return to reality when, with concern in her voice, Elizabeth asked, "Why are you so quiet Charles, is something worrying you. You are not unhappy are you?"

I quickly regained my thoughts and replied, "Of course not my sweet. Your very presence is forever the herald to happiness within my life." As we walked along the terrace together my mind again began to wander but this time back to India, with its heat and noise in contrast to its tropical beauty, and those I had left behind. As my mind further drifted, and to the background of Elizabeth's voice, I thought of 'my ever best friend' and wondered what Moneysa was doing and had she already forgotten about me?

"Don't you agree Charles," was the question that brought me back to reality and my instant reply, "Of course, I am totally with your point of view," was, fortunately, the answer expected from me.

Thus ends my presence in England at the engagement of Charles to Elizabeth. Additional information to which I was privy to was that the wedding was planned for 1781when the Ganton family would return to England following Edward Ganton's retirement in late 1780. In the interim it was agreed that Charles would visit Elizabeth on at least two occasions following approved leave of absence periods.

I became aware that Brother John had a successful interview with the area bishop, and it was agreed that John would return in 1775, when he would be duly ordained as a priest within the Church of England.

Other than repeated paternal promptings to son Charles, to respond to Elizabeth's regular letters, nothing of significance developed despite my close attention to the period leading up to 1775. However, as we shall soon learn, the goodwill dinner held for Brother John, prior to his departure to England for his ordination into the Church of England, soon slipped out of the family vision following further and tragic happenings within the Ganton household.

CHAPTER SEVEN

Storm in India

The wet season of 1775 was, to say the least, untypical and in need of further clarification for all those unfamiliar with this season, that falls between June and September, during which 90% of the total annual rainfall is deposited.

I have deliberately abstained from using the word 'monsoon' because at no stage have I heard anyone around me use the expression which, perhaps, is emotionally inferior to the much used 'bloody wet season.' It must be remembered that the wet season is not a period of unremitting rain, and half of the expected rainfall is deposited during seven days of the three month period, meaning that it is not unusual to have extended dry periods during the so called wet season. This offers some relief following the month of May which is the hottest month of the year and also attracts the highest humidity levels.

Despite presenting you with what is typical data I must again stress that 1775 was an untypically wet season. It opened with heavy rain and three weeks later it was still raining and showed no signs of abating. Indeed the insistent watery salvos that cascaded against the windows seemed to multiply by the day.

"At least Brother John will remember his ordination send off," I remarked to my father who was sorting through some papers on his desk. "Indeed he will," he muttered almost to himself. "Charles, I have two points I want to raise with you. First is the excellent work you are doing within your sphere of responsibility, so much so that the Company directors have earmarked you for rapid promotion and, ultimately, to succeed me when I retire in 1780. What do you think to that?"

Pulling up a chair before him at his desk I gasped out, "In truth, I am delighted to hear that. My love for Company work has trebled through the knowledge that you, and East India Company directors, are happy with my performance."

My father looked beyond me at rain streaming down the windows and thoughtfully said, "That is really good news Charles but we must not forget something else that must be resolved before 1780 is upon us, and it is a critically important question that only you can answer. After your marriage to Elizabeth Salter, will she agree to come and live in India – remember how the hot weather made her ill when she was last here?"

I reflected upon this whilst thinking about Derbie Salter's description of what my life would be in England, as a prospective Lord of the Manor, and that Elizabeth never once referred to life in India as an option following our marriage. "I am unsure of her desires in that direction," I finally admitted knowing full well how my father would respond. "Then you must find out Charles, and you can only do that by responding to her letters. Currently you are sending out one letter to every six received from Elizabeth and that will just not do."

I was saved from further embarrassment by a discreet knock on the door and my father responding with, "Come in Drebar and sit down." The ever smiling Drebar walked in and, with a sigh of relief, sat upon the nearest chair to update us with a list of all the tasks that he and his staff had completed around the house. Not least of these was repairing and mopping up after several leaks that bore testimony to the severity of the weather.

"Thank you my good friend without whom we would be lost," added my father as he walked over to the side table and filled three glasses from the decanter. "Drebar, it is Saturday and you should have stopped work many hours ago not least because you look very tired. Further, it is our secret that you do not object to the occasional glass of medication, in the form of a vintage brandy, which is more than needed this weather," continued father as Drebar happily received the proffered glass. Soon both father and I were drinking to Drebar's health who, not to be outdone, then stood and toasted us and our family. "Thank you sirs," said Drebar, "it is true that I am feeling a little tired and blame the weather for adding rust to my old bones." "Then home to bed immediately," ordered father with a broad smile. "You know where the oil skins are so wrap up well and off you go." We walked with him onto the veranda and watched Drebar, with his head covered against the rain and knee deep in water, slowly wade over what was our lawn and carefully climb the house entry steps, diagonally opposite ours. His final act was to return our hand waves as he entered his house.

"If he is no better in the morning then I will have the doctor look at him. In fact I will be obliged if you will write a note to that effect in tomorrow's diary," father said as he thoughtfully walked back into the house.

Back at my own desk I picked up my quill pen, dipped it into the ink well, and true to my father's intent I made the necessary diary entry. Perhaps father had deliberately arranged several sheets of writing paper, in the centre of my desk, as a ruse to tingle my conscience which, on this occasion, had the desired effect. Thus with a flourish I began to write 'My darling Elizabeth' only to throw my pen down at the sound of running feet and jabbering voices outside my door. Correctly assuming that another rain leak had been discovered, and that Drebar was no longer in charge, I decided to directly supervise whatever was needed to deal with this situation.

Much later my sleep was disturbed as my eyes flickered open, to the sound of the still incessant rain and tree branches that groaned and swayed beneath the weight of the deluge. But there was something else that competed for my attention. I listened very hard and again heard a female voice screaming, "Charles – Charles, please help me." Those urgent words immediately dispelled all thoughts of further sleep. Was it a cry from within a dream – no. I heard them again and again despite the sound of rain beating hard on the window panes.

Leaping out of bed I noticed that dawn was just breaking as I quickly pulled on my breeches and ran out onto the veranda and to my horror saw Moneysa, dressed only in her cotton nightdress, clinging onto the fence beneath a large overhanging bush. She was up to her waist in the water and, it would appear, had given up trying to get to this house and was in danger of being washed away. Quickly I rang the hand alarm bell to awaken my father and summon help from the staff before I leapt in the water and began to struggle over towards Moneysa.

With a look of desperation upon her face she shouted that her father Drebar had died and that she just wanted to be with me. Then she began to cry almost hysterically whilst pleading with me to help her …..."You are all I have in this life Charles ….please help me ….please ….please." Her voice became more and more desperate as I forged through the water towards her …and then it happened.

The hillside was saturated with water and the large bush above Moneysa became unstable and began to slowly topple both into the water and on to her.

I shouted in anguish, "NO - PLEASE - DEAR LORD – PLEASE SAVE MONNIE." Moneysa screamed as, tangled within the bush, she was slowly dragged beneath the water whilst I, seemingly in answer to my prayer, became filled with a strength hitherto not experienced. I tore at the branches oblivious to many deep scratches across my bare chest and arms until, with a mighty heave I lifted out of the water the section of bush in which Moneysa was trapped. I ducked beneath it and held its weight across my torn shoulders whilst pulling away the branches that had tried to drag Moneysa to her death.

Her eyes were closed, and she was shivering badly, but I could not move lest the bush break free from my support and do for us both. I scooped Moneysa up and held her close to my chest in an attempt to keep her warm despite the cooling effect of water which both lapped around us, and poured over us from above. Panic set in with the thought that helpers would not see us within the foliage so I tried to shout, but my vocal cords would not respond. Mentally and bodily I was beginning to weaken as wild and transient thoughts raced through my mind. One moment I felt feeble and inadequate; then I was a latter day Atlas bearing not the world but a large bush upon my shoulders.

Thankfully my delirium ended when a familiar voice restored my senses …"Thank you Charles….please hold me tight ….don't let me go ……I am lost without you …."

After those words Moneysa fell silent and began shivering violently as I became aware of voices around me.

My voice and confidence returned and with a mighty effort I bellowed, "Support the weight of this bloody bush so I can get Moneysa away to safety." The response was instantaneous and with the burden off my shoulders, and carrying Moneysa in my arms, I forged quickly towards the warmth of the house.

Very soon medical help arrived at the Ganton house having first confirmed that Drebar had indeed died in his sleep, and that his widow was in a state of deep shock, and his son Cymol was chanting a litany of Muslim prayers for the dead. Both were totally oblivious of the fact that Moneysa, in trying to get help, had almost lost her life in the process.

For several weeks, and with father's wholehearted approval, our house became a nursing home mainly because Lajila had turned into a recluse following the death of her husband. Her son Cymol, who played a leading role in his father's funeral rites, had become even more involved with mosque activities although father still financed his local education.

"In any event he would have been totally useless at my bedside," were the later comments expressed by his sister.

A bedroom had been converted into a hospital care room and Moneysa received daily visits from the site medical helper who was delighted with her progress. Initially the doctor visited her twice daily and nursed her through what he described as extreme shock, aggravated by loss of body temperature. Less severe, but no less painful, were the many superficial cuts and bruises received from her entanglement in the fallen bush. "I am sure you realise that without doing what you did, as quickly as you did, then she would surely have died," the doctor said with pride in his voice, whilst I struggled to contain my tears. Thus overcome I begged his pardon and retired to the veranda where, with my hands on the rail, I stared in silence at the crater left by a storm driven bush that had almost ended Moneysa's life.

To others the doctor's words may have sounded routine yet they awoke within me a profound realisation of my real feelings towards Moneysa. As I comforted her in my arms, whilst ensnared in that water logged bush, my single objective was to rescue Moneysa or die with her. Our precarious situation had awoken within me the truth that if she was to die then I could not, nay would not, face life without her.

I moved away from the rail determined to think this matter through; yet I was momentarily distracted by the question 'are those real tears running down my face or droplets of rain?' Slowly I walked to the open window of Moneysa's hospital room and gently parted the beaded cord blinds. She was sleeping peacefully yet my mind remained in turmoil. All that had recently happened had caused me to finally recognise that I was in love with a young girl from a different nationality and culture, despite being engaged to marry an English heiress with life as a country squire to look forward to. If my feelings became known and if, perchance, Monnie felt the same towards me, then the repercussions both here and in England would be catastrophic both for family and society.

Later within the comfort of my study armchair, fortified by a glass of quality brandy, I allowed my mind to relax and, as my emotions subsided, I dismissed my earlier wild thoughts as the meanderings of one still suffering from shock. Surely my future has been decided and there was no way back for me? After all why would this young Indian girl have any designs on an engaged Englishman who she thought of only in sisterly terms and, by tradition, her husband would be selected for her. "Wake up Charles and remember that Moneysa loves you only as her ever best friend. Those were her words and do not forget them," I muttered down to my brandy glass.

Without doubt I had been through a stressful time, and no one would deny that. My injuries were deep cuts to my shoulders, arms and chest following my battle with the errant bush and, initially, my appearance resembled that of an Egyptian mummy.

My attitude was one of total gratitude that I had been instrumental in saving Moneysa's life, yet in honesty, I did enjoy my burst of widespread popularity. My line directors in the East India office called me into the board room for praise and drinks whilst my father, with a break in his voice, thanked me for saving Moneysa and said he was sorry for giving me a hard time over my slowness to write to Elizabeth. In fact he took it upon himself, due to my initial disability, to write to the Salter family and acquaint them with what had happened.

CHAPTER EIGHT

A sister for Charles

It was now around November 1775 and both Moneysa and Charles had fully recovered from their ordeal and were working, respectively, at the site senior school and the Company head office. At the request of Edward Ganton Moneysa moved permanently into the Ganton house and her former nursing room was now her bedroom, and private study cum sitting room, for reasons not immediately obvious to me as an onlooker and recorder.

I persevered in this area and, in the fullness of time, I discovered two reasons for Edward Ganton's action.

The first was his fatherly love towards Moneysa who he looked upon as the daughter both he and his late wife Molly always wanted but never had.

Secondly was a cultural problem in that Drebar was dead and, by tradition, his widow and children should return to the nearby village of their origin and rebuild their lives. The requirements were simple in that Lajila should remarry and/or seek an attractive financial settlement through the arranged marriage of her daughter Moneysa who, at the age of 15, was both eligible and admired within the village. Lajila and Cymol had conformed to custom but Moneysa steadfastly refused to leave the Ganton house.

Matters came to a head when Moneysa, whilst visiting her mother in the village, was introduced to a village elder who promptly told her that she was to become his new wife. Without hesitation she rejected her elderly suitor using words that had left him dazed, and in no doubt about her revulsion towards him. In fact her tearful appeal to Edward Ganton, for his fatherly protection, was immediately granted and he advised the village hierarchy that all future contact with Moneysa would be through him.

However, matters came to a head when the Imam and two village elders, one of whom was an interpreter, requested an audience with Edward Ganton which he promptly granted for the following day.

He did not add that both Moneysa and Charles would be present at the meeting, and I presumed they would be there as witnesses to whatever the meeting was designed for. Sorry if I sound vague, but Edward Ganton was an astute business man who parted with just enough information to achieve total and lasting success for the project he had in mind.

Consistent with being an experienced business man he had set out his office in magistrate court fashion, with three chairs lined behind his desk, and an oil painting of a royal looking figure on the wall immediately above and behind his chair. The scene was made complete with the Union flag standing in one corner of the rear wall and an unfamiliar flag in the other; which I researched and found to be the Company flag (period 1707 to 1800) of the Honourable East India Company which I have copied:

Also from my memory of the royal painting I studied various references, and was satisfied that the portrait shown, which is of King George the third (1738 – 1820), was the one that I saw upon the office wall.

When we entered the room I was immediately enthralled by the awesome authority, displayed upon the rear wall, which left no doubt that my father represented a major world power that would both dominate and provide export income to the Indian mainland. Within this tabernacle of authority, and before the entry of the three local leaders, my father invited Moneysa, complete with approved dress and head covering, to sit on his left and I joined him on his right. Both Monnie and I were totally baffled as to the purpose of this meeting but father knew and that was all that mattered.

As an aside I noticed, for the first time, that Charles wore upon his left index finger a rather fine looking gold ring set with a central red ruby surrounded by what appeared to be small diamonds. Interspaced around the ring were small red stones that readily reflected sunlight. It is a fact that Charles paid attention to his appearance which caused me to wonder if this ring was to mark his engagement to Elizabeth Salter, whilst serving to impress the visitors waiting outside?

Upon entry the three men stopped abruptly and, looking aghast, huddled together in hurried and muffled conversation after which the group broke apart.

Then pointing to Moneysa one of them said, "There is a woman."

My father smiled and speaking slowly for the benefit of interpretation said, "Thank you for confirming that fact which means we are in total agreement from the onset of our meeting. Please sit down gentlemen and accept my gratitude for sharing a little of your valuable time this morning. I have a mixture of surprises and propositions that I have thought long and hard about and now, within this group, the time has come for decisions to be made so I will begin with the surprise."

Turning to Moneysa he said in a gentle voice, "We all still grieve the sad loss of your dear father Drebar and the illness of mind in which it has left your mother. At your age of 15 years fate has denied the presence of a father in your life just as my late wife and I were denied a daughter to add to our family joy."

I listened with awe and wondered what was coming next whilst Moneysa looked down at her right hand which she had spread upon the desk.

Placing his hand upon hers my father looked directly into her face and said, "Moneysa, I will be the happiest man alive if you will allow me to become your legal guardian with all the same rights as my two sons. It means you will have a father and three brothers and I will have the honour of calling you my daughter."

In the stunned silence all that came to my mind was that haunting tune that Elizabeth played upon the clavichord. It built to a crescendo and died away as Moneysa gave a sob and momentarily laid her face upon my father's hand. She quickly recovered and looking full at him said, "I have never felt so happy. Thank you, thank you. If you will have me I will try and become the best daughter you could hope for and a good sister to your sons."

In a moment of tenderness my father put his arm around Moneysa whilst she rested her head upon his shoulder.

Our three guests had been struck dumb throughout this scene but now found their voice which was immediately quelled when father raised his right hand and added, "Please gentlemen let me finish then you can have your turn to speak. I have now reached the stage when I can introduce what I called propositions which are brief and to the point.

In my role of Guardian I will ensure, and uphold to my last breath, that Moneysa will have the right to marry the man of her choice only when she is ready to do so. The choice will be entirely hers and not restricted to someone of a particular religion or way of life. I care not if her husband is a Christian, Muslim or Siamese cat worshipper as long as my daughter is happy in the same way that my late wife and I were."

Whenever father refers to my late mother emotion holds back his words but, after a few moments staring down at his desk, he raised his head and continued.

"Gentlemen I have regard and respect for your traditions which, as you know, I have turned to practical effect throughout my years in office. I am aware that Moneysa has been propositioned by an elderly member of your community in exchange for a cash dowry which would have been shared between her mother and the mosque for communal use. My proposal is that you will not lose out financially because I will undertake to rebuild your mosque which was badly damaged in this year's wet season, thus ending your need to worship within a somewhat dilapidated marquee."

For the first time I noticed smiles of approval upon the faces of our guests and one began to speak only for father to cut in and ask his forbearance for only a few more minutes.

"Finally I will retire from the East India Company during 1780 and have plans to return to my native home in England accompanied by my sons and new found daughter Moneysa."

With that Moneysa mouthed a hushed 'hurrah' whilst father poured a glass of water and quickly drank it. Our visitors, with heads bent towards each other, were engaged in deep conversation and father put them at ease with his non-committal, "Take all the time you need gentlemen."

In due course the interpreter, who was their elected spokesman, stood up and read from the hurried notes he had prepared at their dictation.

"Sir, we are grateful for your hospitality and your kind reception of our persons. Also we will always remember you for your continuing generosity both in providing work, giving food and financial support to our village followed by your recent kind offer to rebuild our mosque.

Our only concern is for Drebar's daughter, Moneysa, who was born a Muslim and, as such, can never leave the arms of Islam without incurring severe punishment both in this life and the next."

Father cut in with, "I thought I had made it clear that Moneysa will at all times make her own decisions, although guidance will be available if asked for, and if she wants to practice the Muslim faith then every help will be given for her to do so. With regard to the punishment to which you refer it will not be applicable in England and, if my ward is threatened before we leave, then your village will attract the attention of a unit of Dragoons less than one hour's ride from here."

Somewhat taken aback the interpreter mumbled, "Sorry, I did not intend what I said to be taken as a threat ....may I sit and talk again with my friends?"

Father nodded and then smiled at Moneysa and me.

About ten minutes later following a hubbub of voices and furious note taking the hard worked interpreter again rose to his feet.

"Sir," he began. "My friends have stressed that they meant no harm towards Moneysa or any members of the English community who have brought so much benefit to our lives. In truth we are concerned about her spiritual welfare and wondered, with respect, if when you return to England then perhaps her brother Cymol, who is a devout Muslim, could accompany you and hence support his sister in spiritual matters?"

Before replying father bent his head towards Moneysa who whispered something in his ear.

"I accept what you have said upon the violence issue and that matter is now closed. With regard to your request for Cymol to move with us to England then I am happy to report that Moneysa would welcome his presence together with their mother if she so desires. Should her mother choose to remain then I will arrange for a regular support income to be paid to her."

Essentially that was the end of the meeting and the visitors remained for cups of tea and polite conversation in the cool shade of the veranda.

At a later date I was present during periods of conversation from which I was able to elicit that Edward Ganton had quickly obtained full legal agreement for him to become Moneysa's guardian and that, true to his promise, work had commenced upon the new mosque building in the nearby village.

In a twice repeated statement father stressed to Moneysa and Charles that he would be the one to tell the Salter family about the guardianship order, and he would do this when the families were united in England in the year 1780. He said he preferred face to face situations when very important items were to be announced.

If Charles Ganton spent further periods in England with Elizabeth as previously agreed then he did so without my presence but, in retrospect, I suspect that he remained in India deeply engrossed in his new responsibilities within his father's office, until the family returned to England in 1780.

Contained in the many letters that Elizabeth despatched to Charles were messages for Moneysa which Charles would read aloud to her. In more recent communications these messages began to appear in the form of separate letters to Moneysa, which were received with great delight, since they were the first letters anyone had ever written to her. This, in turn, gave Moneysa her first experience of letter writing, and ownership of a dictionary, which further enhanced her significant verbal skills. I must add that Moneysa treasured her dictionary which I felt certain had been borrowed from the Company office because the worn gilt print on the cover suggested much handling. It was dark red in colour and all that remained of the cover title were the letters 'J..nso....'

Moneysa loved to read her letters from Elizabeth out loud to Charles and her guardian father, who she affectionately referred to as 'Papa'. Not a word was missed and punctuation marks were faithfully included which held her audience entranced when, in her musical accent, she read out such expressions as ....'My dear Moneysa comma ....' and 'it is a cool yet sunny day full stop.'

In particular was Elizabeth's great distress and concern over the bush incident which almost claimed Moneysa's life, followed by an outburst of delight, from Elizabeth, when she learned that Moneysa was to come and live in England. She had immediately instructed her dressmaker to plan a wardrobe containing a variety of English fashions to be ready for Moneysa's arrival in 1780. However, before *work could begin Elizabeth requested certain measurements that were essential to the project. In the absence of other females the site medical helper, who had previously nursed Moneysa back to health and also did community work for the Anglican Church, willingly agreed to measure and record the dimensions required.*

Finally Elizabeth expressed her great joy that Moneysa was now living in the Ganton house wherein it was her belief that she would have greater security, although she remained unaware of the now active guardianship order. She closed by reminding Moneysa that she was very special to both families and that she was always in their thoughts.

This expanded scheme for letter writing put Charles under greater pressure to respond more quickly which, perhaps, is what Elizabeth may have had in mind?

CHAPTER NINE

Final months in India (1778 – 1779)

When my father decided upon a certain course of action he was not slow to set his intent into motion, which is why he was such a success in his work. Hence it was no surprise to me when, over the breakfast table, he unexpectedly announced, "To honour the fact that we have worked very hard, and that it is Moneysa's 17th birthday, we will take a few days relaxation amidst the trees and cooler air. After all it is 1778 and we will soon leave India, perhaps for ever, when I retire in 18 months time. So let us enjoy what may be our last opportunity to relax in our mountain retreat."

Which, two days later, is exactly what we were doing as Moneysa and I enjoyed breakfast together on the veranda set in our forest location.

The tranquillity of that morning was broken only by the clink of our china cups until Moneysa declared, "In one way I will not be unhappy to leave my land of birth." I noticed a look of sadness upon her face as I asked, "Why is that?"

Inner grief had stilled her tongue as she arose and slowly walked down to the lakeside, and sat upon a viewing bench, that had been set in place since we last came. From the veranda I called to her, "I am here to help you Monnie. Do you want to be alone or shall I join you?" She turned and looked back at me then, with a half smile, she tapped the seat alongside her which was her way of saying 'yes.'

For a while we sat together in silence until, with a sigh, Moneysa began to share with me her concerns. "The attitude of the villagers is making me very sad Charles," she murmured almost to the lake. "When the news broke that I am now a legal member of an English family and also the guardian daughter of Mr Edward Ganton, which is for me the greatest honour I ever would have expected from this life, they in turn have chosen to treat me like a leper."

Whilst she was helping herself from the dish of grapes I had brought with me I added, "And it is my greatest honour that I can call you sister." She smiled at me and popping a grape into my mouth said, "Thank you my brother." At the same time I noticed the lake ripple to a sudden gust of light wind and realised, purely as an abstract thought, that the wind chimes were no longer in the trees.

"They have never threatened me nor would they dare after what Papa said, but as you know, for several years I have tried to help families who were sick, short of food or had other problems. Now they refuse my help and say that I have turned away from Islam and India. They often scream at me that I should repent and come back to them, dressed like a Muslim woman should, and then agree to marry a man from the village."

A look of total defiance came over her face when she declared, "I will never allow anyone to tell me who I must marry and Islam is filled with oppression towards females."

Pointing to a scarf which went around the top of her head and beneath her chin and finally hung over her left shoulder she said, "Take this headscarf, called an Odhani which I am told to wear in order to be modest and so prevent men from becoming excited at the sight of my hair." Whilst she was speaking Moneysa began to remove her Odhani and, throwing it over the back of the seat, she ran her hands through her long black hair so that it hung over her shoulders and down to the centre of her back. "Does my hair excite you Charles," she added with a wry smile, as I rapidly nodded my head in exaggerated enthusiasm.

"When I get to England I will never wear that thing again. Elizabeth said she will show me how to make my hair hang in ringlets like hers," declared Moneysa, with a smile, as she placed another grape in my mouth then ate one herself. "I know that Papa will like to be reminded of his wife through my chosen hair style."

Thereafter Moneysa never again returned to her native village and remained within the township provided for English residents. She paid a daily visit to her mother and brother who, for reasons unknown to me, had moved back into the Company house. Also she kept her religious obligations alive by attending house devotions celebrated by Cymol on special occasions.

Most of her day time was spent within the Ganton house studying spoken and written English together with receiving lessons in playing a clavichord that had been hired for her. In the evening she would dine with Papa and his son after which, she would have another chess lesson on the veranda from Charles, who she vowed to beat before the time came for them to go to England.

Up to Christmas 1779 life in the Ganton household passed smoothly and the Christmas celebration meal was a joyous occasion held in the presence of the newly ordained Brother John, who had returned via America, and was to

*accompany the family back to England. I was drawn within
Charles briefly whilst Moneysa was practising the clavichord
leaving Charles alone with his father and brother.*

"You fully deserve the honour the East India Company
has bestowed upon you Charles," announced my father.
Looking somewhat bemused Brother John asked, "What
honour?"

With a big smile father explained that an offer had been
made, in writing, for me to take over his former post with
effect from the first of January 1782 thus giving me time to
become accustomed to marriage whilst making arrangements
for the transfer of my household back to India.

Firmly shaking my hand Brother John wished me every
success and then asked if Elizabeth was happy to spend her
married life in India? Inwardly I cringed knowing full well
that father would not let me get away with a half answer,
which he quickly confirmed.

"Surely you have asked that question during your
exchange of letters Charles?" he asked with a depth of
meaning in his voice.

"Many times father but I have not got beyond her
ignoring the question altogether or dismissing it with a
vague 'we will talk about that when you come to England,
Charles.'"

*Time appeared to accelerate and early in the new year of
1780 there were the retirement dinners which Moneysa, as
the ward of Edward Ganton, was able to attend even if she
was the only Indian national sitting at a society table.*

*Her intelligence and quick wit, derived from her father,
Drebar, meant that she gave good account of herself and
really shone when many others were feeling the effects of
alcohol, which was a commodity that never passed her lips.*

The house furniture was Company property so only *clothing and personal items were packed, and despatched ahead to the dock warehouse, awaiting embarkation. On the night before the family's departure there was the thank you dinner for the household staff which was an emotional event because, without exception, the staff loved the Ganton family including Moneysa, its most recent addition. At the agreed time it was all over, hands were shaken and tears were shed, then the family retired for their last night in India.*

For several years it had been my tradition to awake early and take a walk along the veranda, breathing in the clear air of dawn, and this our last day was no exception. However I had just set foot outside when I became aware of a figure standing at the end of the veranda, seemingly gazing at the scenery whilst adjusting her hair.

I quietly approached and whispered, "Good morning Moneysa."

She turned, smiled and replied, "Good morning Charles. I was saying farewells to my birthplace and the happy memories of my lovely Papa Drebar."

I agreed that none of us would ever forget him and then I paused as I gazed at her face in the developing light of dawn. "Please know this Moneysa that I will never forget you whatever may happen to us in the future." She lowered her head and suddenly began to cry gently, as if to herself, and as I moved towards her she rushed into my arms.

My "Do not be upset Monnie…." was halted by her quick reply, "They are tears of happiness Charles as a mark of our deep friendship that began almost 15 years ago and is still growing." With that she kissed my shoulder where her head had been and, restored to her genial self, announced that she would wake up her mother and brother and then return for our morning feast of grapes on the veranda.

CHAPTER TEN

Final journey from India in England

It was the year 1780 as we embarked upon yet another voyage from India to England; only this was our first sea journey as part of a convoy with several other merchant ships all escorted by two mighty 74's, one of which was flying a Commodore's pennant, and several frigates that were the eyes and at times the teeth of the squadron. This was because of the clever buccaneering antics of fast and well armed American frigates who were wreaking havoc on our shipping, and even the English coast line as they pushed hard with their War of Independence.

However we quickly became accustomed to holding on to whatever was static in a world of creaking timbers, flapping sails and the curses of sailors as they fought to minimise the wild antics of a ship, in full sail, ponderously plunging on before the wind.

Brother John, Moneysa and I were fortunate in that the violent motions of the ship produced no ill effects within us but our father, together with Cymol and his mother, often felt disturbed and compelled to remain in the shelter of their quarters until the weather grew less severe.

In many ways we were honoured passengers aboard what was once a large three decked ship of the line, now 'cut down' to enter service as an East India Company merchant vessel; better known as an 'Indiaman.' On several occasions our party of six were invited guests, at the Captain's dinner table, after he discovered that our three Indian companions were not servants but, to quote my father, "They are adopted members of my family."

According to our experienced Captain he expected that, weather wise, the journey would be trouble free with the wind consistently in our favour. With modesty he claimed that it would confirm his good judgement to set sail, from India, in early May of the year when the weather was most favourable.

His decision meant we had a peaceful passage around the Cape and through the Bay of Biscay with our only major anxiety being the receipt of a signal, from a passing English frigate, advising us that we were now at war with France.

Our Captain had shrugged off this information as yet another minor skirmish with our traditional enemy, and went on to express his alarm that England was taking far too long to defeat the rebels in America.

Helped by good sailing conditions the journey lasted for around 18 weeks during which John and I spent much time, walking the lee side of the ship, discussing theology and his plans for the future either as a parish priest or a missionary in the colonies.

In the early days of our journey, when the weather was warmer and the sea less rough, Moneysa dressed in her sari and without her headscarf would often join us on the deck, in her words, "To watch over her older brothers." John and I were constantly amazed that despite her youthful age of 19 years she had the knowledge, and confidence, to richly add to our store of discussion topics. I clearly remember her view that compassion towards the needy dispensed with 'dusty theology' be it Islam, Hindu or Christian based.

This never failed to stir Brother John to launch upon the Lutheran 'justification by faith alone' edict which Moneysa, with a mischievous smile, countered with, "Am I alone in having faith in a God who wants me to help the poor?" These were not idle words because prior to her becoming father's ward she was always busy visiting the sick and troubled in her home village, and the neighbouring region but, as I explained earlier, those same villagers later turned their backs upon her as a traitor to Islam.

Almost as an aside I must share with you one clear memory of Moneysa appearing on deck, when the weather was windy and cold, wearing a large borrowed sea coat wrapped around her. In order to support herself she linked arms between John and myself as we, despite the weather, began a threesome walk along the deck.

When the ship swayed from side to side our threefold unity held firm cushioned, in turn, by John bouncing off the starboard safety rail and I from a line of coiled rigging rope. Predictably, there was only one outcome namely that of total confusion and merriment as we eventually collapsed in a tangled heap on the deck.

Few would argue against the fact that her developing personality, matched with a lively mind, was in stark contrast to her older brother Cymol who, although regarded as a family member, remained a respectful servant and, though he never openly said it, lived the philosophy that Moslems and Christians could never mix. His work outlet had been in the local village Mosque having been appointed junior Imam with pastoral responsibilities, which were extended with his new commission to travel to England as spiritual advisor to his sister. So far he disapproved of her walking the deck without head covering but his protests were literally lost to the wind.

Sometimes in the cool of the evening my father would venture on deck and add his wide knowledge to whatever we were debating but, as we often laughed, he had the knack of steering the topic around to his love of the Moravian faith and, in particular, his strong adherence to the doctrine of Predestination. Also on our agenda was the news received from strongly Protestant Dutch East India officials, when we docked in Cape Town, of a recently passed 'Papist Act' that scrapped certain penalties imposed upon Catholic subjects during the reign of King William III. Already there had been minor skirmishes in London, involving damage to Catholic houses, and full scale riots were feared in the near future.

Less frequently Cymol would join us wearing his seamless long collarless shirt, over white trousers, complete with a circular white prayer cap which was traditional dress for a devout Moslem. Although his sister Moneysa had an excellent knowledge of the English language, resulting from my father paying for her education to the same level as both John and myself, Cymol remained suspicious of English (Christian) delivered education and, supported by my father, was taught exclusively in a local mosque school.

His mother Lajila rarely came on deck and was happy to sit in her own silent world or carry on with a sort of floral pattern embroidery and, when anyone praised her work, she would point to it and say something sounding like 'cutch.' Her knowledge of the English language was on par with my strength in the Urdu tongue, which made for limited conversation without Moneysa to act as translator.

However our regular Sunday services were free from verbal discord and followed the Book of Common Prayer in accordance with the traditions of the English and Protestant state church. In the opening weeks of our voyage the service was held from the quarterdeck with the entire crew assembled on the main deck. Naval tradition meant that the Captain led the service although father and Brother John took it in turns to preach above the sound of flapping sails and the creaking of the timbers. In colder and rougher weather a service was held in the Great Cabin with only selected crew members present.

Moneysa regularly attended these services, much to the disapproval of Cymol who consistently lived his devotion to Islam in their fixed time prayer sessions, having determined from the helmsman where east and hence Mecca could be found.

Despite the relative hardships of several weeks at sea our family spirit did not wane and evenings would be spent, dependant upon the weather, either on the deck or below being entertained by Indian folk songs sung by Moneysa accompanied by Cymol playing the Sitar or a small hour glass shaped drum fastened around his neck. I believe this instrument bore a name that sounded like 'Dumara.'

Forgive me for interrupting but I wish to stress a point with you.

I know you will appreciate that if I were the author of a fictitious 'novel in process,' rather than the biographer of Charles Ganton, then I would have made much more of a lengthy ship journey from India to the newly built East and West India docks in London. Most authors would not hesitate to include a sea battle or a storm of hurricane proportions.

Be assured that at no time was I tempted to include such readable and graphic incidents because, in fact, they did not occur. It has been very important to me, throughout the decades since these memories began, to carefully retain this developing history, free from the imagination of Charles Cane, which may be the reason why it has taken over sixty years for this distant, but real life story, to finally appear in print for your consideration.

What you are reading are the memories which Charles Ganton chose to retain, since they meant something to him, and are now entrusted to me as he relates his story through my pen.

When the time came for us to say farewell to our Captain, and leave his ship moored to a quay side strewn with barrels, horse drawn carts and greasy cobble stones our hearts were beating fast because of the occasion. We had, together with our beloved and adopted family, come to stay and soon I would be the husband of Elizabeth and, perhaps, a future squire in the making. As I glanced towards Moneysa I felt that, as an added gift, I had brought the joys of India with me.

But we were not yet in the countryside. What made an early impact upon us was the noise and bustle of the dockside in the flickering gloom of wall mounted oil lamps and the stench of open drains with rats freely swimming in the murky water. Gloomy buildings overhung narrow streets covered with muddy straw that was home to beggars, thieves and vendors of all manner of goods ranging from faded flowers to dubious bread cakes whilst their less enterprising colleagues, awash with gin and grog, staggered or crawled their way to oblivion. I once overheard a coach driver explaining how difficult it was to pick their way through dockland streets and despite cracking their whips, and hurling obscenities at the throng, accidents did happen beneath the coach wheels; leaving the injured or dead to be cleared away by feral dogs and ever obliging rats.

It was a dreadful scene to behold and just as father was about to close the carriage curtains Moneysa gasped in horror at the sight of a drunken woman holding her baby by its leg as, one handed, she fought with and screamed abuse at a man; all for no obvious reason.

"I am pleased that alcohol plays no part in Muslim and Hindu lives," retorted Cymol with a hint of challenge in his voice. For once we had no answer other than to silently record the worth of his words.

However the ever resourceful Brother John skilfully changed the subject when he nudged me and said, "At least we have not been greeted by those wretched bells on this occasion," to which I heartedly agreed.

Although it was early September in 1780 cold penetrating mists already held both London and us in its grip, causing us to recall the distant warmth we had left behind. Happily our Indian staff, between moments of weeping over our departure, had, thoughtfully, packed cloaks and warm coats in our trunks. We were thankful to don these items before disembarkation.

Thus the journey began which, to me as your narrator, was very disjointed in that Charles Ganton clearly had nothing of significance to report. Although I was present with the family during the stage coach journey that led them from London towards their new home, wherever that was to be, I was 'held' as a spectator for reasons that still are not clear.

Obviously the Ganton family knew where they were heading but, as I have previously indicated, I could not ask questions and must be content with recording what was said, or what significant points central to the mind of Charles Ganton may draw me into his person.

I did note that the sun began its process of 'setting' upon the left hand side of my position, within the coach, thus telling my mental compass that we were travelling in a northerly direction. I was conscious of the incessant noise of coach wheels, and rocking of the carriage, as our four horse driving force literally tore through the countryside to the sound of the driver's post horn as our coach approached crossroads, or when stopping at appointed roadside inns in order to change horses and allow us to refresh ourselves.

With regard to our destination I twice heard, above the noise of wheels upon uneven roads, Edward Ganton refer to 'Bridge' but further qualification was lost due to the prevailing noise of our journey. I established we were to be the guests of Derbie and Elizabeth Salter and their daughter Elizabeth who was betrothed to Charles. At one stage Edward Ganton reminisced how he and Derbie Salter placed a high value on their lifetime of friendship that was measured by 'turn about' family reunions held in India and England on more than one occasion.

I was staggered to learn this and that Charles Ganton, for reasons known only to him, had found no motive to mention these sequence visits in his dictation for posterity. Alternatively I may have misunderstood the gist of the conversation due to the noise and motion of the fast moving coach. Nevertheless I felt bound to draw your attention to my concerns albeit they are of no real consequence to the main flow of my narrative which, perhaps, may be the reason that Charles did not waste his energy and time reporting what was perhaps perimeter detail.

To my belief the significant feature of these reunions was the rather one sided romance which blossomed between Elizabeth Salter and Charles Ganton and their engagement to be married, in England, when the Ganton family finally left India.

Our previous freedom of the deck was now severely restricted to the confines of horse drawn transport. On one side of the coach father sat between his two sons and I faced Moneysa who, with Cymol, sat on either side of their mother. Fortunately there was an ample supply of coach blankets to cover our legs and even pull up to our necks if we so desired. We yawned, dozed for a while, talked, read or just sat lost in thought. What has kept alive the memory of this otherwise inconsequential journey was one incident that was born from humour and, perhaps, went on to sink its roots in prophesy? Moneysa broke the silence when she said in pretend seriousness, "Charles, please keep still and I will draw you." The coach windows were heavily coated with condensation and, with artistic bravado Moneysa, using her finger, drew my face upon the window. It took the form of a large circle with two small circular eyes, an upturned 'V' for a nose and an almost ear to ear half circle smile. Beneath the face she traced the initial 'C.'

Laughter followed and, as it died away, the high level of humidity had its effect upon the window drawing. The boundary of one of the caricature eyes broke free and ran down the face as if shedding a tear. Immediately Moneysa said, "Do not cry dear Charles for now is the time to be happy. Sadness belongs to tomorrow."

I smiled, but that simple incident left an unexpected chill within.

To a long blast on the post horn the coach rumbled to a halt. Eagerly Ganton senior leaned forward and, opening the coach window announced, "We have arrived," followed by acclamations of "Thank you Lord" from John and "Allah be praised" from a travel worn Cymol. Such was the joy of the passengers that they paid no attention to a stream of obscenities from the drivers as they cracked their whips at a group of dogs yapping at the horse's legs.

Above the sound of horses snorting and the coach grinding to a halt I heard a loud rustic voice clearly shout "Greta Bridge," which was repeated a few moments later followed by an invitation to disembark and head for the welcoming glow of the coaching inn.

CHAPTER ELEVEN

Reunion at Greta Bridge

We slowly descended from the coach into the icy embrace of a cold northerly wind that brought tears to our eyes, and speed to our feet, as we rapidly crossed the inn yard. As I stood aside for the ladies to enter a reception room I glanced back at a group of men, under the supervision of uniformed coachmen, who were transferring our belongings onto the storage areas of two ornate coaches waiting nearby. My muttered, "Thank you for your labours" was immediately lost in a wraith of condensed breath that faded into the cold work zone I had gratefully left behind.

Quickly we were directed to a door that led into a private guest room which had been prepared for our reunion with the Salter family and invited guests.

Sensing our joint apprehensions of what lay within father paused, turned, and gave each of us a smile and a nod of encouragement, after which he knocked and opened the door wide for us to make our long awaited entrance.

The gratifying sight of logs piled high upon a convivial fire, with its radiance reflected on the many welcoming faces around us, restored our warmth and confidence which combined to draw us into the spirit of good will that reigned in that room.

What a reunion it was.

I would gladly wager the national debt that no other would surpass it in terms of happy voices, tears of expectation and the sheer joy of being together again. It was a mercy that father and his friend Derbie Salter did not shake off each others arms, or indeed lose contact with their feet, as they closed together in a merry jig around the floor; thus throwing aside the reserve normally expected from traditional family leaders. Everyone, be they a total stranger or distant friend, descended upon us with the intention of introducing themselves, and to learn more about us as future members of their social community.

In the midst of this joyous turmoil Elizabeth pushed her way over to me, held both my hands and, pretending to study my face declared that I had grown younger. With a quick kiss upon my cheek she was over to Brother John, leaving me with an elderly man who regaled me with the time he played cards with the prime minister.

Next was the delightful sight of Elizabeth and Moneysa with their arms wrapped round each other crying with reunited happiness, and Elizabeth declaring that Moneysa was now an attractive young woman who was destined to become the target and heartbreak of many a young man.

Then the two families embarked upon an interchanging pattern of greetings in which Moneysa, Cymol and their somewhat bemused mother were fully involved.

Finally the excitement of meeting was replaced by what can only be described as a thoroughly genial group, seated round a traditional English inn fireplace, enjoying their newly restored presence amidst friends new and old. Servants rushed around with trays of refreshments then discreetly sank into the background as the two family heads prepared to address the gathering before them.

Elizabeth caught my eye and smiled as her father adjusted his beloved wig and rose to his feet with the expected, but sincerely meant, words of joy and gratitude that our families were finally together and, by the grace of God, would so remain for many years to come.

For the benefit of many non-family members present he described that my father and he had been close friends, for more years than he could remember, and the pinnacle of their friendship was that the two families would soon be united through the marriage of his daughter Elizabeth to his son Charles.

I did not fail to notice Elizabeth discreetly dab away tears born from the emotion of the moment, but these turned to 'downfalls of joy' following the unexpected announcement that, as an early wedding present from her parents, a house had been purchased in her name.

When silence was restored he moved on to his next gift which, subject to the approval of its now current owner Elizabeth Salter, was that the Ganton family could if they so wished, use this property as their first residence in the county until they had chance to look around the area.

He then, to a ripple of applause, explained that plans were in place for our marriage to be solemnized during the spring of next year and, to loud cries of delight, he announced that it would be a county event with no shortage of titled guests present. Unable to suppress her emotions any longer Elizabeth burst into tears of joy as I put my arm around her shoulder whilst trying very hard to contain my own emotions for, after all, I was destined to become the stiff upper lipped head of the household. Soon Elizabeth returned to smiles and, amidst applause, Derbie Salter sat down and poured himself a generous glass of port wine to mark the occasion.

Much to my surprise, and with tears still present on her face, Elizabeth stood up and thanked her father and mother for being such loving parents and how proud she was to be their daughter. Her concluding remarks, although spontaneous, won over many hearts, young and old, with "I would like to assure all present that the Ganton family are welcome to live in my house, for as long as they wish, at a rental charge of constant care and kisses from my husband when I take residence as Mrs. Charles Ganton.

The originality of her terms of residence attracted a hilarious response, from the many that descended upon Elizabeth and me, and their goodwill was shown through hands slapping my back aided by a range of voices hollering good wishes in my ears.

Yet I felt strangely distant from all that was happening. I was fully aware of all that had been said but I was not part of it because my inner self had mentally drifted away. I was nothing more than a distant spectator to the slow motion happiness of someone else, whereas the real me was wandering along a forest path humming lullabies to Moneysa, who was asleep in my arms. It was so peaceful and I so much wanted my walk with Monnie to never end, but it was not to be.

My reverie ended when someone shook my shoulder and a male voice bellowed, "Wake up Charles, too early for sleep. We are waiting to hear from you." I returned to reality when another well wisher thrust a glass of wine into my hand which I instantly drank and, with false bravado rose to my feet.

Noting Elizabeth's smile of approval I thanked Mr and Mrs Salter for their good wishes and generosity that had reached its pinnacle with the gift of their daughter as my future wife. Then on behalf of my own family I agreed to the tenancy conditions required by Elizabeth, and stressed that it was always my policy to pay all my commitments in advance of the required date.

With that, and to the delight of all present, I pulled Elizabeth to her feet and promptly kissed my future wife to a burst of cheers, laughter and applause that may have been heard throughout the entire county. After she had regained her breath and composure Elizabeth thanked me for my prompt attention to requirements, but did add that interest may be required at a later date.

Here there was a lull in the proceedings, and genial chatter took over, as father and Derbie Salter huddled together in quiet conversation whilst I sank once more into silent thought; particularly over my recent public display of tenderness towards Elizabeth.

That inner voice was again, from its throne of conscience, challenging my every action. "Charles was that public display of affection towards Elizabeth genuine or just a way of reminding yourself that Moneysa must now begin to lose prominence in your life?"

Some distance away I could see Moneysa in conversation with the parents of a young man who had just been introduced to her; seemingly happy and unmoved by my public show of affection towards Elizabeth.

"After all Charles," my private tormentor continued. "You grew up together and are looked upon as brother and sister. Soon she will fall in love, marry and move out of your immediate life as you, when husband to Elizabeth, will move out of hers. Your once ever best friend will become just another face from the past."

Suddenly everyone was clapping and I immediately joined with them in total ignorance of what it was about; yet it did release me from myself.

Then I was aware that father had begun his address that covered his version of most of the points raised by Derbie Salter, together with his earnest wish that my mother could have been present upon this day of all days.

He then gained the deep interest of everyone present with what he called 'the era of Drebar and his family' and how, prior to his death in 1775, the entire family regarded him not as a servant but as the very backbone of the family.

"In fact he will never die while we have his daughter, son and widow with us today," added father as, with an inward movement of his arm, he symbolically drew Moneysa and her family into the centre of his life.

"However after Drebar's death they were required, by local tradition, to return to their village of birth which, reluctantly, they agreed to do."

Father paused to both quench his thirst prior to revealing all that had happened following the death of Drebar, which had remained a family secret waiting this day.

"Lajila was faced with the option of finding another husband or arranging suitable terms for the marriage of her daughter to a village elder," father said as he paused to survey the many shocked faces before him, and the realisation that he had his audience hanging on his every word.

He slowly played to the emotions of all present when he stressed that almost immediately an ancient village widower offered Lajila a sum of money, and a small plot of land, in return for the hand of her daughter in marriage.

This was met with a gasp of amazement that such transactions really happened and the young man standing close to Moneysa, with arms folded, adopted a protective role that was obviously to the fore of his mind.

In true theatrical style father judged that the time had arrived to begin to defuse the passions he had generated as, with a smile, he assured them, "That Moneysa, despite her then tender age of 15, was not going to agree lightly to such a deal. He described that even then her knowledge of the English language was excellent, to the point of including some of the cruder expressions of our speech, that were made all the more humorous when delivered in her lovely accent," concluded father as, with a smile, he sat down and viewed their stunned silence.

"Do you really wish to know what happened next?" He asked whilst suppressing his urge to burst out laughing.

As with one voice his audience responded with a very loud, "Yes please."

Father had successfully whetted the ears of all present except for Moneysa, who visibly wilted at the prospect of her un-lady like remarks being made public.

Knowing what was to follow I fixed my gaze upon Moneysa who, sensing the embarrassment to come, turned and with a muttered, "Oh no," ran and hid her face on Elizabeth's shoulder.

Father went on to describe that in no uncertain terms she had dismissed her would be suitor and, beside herself with rage, had run from the village and straight into his study, having brushed aside two amazed house servants in the process.

After a token half curtsey she told me what had happened and declared betwixt tears and anger, "That she would never marry that fat old man whose breath was as foul as a dog's fart."

With that the entire company erupted into torrents of laughter and, after initial embarrassment, Moneysa joined in the mirth. A full five minutes elapsed before the gathering of family and friends settled down, free from giggles, and more at ease now that the curtain of sadness and death had been raised by united laughter and joviality.

At this stage of his address father paused whilst a waiter filled his wine glass, after which he quickly reduced its content to half level, and continued with, "My friends I will now share with you one of the most important decisions I have ever made. Following the tragic death of her father, Drebar, and the vulnerability of his 15 year old daughter to the rules of tradition, I decided to apply legal stability to our simple acceptance of Moneysa as a family member.

Thus, in accordance with the English family law system, I am now the legal guardian of Moneysa and I call her my daughter with the same affection as if she were the daughter that Molly and I were denied. This means that I will soon regard myself as the proud father of two lovely daughters, Elizabeth and Moneysa which makes me the happiest man alive."

This announcement was greeted with loud applause and the clinking of glasses as toasts of goodwill were proposed.

When relative silence fell upon the group father announced that he could not sit down until he had publically declared his thanks to Elizabeth for her part in uniting the two families. Looking at Elizabeth, and noting her smile of gratitude, he went on to ask for her help in another very important area.

"As you know Moneysa is very keen to try out the latest fashions that grace the female wardrobe and I look forward to seeing her dressed as we have never seen her before. Also it would suit Moneysa to have warmer clothes to wear that were, hitherto, unnecessary in the Indian climate."

To the delight of all present Moneysa, in her rich musical accent, replied with an impassioned, "Yes please, Papa."

Father then invited every one to refill their glasses and began with, "Ladies and gentlemen please be upstanding with me in a toast to Elizabeth, Charles and Moneysa that they will be abundantly blessed in their lives ahead."

After the group response father turned to hurl his glass into the distant fireplace but, in the interests of safety, he thought better of it and returned it to the table.

Quickly, and much to my surprise, Elizabeth stood up and confirmed that come tomorrow Moneysa would be introduced to her new wardrobe and additional clothing was available for Cymol and his mother if they desired to wear them. She went on to explain to Moneysa that she had brought the first of her new garments with her because it was very necessary in the current cold English weather.

That was the prearranged signal for a staff member to appear carrying a lady's woollen, silk lined cloak and hood edged with fur.

From my viewing of the coat I was able to research and tentatively identify the item as an 18th century cloak known as a Pelisse.

With a cry of delight Moneysa rushed forward, tried the garment on, and after three twirls of excitement declared, "It is a perfect fit," and rushed over to thank Elizabeth with a kiss upon her cheek. Still admiring the coat Moneysa stroked it with both hands, held it to her face, and said that for the first time she was without words.

Suddenly she reached up and removed her Odhani allowing her long black hair, which literally shone in the room light, to fall upon her shoulders and part way down her back. I heard a suppressed gasp of admiration which turned to gentle applause when Moneysa rolled up the Odhani and presented it to Elizabeth who received it with grateful thanks.

Perhaps I was the only one to notice Cymol slowly shake his head and stare down at the table in front of him.

At around midnight the reception party began to disperse into the freezing night air and I was invited to ride along with Elizabeth in the Salter family carriage which, after standing outside for several hours, was as cold as an ice container.

Elizabeth and I simultaneously sat down together only for me to leap up when the icy nature of the seat made its presence felt in my lower regions. "Having all these fashion layers around me does have an advantage," declared Elizabeth with a laugh.

Mr and Mrs Salter gingerly sat down facing us and, in an instant, two servants had the travelling blankets around us and our feet snugly in a half blanket containing a ceramic hot water bottle. Beneath the blankets Elizabeth held my hand tightly and remarked that it was a little cooler than in India, to which our teeth seemed to chatter their agreement as we began our journey to my new home.

"That was a very brave thing you did in saving Moneysa from drowning Charles," remarked Mr Salter.

I tried to shrug the compliment off with a smile whilst adding, "At least the water was warm, unlike the air around us at the moment."

A mixture of tiredness and contentment stilled our tongues as we drifted into a half sleep until, without warning, the sudden blast of the post horn caused Mr Salter to remark, "Home sweet home," as the scrape of iron gates upon gravel told me that we were about to enter the driveway to the Salter family residence.

CHAPTER TWELVE

The Ganton family at Salter Grange

In no time both families were seated, in peaceful harmony, around a roaring log fire set in an ornate drawing room that offered, following the gentle pull of a bell cord, a wide range of drinks to suit all tastes.

It was not long before an uncomfortable looking Cymol begged leave to retire as it was time for his mother to go to bed. Instantly all the men stood as mother and son were shown to their respective rooms by one of several maids who had been allocated, by Derbie Salter's butler, to act as personal servant to the visitors he had placed in their care.

The men had hardly regained their chairs when Elizabeth stood up and declared that she and her mother were to introduce Moneysa to her new clothes. Immediately Moneysa sprang to her feet and, filled with joy and excitement, she waved to all the men as she was swept upstairs by the two Elizabeth's, followed by Ruth, who had been chosen to be Moneysa's exclusive maid.

As if from nowhere a servant, bearing a tray complete with a brandy decanter and four brandy glasses, quickly appeared and the men settled down to seriously consider a variety of irrelevant topics, as they fought to retain their eyelids in an open position.

Eventually we retired at what was, for me, a late hour and sleep was my welcoming partner within a truly luxurious bed.

Charles Ganton was a man of habit which did not change during his residence in England.

He liked to rise early and have a bath in his wooden tub, or a standing wash down which, in the Indian hot and high humidity season, was essential to his daily wellbeing. Of course there was no shortage of Indian servants to carry large containers of hot water, in shoulder yoke manner, from a detached boiler room which contained a large metal drum heated over a wood fired stove.

He frequently commented that on his visits to England he enjoyed the comforts of the Salter residence except for its lack of washing facilities which, at the best, were restricted to the traditional bowl, jug and wash stand in each bedroom. Charles had stressed that these receptacles must be filled with hot water to accommodate his need of them at 5.00am each day.

As an aside I must add that this was my second only visit to England, whereas Charles seemed to infer that there may have been more. Be that the case then, for reasons unknown, Charles did not declare them within his dictated narrative.

Out of interest I researched the attitude of 18th century gentry to daily washing and found them to be severely wanting. I concluded that cleanliness was not a very important issue at the time and many preferred to combat body odours with an abundance of perfume or scented powders and oils.

It was 6.15am and much to the amazement of junior servants, who had been busy since at least 4.00am, I wished them the blessings of the new day as I strode out of the double front doors, down the wide stone entrance stairway and on to the gravelled driveway. It was very cold and my condensed breath followed me like a wraith afraid to leave its founder's presence.

To the rear of the house I could hear snorting and muffled shouting as the horses were being moved from the warmth of the stables into a nearby paddock. The sound of their metallic shoes in the paved stable yard appeared to be amplified on that calm, frost coated morning; but I took heart as the approaching dawn began to resurrect the eastern horizon and early birds told of life within dark and frost coated bushes.

Following a bout of stamping my feet and blowing warmth into my clenched hands I turned and looked back at the Salter manor house which, in the half light, was a picture of magnificence as was, in the envious eyes of many, my status as fiancé to Elizabeth who was heiress to all I could see, not forgetting hidden wealth carefully preserved and invested by dusty family solicitors. Yet the same recurring question plagued me in the form of, 'Is this the life style you really want to practise along your pathway to the grave?'

With my mind as sharp as the ice around me I reviewed my relationship with Elizabeth. After all Christmas Eve in 1771, when Elizabeth and I were 17 and 19 years old respectively, was an almost magical time to fall in love. More so when immersed in the beauty of Indian surroundings and the glory of the season, which eclipsed any talk of where we would live when joined together. Would not talk of this nature be tantamount to heresy against the fairy tale life we had chosen for ourselves?

Also in those days I was still a student and not averse to the prospect of life without serious purpose; but now I had proved myself to the senior directors of The Honourable East India Company, who had rewarded me with the promise of high command in a work discipline I am passionate about. The thought of walking away from my employers, in favour of social idleness, was becoming more and more abhorrent to me such that I resolved to discuss the matter with Brother John, in his role of confidant and spiritual advisor.

As I walked back towards the house I felt depressed over the fact that Elizabeth enjoyed her present life style and was unwilling to discuss living with me as my wife in India. My depression deepened at the prospect of a family meeting designed to address this problem, which was planned to take place before the end of the week, causing me to stumble over the top step to the discomfort of my already frozen great toe.

With the door closed it still required a full ten minutes to restore warmth to those inner parts despite the attentions of a glorious log fire, on full draw in the dining room fireplace, above which a Salter ancestor, immortalised in oils, frowned down upon those who had cause to be in his presence.

Standing with my back towards this warmth I judged, from the urgency of footsteps above me, that both families were in their various stages of preparation and some had already congregated outside the closed door. I could hear subdued voices and muffled laughter as the party assembled; yet for reasons unknown they chose not to join me immediately in the dining room and were, perhaps, waiting to enter as a complete family unit.

Suspecting that Moneysa had another one of her 'fun surprises' in mind, and derived from years of experience in this area, I decided to stand fast and await the outcome which began with a gentle knocking on the door. With a voice in character I invited those without to "Come in" and immediately the double doors were thrown wide open and I had a fleeting view of smiling family members and giggling maids in abundance.

Then a radiantly happy Moneysa walked slowly into the room, stopped before me and turned a full circle before saying, "Hello Charles, am I still your ever best friend?"

In truth a heart composed of stone would have shattered with the love and loyalty that Moneysa, her hands held slightly apart, appeared to offer as she repeated those oft used and much treasured words. It was very clear to me, and perhaps all present, that my opinion of her appearance meant everything to her. Instantly my inner turmoil fled as I gazed upon her in a few moments of suspended time, while the haunting tune which Elizabeth named 'our melody' briefly filled my mind.

I would fail in my task if I did not attempt to describe to you what Charles saw that affected him in the way he described. Moneysa was wearing a close fitting, dark blue cloth redingote with two shoulder capes, a wide collar and long sleeves, fastened at the waist. The sleeves were edged with pale blue frills offering a pleasing contrast to her small yet shapely brown hands. This long outer garment revealed a lace fichu at the neck and the skirt of her blue taffeta gown was enhanced with a frilled hem. She wore a simple veiled bonnet over her rich dark tresses arranged in curls with ringlets over her right shoulder.

Charles appeared mesmerised by Moneysa's appearance which is understandable since he had never seen Moneysa wear anything other than an Indian sari and Odhani as they grew up together. You will recall that Molly, the late wife of Edward Ganton, always wore her hair in ringlets to please her husband who had often told Moneysa of his love of that particular hair style. Hence it was not surprising that, out of her love for Papa, Moneysa chose to adopt a similar fashion.

I must not forget to add that Moneysa wore a necklace bearing a dark red pendant which, I later learned, had belonged to her late grandmother (mother of Drebar) and was worn entirely at her insistence, against the advice of her maid, dresser cum hairstylist Ruth, who considered the necklace to be 'out of place.'

The tune faded and I heard my seemingly distant voice becoming clearer with, "I will forever be your best friend Moneysa; that is if a beautifully dressed and eligible young woman like yourself has any time left for the dull person standing before you."

Moneysa, playing her audience, stood in pretend thoughtful mode with her hand touching her chin and looking down at the floor, before giving a confident, "All my time is yours Charles but with one condition."

Clearly the entire gathering was agog to hear just what her condition was to be as I jovially replied, "Then tell me about your proviso in order that I may grant it."

With a wide smile her instant answer was, "That I can continue to steal your grapes without you chasing me around the garden."

Everyone present appreciated the surface humour whereas I was left struggling with a new surge of inner turmoil as I fought to understand all that was happening within me. Looking at Monnie I could sense that we were both oblivious to other people as we stared at one another as if we were strangers meeting for the first time. Where was the five year old child holding a strange woollen creature by its long neck; with ease I recalled an eleven year old girl who I saved from drowning; but now Moneysa was a twenty year old Indian national looking radiant in English dress and, seemingly, a new bond was drawing us even closer together. Was it that our friendship had matured from a simple brother and sister childhood relationship to an all embracing unity of emotions, with eternal consequences?

Steadfastly we looked fully into each others eyes as if searching for answers when the spell was broken by Mr Salter, ringing a hand bell, which was the signal for us to take our places at the breakfast table. Our host sat at one end of the table with Elizabeth and myself at his right and left sides respectively, whilst father occupied the other end with Moneysa and Brother John as immediate companions. Yet I could not turn my eyes away from Moneysa, who suddenly was no longer 'little sister,' but a beautiful young woman who returned my fixed gaze with a smile that filled my life with renewed hope and comfort.

At the risk of repetition I will remind my readers that, where possible, I attempt to prove the accuracy of what I see and hear in order to confirm the legitimacy of my narrative. Within this remit the breakfast scene gave me a further opportunity for research mainly due to the questions asked by Cymol, in his search for food that was compatible with Islamic traditions both for his mother and himself.

Adjacent to the wall at the greatest distance from the fire was a mahogany buffet table with pedestal legs and five cutlery drawers. Set in the centre of this table was a silver lidded tureen, complete with two handles and four curved legs that contained an ample supply of fried bacon. Access was gained by sliding rather than lifting the lid.

Nearby was a free standing table upon which was a silver hot water container, in the design of a trophy cup, but with a tap situated at its base. There were several other items which were less visible, but I was able to confirm that the three reported sightings were consistent with the Georgian period around the year 1780.

Without doubt it was a substantial breakfast and although the sideboard was set out in buffet manner, it was not used as such, given that nine sitting around the table were skilfully catered for by four very experienced and attentive servants.

Beautifully hand written menus were displayed on the table but, unfortunately, I was never in a position to read them hence I was grateful to Cymol, whose afore mentioned questions, gave further documentary evidence in support of my narrative.

Sadly he got off to a bewildering start when he caught the attention of a serving maid and, in a moment of confused language, asked her a question in Arabic which caused great bafflement to both the servant and many sitting around the table.

Immediately Moneysa took the initiative and reminded her brother that he was not in the mosque but sitting around an English breakfast table where Arabic was not regularly spoken. She then provided the girl with the following English translation, "Please tell my brother what food is available." The servant's reply enabled me to record some of the menu items that graced an 18th century breakfast table including bacon, sardines, smoked herrings, sausages, potato dishes, fresh bread rolls, marmalade and a variety of jams followed by tea, coffee or vintage brandy.

Understandably Moneysa and her family declined both bacon and sausages but made up for it through various other items provided according to their needs.

Following that rather substantial breakfast we declared what our individual plans for the day were to be, after which we retired to our separate rooms to rest awhile until the late autumn sunshine had dispelled the frost. My bedroom contained a small but effective log fire, with tongs at hand and plenty of wood in reserve, bearing tribute to my new world of comfort in which my every need was catered for. Compared with the Salter amenities my way of life in India was relatively basic and yet, I mused, all I have is a constant yearning to go home to the country in which I was born. I stretched out in the fireside armchair and tried to come to terms with reality as my eyes, fixed upon the ceiling, followed a spider seemingly searching for a corner in which to hibernate. I laughed to myself as I recalled that, in India, spiders were the least on a list of uninvited house visitors which was headed by monkeys. Those creatures walked around towns and villages scavenging for food and, on several occasions, I had to chase them out of my bedroom and be faced with the dilemma: 'closed window means hot room but no monkeys.'

"What the hell am I thinking about monkeys for," I said out loud as I leapt up and walked over to the window. "Think of today Charles and recall the agreed programme."

Elizabeth and I were to be driven, in a two horse chaise, to view the house which Mr Salter had donated as our wedding present which, as I understood, was a fair distance away. Moneysa was to have her daily instruction session with Brother John to enable her to be admitted as a member of the Church of England during the next few weeks. To date Cymol was totally unaware of this development but it was consistent with the terms of the guardianship agreement.

As for Cymol he and his mother had retired to their double room which was separated by an inner connecting door. Lajila was, in mental terms, in a poor way as she only recognised her son, and now that Moneysa's dress style had changed she may wonder who her daughter was.

"Not so with me," I muttered out loud, "I still remember Moneysa as an obscure young village child who wandered into my life and we effectively grew up as brother and sister but now, but now. Oh, come on Ganton and get ready to accompany your wife to be," I literally snarled to myself as I plunged my face into a large basin of water on the washstand.

The outcome of the visit made by Elizabeth and Charles to their future home is unknown for at no stage was I drawn into their presence. You will recall from my opening scenario that Charles Ganton spoke out aloud his story in trust that it would somehow be preserved awaiting the advent of this narrative.

Remember that Charles Ganton was not merely reciting his entire life story but expounding only those happenings that were of great importance, or relevance, to all that had followed him to the end of his life; including eternal matters that he had not the time or understanding to resolve.

Accepting this I must assume that he deliberately chose not to comment upon their joint visit, to what was to have been their matrimonial home, because it had no direct bearing upon what was to come.

CHAPTER THIRTEEN

Problems for Elizabeth and Charles

After breakfast and before we each went our separate ways, Brother John gained permission from Mr Salter to make a very important family announcement which went as follows: "You have been aware that, for some weeks, I have been giving almost daily tuition to Moneysa in the form of a catechism of the Christian faith. I must add….. nay stress …. that I have also derived great value from these sessions since her lively and intelligent mind would test the ability of even the greatest church theologian."

This was followed with light laughter and tapping of the table top with tea spoons whilst father, who was sitting alongside Moneysa, gripped her hand and in a voice filled with pride whispered, "I am proud of you Monnie."

Brother John noticed that Cymol was sitting in silence with his head lowered and hands clenched before him.

"I must add," continued Brother John, "that I did inform Cymol of the situation before I asked leave to make this announcement, and I assured him that Moneysa was not pressurised into seeking membership of the Christian faith.

Moneysa has asked for a private ceremony of admission so, with the agreement of my father and a transport request to Mr Salter I plan, this day, to take Moneysa along to the Foxton parish church wherein my friend the Reverend Cotney will baptise and receive her into the Anglican Church; thus granting her full rights of Communion."

Immediately Cymol helped his mother to her feet and begged permission to leave the table, which they did in complete silence, broken only by a sob from Moneysa.

Father put his arm around her as she thanked Brother John for his excellent tuition which, in her own words, "Was given to one who never accepts important matters without argument; more so when faced with leaving the faith of my beloved father, Drebar."

I again use her actual words when she continued with, "I prayed to God and I have felt the warmth of his call to do what will happen this day. I am sorry that my brother does not agree with me but it is my choice to walk along the path that leads to my destiny."

Her message was followed by many words of support after which Moneysa thanked everyone in turn and last of all she looked at me, smiled and said, "Without my ever best friend, Charles, I would not be here today."

Her eyes filled with tears and I became aware that my sight had become strangely blurred, and that all I wanted to do was to hold her close, and tell her over and over again, that I …. "Are you ready to wave them goodbye Charles for it is a fair ride to Foxton and the roads are very difficult," came the gentle voice of Elizabeth as her hand slid into mine and drew me towards the door.

The Salter family, father and I stood together and waved every blessing upon Moneysa and Brother John as their two horse chaise, with the driver astride the left hand horse rather than upon the rear driving seat, which afforded only limited vision of the poorly surfaced road, moved off to meet their appointment with the Reverend Cotney.

We, in turn, moved back into the warmth of the house and, in particular, to the inviting fire burning in the oak panelled hall fireplace.

"Elizabeth, you have an excellent opportunity to show your skills upon the clavichord whilst entertaining Charles and your mother in the comfort of the music room. Please excuse Mr Ganton and myself while we discuss certain subjects prior to our meeting in the drawing room in about two hours time."

Thus said they departed and left me dreading the forthcoming family meeting, mainly because I did not want to offend the Salter family or damage the lifelong friendship between Derbie Salter and my father. Elizabeth's playing was restful and soothing but was no match for the bouts of mental tension and uncertainty that were assuming nightmare proportions in my mind.

As the families assembled for the meeting I was unaware of any latent tension in the Salter house drawing room, as they praised Moneysa for showing her strength of character in becoming a Christian against a background of strong traditional ties to another faith.

In the relaxed air of general conversation, and without evidence of prearranged chair management, Charles and Elizabeth sat together facing Derbie and his wife Elizabeth, whilst Edward Ganton sat to one side in an armchair.

There was a moment's pause for Derbie to summon his butler and instruct him that on no account must anyone interrupt this family meeting; he bowed his understanding and quietly withdrew from the room.

Then Derbie, with the restrained authority of his position as district magistrate, which at times reflected in his mannerism, addressed Charles and Elizabeth as if they were in the dock.

"The matter that is to the fore of my mind is not so much measured in terms of criticism but, rather, of surprise that after eight years of engagement you have carefully avoided the question of where you will live following your marriage next year.

As your respective fathers we are more than a little concerned at your attitude which, if not quickly corrected, will leave us with no alternative other than to postpone your marriage.

Please take your time and present to us your concerns which will be heard with parental love and hopefully resolved from our joint wealth of experience in this life."

I looked towards Elizabeth and, as if by instinct, we smiled and joined hands as I asked leave to be the first to answer her father's questions.

"Let me dispel any concerns you may have that lengthy periods of separation may have weakened the bond between Elizabeth and myself, and I would ask you to accept the reality of a spiritual union of like minds that holds us together.

Such a union generates thoughts of love, goodwill, compassion and concern that can travel across land and ocean as if within the blink of an eye; yet arrive as fresh with the recipient as with the desires of the sender."

I paused and looked at the faces before me and noted their deep interest and apparent desire for me to continue.

"During the last eight years, as my father cum mentor will confirm, I have achieved singular fame as a junior manager with the Honourable East India Company and have been offered a senior position which I must accept or decline before January 1782. For my part I feel called to serve the commerce of our great nation using the talents which I firmly believe God has given to me, and I know they will be enhanced if Elizabeth will unite with me as my wife, confidante, companion, mother of our children and friend throughout our lives together; all of which I ask you to accept as my sincere response to your questions."

Throughout his address I was aware of nods of approval from the family and an increased sense of emotional discomfort displayed by Elizabeth who, with her hands now clasped tightly together, thanked Charles for his honest reply which was to be expected from one who had given her the greatest honour possible by inviting her to be his wife.

She then reminded those present of the great discomfort she felt when, at the onset of her first visit to India, she became the victim of high heat and humidity levels which induced bouts of sickness, severe headache and acute fatigue such that, in her own words, she began to look upon death as an optional release. Elizabeth then thanked all for recognising her predicament and, in particular Mr. Ganton, for arranging the move to his mountain retreat where prevailing weather conditions were just bearable on condition that she wore minimum amounts of clothing.

Pausing to wipe her eyes, and with an emotion filled voice, she stressed that her love and loyalty to Charles, as his wife, would be of little use if she succumbed to weather extremities and departed this life well in advance of her allotted life expectation.

The logic of what Elizabeth said seemed to have a profound effect upon my father as he stared down at the floor, perhaps accepting that Indian weather extremities may have been responsible for the untimely death of his wife, my mother Molly?

Looking fully at me Elizabeth put one hand upon mine and declared that she loved me, and wanted to become my wife, but only if we could live in England for the reasons she had described to everyone. She felt certain that the wide range of estate and social duties would provide me with challenge enough to meet my abilities whilst affording absolute work satisfaction.

Additionally, Elizabeth offered permanent accommodation for both my father and her friend Moneysa, who she thought would soon be snapped up by one of several wealthy and eligible bachelors in the area; whilst Cymol and his mother would be provided with nearby cottage accommodation if so required.

All this was followed with at least two minutes silence which was broken by Derbie Salter.

"We are grateful that the problem has been exposed and would appear, from health considerations alone, that the marriage can only take place if Charles will consent to live in England.

Both Mr Ganton and I realise that such a momentous decision cannot be resolved immediately and I, with my friend's prior agreement, do formally suggest that the matter can only be resolved by Charles and Elizabeth alone. We further suggest that they spend the weeks leading up to the Christmas period considering their respective stances, and be in a position to announce if or not the wedding will take place no later than in the Spring season of next year.

Finally we think that effective dialogue may be better served if, with Elizabeth's approval, Mr Ganton and his family move into the proposed matrimonial home thus allowing us to visit one another as guests rather than room mates.

This suggestion was readily accepted by all present and Elizabeth willingly agreed to loan her property for this purpose with, in her words of humour, "Without rent or bill of lease."

Thanking all for their contributions Derbie Salter finally asked permission to read through a proposed list of guests, should the wedding take place, and invited comment upon any omissions or unsuitable invitees. After three names had been read he paused on hearing a discreet tap upon the drawing room door.

With a frown he ignored the interruption and continued reading through the names only for much louder and repeated knocking to elicit from him an angry, "Blast," followed by a bellowed, "Come in."

With that his butler, looking pale and clearly shocked, stood inside the doorway and begged permission to speak with Mr Salter in private.

As the door closed behind him the rest of the gathering looked at each other and, in muttered terms of concern, agreed that it must be a matter of critical importance for an experienced butler to disobey his master's orders and break into the sanctity of a family meeting.

CHAPTER FOURTEEN

Disaster on the Foxton Road

Consistent with everyone present I too looked expectantly, as the drawing room door opened, and a worried Derbie Salter walked slowly and thoughtfully into the room and continued over to the window as if looking to the elements for inspiration.

Suddenly he became his active self, turned and addressed us in a firm but concerned voice with the news that a terrible accident had occurred on the road home from Foxton. He explained that the road was notorious for deep potholes and that the chaise had hit one causing the carriage to tip over; resulting in the Reverend John and Moneysa being thrown down an embankment on to shale covered ground.

A gasp went up followed by a clamour of questions asking after the welfare of the passengers which, according to the driver, was that John had hurt his back and Moneysa was lying unconscious.

They had wrapped her in blankets from the chaise and made her as comfortable as possible whilst he, the driver, uncoupled a horse and rode with all haste to alert a Foxton doctor who immediately, accompanied by his wife, had driven their carriage to the scene and transported the still unconscious Moneysa and the Reverend John to his surgery. With that the driver had ridden post haste to report the accident to his employer Mr Salter.

Immediately I leapt to my feet and with a voice that sounded strange even to my ears I said, "I saved Monnie's life once before and by the grace of God I am ready to do it again." Turning to Mr Salter I reminded him that I was an experienced horseman and requested a mount so that I could accompany the carriage driver to the place where Moneysa was.

He immediately agreed and within five minutes we were riding together as if all hell was at our heels.

With head low I gazed intently at the road ahead and only briefly turned to observe the shattered chaise lying on its side, on the rim of the road, as my companion indicated with repeated pointing of his left hand that we were about to turn into what looked like a village street. I was aware of a village green and squat church tower as I followed my guide to the right, and down a short drive, then reined to a halt outside a modest cottage which served as surgery for the local doctor.

The door was opened by a kindly looking man who received my, "I am Charles Ganton and I understand that you are caring for my injured sister and brother," with a smile and invitation to enter. Quickly he led me into a small drawing room, where before a warm fire sat a rather dishevelled Brother John, with his left arm supported in a sling.

"Do not worry about me Charles," he remarked. "I am complete other than having a selection of bruises and grazes that are of no consequence. Please find out how Monnie is and let me know."

With that the doctor ushered me into a small side room which contained a single central bed placed between a small side table and a plain wooden chair. Other furniture consisted of a padded bench seat, cupboards containing shelves of medicines and bandages, a wash stand with the usual facilities and an open clothes cupboard in which I could see Moneysa's beloved new dress looking soiled and torn but, thankfully, free from bloodstains.

I sat beside the bed and gazed intently into Moneysa's face as she lay there, quietly breathing, with her curled tresses upon her shoulders and her arms resting above the bed covers.

The voice of the doctor broke into my thoughts with, "I believe that she is in a state of deep shock for which the best cure is rest, and the sound of voices that she both knows and will respond to," and I smiled as I assured the doctor that my voice had been created for that very purpose.

The doctor went on to explain that his wife had removed Moneysa's outer clothing which enabled him to confirm that nothing was broken and her heart and breathing were working well, and her only obvious injuries were a small cut on her forehead and bruises of a relatively minor nature.

"Please remain with her Mr. Ganton and use your voice to best advantage whilst I ask my maid to serve you and your brother with a hot drink."

It was incredible how a deep yet peaceful silence had so dramatically wiped from my mind the thunder of horses' hooves and a heart- pounding dread of the carnage I expected to find. I was so very relieved that Brother John was fine and Moneysa was alive and bodily well, yet locked within herself behind a door that only she could open.

I slowly raised her hand and stroked her finely formed fingers as my mind returned to 1775 and the horror of torrential rain, with the sight of Moneysa being dragged beneath the torrent by an unearthed bush.

Although the circumstances were different I still felt the identical urge to save her because I … because I … "Why, Charles, do you want so much to save this young woman from India," I cried out aloud to myself yet controlled my emotions as I suddenly became aware of the maid standing with a tray in her hands.

"I beg your pardon for interrupting sir, is all well with Miss Moneysa and yourself?" I nodded and thanked her for her concern and asked her to leave the tray upon the bench, then to tell Reverend John that all was well with Moneysa.

Now I was faced with two questions, "Is all well with Miss Moneysa and myself and why do I, some seven months away from my marriage to Elizabeth, feel so devoted to this young woman from India and, more to the point, if I do know then why don't I tell her and the world about it?"

I slowly bent over her and let my hands run gently through her rich black tresses as I whispered in her ear, "Moneysa, it is your ever best friend Charles begging you to wake up because …… because I………"

Suddenly mist filled my eyes as the word 'because,' which had long been captive within the depths of my inner self, broke free in homage to the sleeping Moneysa with the words…….. "Because I love you and I was a fool not realise that from our first meeting when, as children, our love was born awaiting the maturity of time."

I looked down at her face so still and serene as my head slowly came to rest upon her shoulder. I kissed her hair as I murmured, "Monnie, please come back to me."

It may have been a matter of minutes, or an even longer period of time, which are both inconsequential against the fact that I suddenly became aware of fingers gently running through my hair. Turning my head I beheld Moneysa smiling at me and thanking, "Her ever best friend" for yet again restoring her life.

In a brief period of silence, with our faces so close together, reality was without meaning as I blurted out, "And thank you for saving me from the unthinkable loneliness of life without you Monnie."

Her eyes filled with tears as she whispered the words, "Charles and so it is ….." which stopped when I gently put my finger upon her lips, in the traditional 'shush' manner, as I quietly replied, "Let us tend the bud as we await the flower that will never fade."

Then trying to restore my business style manner of speech I asked her, "Are you feeling fully recovered?" Moneysa confirmed that she felt a little stiff but otherwise in good health and was grateful for her many undergarments that had cushioned her against serious injury; whereas the single layer thickness of her sari could have meant disaster for her.

We talked albeit gabbled together happily in the joy that all was well which perhaps prompted Monnie to ask, "Charles, will you permit me to do something?" Without hesitation I replied, "Of course you may" which was barely said before Moneysa reached up behind me and gently pulled my lace tied pig tail, that hung below my collar, whilst adding a soprano pitched 'ding-ding' to the pulling action.

"Be careful," I added as I held one of her long black tresses and gently pulled it to a sombre 'dong-dong' set in the baritone range.

In no time at all we were performing a composite melody of 'dings and dongs' that soon had us both, with arms around each other, literally howling with laughter as the door opened to reveal a surprised doctor, Brother John and housemaid standing open mouthed upon the threshold.

"May God sustain my soul," exclaimed the doctor, "Apothecary, learn well from what you see. Put away your books and medicines and know that true recovery is the product of happiness as witnessed before each of us this day."

Within the hour a post horn announced the arrival of the Salter family coach and a tearful reunion commenced with Moneysa being warmly embraced by Papa, and then Elizabeth, who quickly cleared the room when she announced that she would help Moneysa to wash and dress into clothing brought along for the occasion.

Whilst waiting for the ladies to join us in the warmth of the drawing room we learned, via an account given by the driver to his master Derbie Salter, that Brother John was influential in minimising Moneysa's bodily injuries. This was due to his prompt action in gathering her in his arms, as the coach began to tip over, and twisting his body around so that when they hit the ground he made the first contact and Moneysa was cushioned by his relative bulk beneath her.

The force of the impact caused her to bounce off him and continue to roll down the hill leaving Brother John with a badly grazed shoulder and muscular discomfort. We all thanked a somewhat embarrassed Brother John and sealed our gratitude with a well deserved round of applause which, out of curiosity, caused Moneysa to discreetly pop her head around the door and ask, "What was that for?"

The journey home was followed by Moneysa and Brother John being examined by Derbie Salter's family doctor who noted a small cut on Moneysa's forehead otherwise she was declared fit and well. He decided that he would come daily to check her progress and dress Brother John's cuts and grazes.

Following dinner and relaxation before the drawing room fire the family were reminded that they were tired after an event filled day, by the appearance of Ruth who, after a half

*curtsey, announced that Miss Moneysa's bed warmers were
in place and should she lay out her night clothes?*

CHAPTER FIFTEEN

Elizabeth and Charles resolve their problems

Hence that memorable day had reached its end. I was aware of a short passage of time which may have been as long as two weeks, judging by the rapid fall of leaves.

October had arrived marking the departure of the Ganton contingent to the house loaned by Elizabeth; as recently agreed at the family meeting. Before their departure I must record two events that were meaningful to Charles.

The first involved Elizabeth, in the presence of Charles, telling Moneysa about house parties that were held during the weeks leading up to Christmas and that she would teach her how to dance.

"And do not forget lessons for me Elizabeth, because I am still baffled by the steps and rely mainly upon instinct and luck," I remarked.

"He is being modest so take no notice of him.

You look very thoughtful Monnie, are you alright? You are not worried about the dancing are you?"

After a momentary pause Moneysa cheerfully replied, "No, not at all. In fact I love parties and dancing but I was wondering about those people."

Taken off guard Elizabeth briefly looked at me then asked, "What people?"

In an unusually sad voice Moneysa explained that when she was travelling to Foxton she saw a number of small stone houses that had doors and windows missing but people were living in them and some had young children.

Their clothes were in rags and they looked hungry, cold and unhappy and, with increasing enthusiasm, she suggested to Elizabeth, "How happy they would be if we invited them to our parties then they could celebrate the joys of Christmas with us as their friends."

Elizabeth looked at me in bewildered desperation, which turned to relief when the dinner gong began its urgent roll for our immediate presence at the table.

The second event occurred during the evening before the Ganton family departed for their temporary new home owned by Elizabeth, and took place in the library from which there was a commanding view of the hills and woodlands. Elizabeth, standing at the window, invited Charles to join her watching the shooting stars in the night sky.

I walked behind Elizabeth and put my arms gently around her waist and she responded by resting her head on my shoulder and placing her hands upon mine. "It is a pity that we cannot drift away together in that sea of stars," she murmured as she gently stroked the back of my hand and, before I could think of an appropriate reply, she said, "But once more I am dreaming about something that cannot happen."

"Don't forget that we are young and all things will be possible when we are married," I added by way of compromise. She did not answer and was happy to lie back in my arms and view the heavenly display above, which gave me the opportunity to raise the question that, no doubt, was to the front of her mind as it was in mine.

"Elizabeth, have you thought again about returning to India after our wedding? I know that all will be well if only you will say yes to my offer. Please do not dwell upon 'what may happen' and think only of the constant love and attention that will be yours as my wife and mother of our children. I will always place you at the centre of my life as your husband, provider and companion in our later years together."

Elizabeth stiffened slightly then relaxed as she turned and faced me.

"I know you would Charles as I in turn would centre my love entirely upon you. You are my first and last love and I am not being overtly dramatic when I say that no one will ever fully replace you in my life. As your wife I want to live with you Charles and not leave you a widower to grieve over my grave, whilst recalling how different our lives could have been."

Elizabeth paused to take hold of my hand, almost as an act of compassion, as she followed with, "Can you not see that the same illness that struck down your dear mother could similarly end my life before its appointed time? It is a known fact that the extremities of the Indian climate are particularly unkind to English women.

Please stay here with me Charles. I know that by comparison life will be less challenging for you but, together, we will work something out that will satisfy your leadership skills within an estate that covers all of the countryside you can see from this window."

Elizabeth faced the window as she awaited my reply as I, unable to give the answer she yearned for, stood alongside her hoping for heavenly inspiration.

Without doubt I could understand the strength of her logic but that was not enough; for the simple reason that the call of the East India Company was, to me, even stronger. Surely there was a way that I could convince her that she would not die as my mother did but, despite my optimism, I thought it very unlikely that she would change her mind.

In the ensuing silence her voice cut into my thoughts, "Darling Charles your silence is an answer in itself and I admire your dedication to the life awaiting you in India. We both agree that our love for each other is foundation enough for our marriage but, sadly, it would be no marriage at all with you working in India whilst I sit here awaiting your next letter, and thinking of the happiness we have surrendered."

As we stood in silence gazing at thousands of light filled specks in the black sky I suddenly felt apprehensive as the fact that our expected marriage, and the longed for unity of our families, appeared to be over.

I turned and faced Elizabeth, gripped her hands, and asked, "But what of our engagement Elizabeth?"

I dwelt upon a single tear that had begun its downward course as she looked at me, gently touched my face, and almost whispered, "Darling Charles, it would be a woman bereft of all emotions that could not find it within her heart to love you.

Do you remember that December night and the haunting sound of the wind chimes at the Indian lakeside and the words I confessed to you in that scene of beauty?" Elizabeth paused, smiled then said, "Please hear them again Charles for they echo the same truth and fervour that will always be with me."

With a break in her voice Elizabeth went on to remind me of those very words ….. "In fact from the moment we first met I knew that I was in love with you and just hoped that you would find it within yourself to love me. I believe that sincerely, yet briefly, you loved me at that lakeside, only for your fervour to fade as clouds covered the moon and the last chime faded away."

I held her in my arms as she burst into tears from which she soon recovered and looking me full in the face said, "Although I now release you from our engagement remember that I will always love you Charles, and whatever happens I want to be your special friend until we both leave this life."

Almost with a sense of panic I held Elizabeth as I stressed the strength of my love for her only for her hand to gently cover my mouth as she almost whispered, "Please Charles, I was honoured to be held within your love for a time so short yet rich in happy memories.

There is little wonder that my favourite flower is one that blooms in the morning and withers in the evening yet the fragrance of its memory lives on in the lives of those captivated by it."

There was nothing more to be said as we held each other in silence, and paid little heed to a shooting star that traversed the night sky before us.

The reference made by Elizabeth to a flower that blooms in the morning and withers in the evening was something new to me and, following a subject search, I discovered that it is called a 'Day Lily.' Also imagine my surprise when I further discovered there is a member of the Day Lily family that bears the name 'Elizabeth Salter.'

Now composed, we sat gazing at sparks leaping chimney bound from the log fire before us. Then almost as if she was speaking to herself Elizabeth said, "I suggest that we do not report our decision to my father until after Christmas, which was his wish, but let us try and enjoy the season during which I earnestly pray that you will change your mind and remain with me."

I sat staring into the fire until inaction drove me to my feet and, with hands over my mouth in prayer fashion, I walked over to the window, where consumed with desperation, I said out aloud, "But what about that simple yet eternal word known as 'love' which has become victim to our situation?"

In a quiet yet commanding voice Elizabeth stilled my words with her request for me to, "Stop pacing about and come and sit down with me."

Dutifully I moved towards the fireplace and sat facing her from an armchair.

"Charles, there are many who would claim that our proposed union was a family planned event with the single aim of uniting our families without reference to love which, if evoked, would have been an added bonus. Even then it would be a type of love born from a family pact rather than from the heart.

We are fortunate Charles in that our love is the door through which family aspirations could become a reality."

Perhaps Elizabeth noticed the puzzled look upon my face when I responded, "I agree with you but I cannot follow where your thoughts are leading."

Elizabeth smiled as she said, "That is another reason I love you Charles because of your constant desire to get to the heart of a conversation without wasted words."

I grinned, nodded my agreement and asked her pardon.

"There is another type of love and I suggest that you talk with Brother John about it."

With raised eyebrows I asked, "What is the love you speak of?"

Instantly she replied, "The love that exists between Moneysa and yourself."

I felt as if a bolt of lightening had suddenly shaken my life. I made to rise to my feet and pace the room but in deference to Elizabeth's plea to the contrary I remained in my chair.

There was urgency in her voice as Elizabeth stressed that not only she but her mother and, to some extent, Brother John may be aware of this love.

Indignantly I retorted, "Are suggestions being made that Monnie and I are having clandestine meetings which would be an affront to all that we hold as pure, open and honest before God and our families?"

Urgently Elizabeth leant forward and gripped my hand as with sincerity she stressed, "No one has ever even hinted at such impropriety which is foreign to the moral fibre that is evident in the life of Moneysa and the families we represent. No one can define the union between you and Moneysa other than through observations."

Mentally I recalled my inner feelings as I sought to awaken Moneysa after the recent carriage accident and began to capture a little of what Elizabeth was saying.

"Please walk with me through times past Charles and remember just a little of what I have seen, or been told about, starting with that little girl who gave you her doll.

Ever since then, and regardless of how many others were present, you would both be drawn together either in mischievous chase about, deep conversation or the time when you sang a lullaby to your sleeping Moneysa as you carried her home.

Your brave actions in fighting with an uprooted tree and a raging storm to save her life in that torrential flood became a legend in its time and, with one voice, those present declared that you would have perished with her rather than abandon your Moneysa to that wild storm.

Recently when you heard of the Foxton carriage accident you galloped your horse to where she was, without regard for your own safety, because your sole objective was the welfare of the one who has captured all our hearts.

My visit to India gave me two precious gifts that circumstances will never take away from me, regardless of difficulties and storms that may lie ahead in each of our lives.

India had its blessings in that it led me to Charles and a charming young woman called Moneysa who I love as dearly as my own sister, and whatever the future holds I resolve to remain with you both as your close friend.

I do not betray confidences when I remind you that Monnie, in a host of different ways, frequently refers to you ranging from holding a new dress up to the light and wondering 'if Charles will like me in this?' to the time when she announced, to me, that she would only agree to marry a man who was like her ever best friend Charles.

I must stress that she has never given a hint of resentment that we are, or were, engaged to be married and that she just wanted to remain within our circle of family friendship. Sorry that I have gone on at length Charles, but that is what I meant when I spoke of the love between Moneysa and yourself."

Once again I made myself remain in my chair as I thanked Elizabeth for presenting to me a picture so clear yet, however, it was devoid of one important and significant point.

"What you fail to grasp Elizabeth is the love I have for Moneysa is that of a brother to his sister. It is love that developed from the fact that we grew up together, in the depths of India, and such a bond can never be broken."

Elizabeth put her hand to her mouth as if arranging her words for effective delivery which, when spoken, had a chilling truth to them, "Charles, please remember that you are no longer children playing games in India. You are adults and the Moneysa you now see is not your sister but a young woman who is in love with you."

I moved to speak but Elizabeth held up her hand and continued, "Your definition of the love bond between you will soon be put to the test when the pre-Christmas dances and parties commence.

The dress Moneysa will wear, together with the natural beauty of her black hair and dark brown skin will outshine every other female present, including myself, because we rely entirely upon body supports, padding and heavily powdered wigs.

Surely you can see that Moneysa has a level of beauty and charisma that will devastate all eligible young men, who will offer to serve her every need, lest their hearts will break should they fail? Watch all that Charles and then, at the end of the evening, ask yourself if you still love Moneysa only as your sister, and that you would happily see her in the arms of another man?"

I stared at Elizabeth and searched for words that were not to be found. I stood up and raised my hands, only to let them fall loosely by my side.

Turning, I thanked Elizabeth for her frankness then walked over to the window to gaze again at the twinkling stars, as I silently conceded that the truth, within her words, had totally defeated my half-hearted reasoning to the contrary.

For once in my life I was without reply which, under the circumstances, was no bad thing.

CHAPTER SIXTEEN

The tenants of Ganton Hall

In many ways it was good that space was placed between Elizabeth and me so that we, in our individual ways, could ponder our future relationship either as husband and wife or, no less importantly, as very good friends.

The exodus involved two coach journeys which was quite remarkable considering that we had no furniture but plenty of clothing, mainly due to the large wardrobe of 'essentials' that Elizabeth had given to Moneysa. Also her personal maid Ruth had been seconded to live at Ganton Hall in order to take care of Monnie's needs and help her to prepare for the party season ahead.

Ruth, who was much older than Moneysa, had adopted the role of a mother figure to her and a firm bond of friendship had developed between the two.

When I first saw the house its appearance pleased me and its accommodation, although smaller than the Salter residence, was hospitable to the highest degree. It was an old property that had been built in the early 17th century and creaking floor boards paid tribute to its age. It was a square set house, approached from a U shaped driveway, and entry was via a pillared, covered porch with double doors giving access to the reception hall.

The view upon entry was dominated by a large fireplace set in the centre of the left wall with oak bench seats in close proximity to the fire. To the immediate left were double doors leading to a library cum reception room. Ahead was a staircase with four wide treads that turned to the left and continued to the first floor. There were doors in both corners of the hall that led to a connecting corridor and hence to the kitchen and other rooms at the rear of the house.

One of those rooms was a sitting room that led into an orangery which, sadly, tended to leak when it rained hard. Immediately on the right of the hall were double doors to the dining room. Beyond the dining room were two rooms, accessed from the central corridor, that were reserved for men and women to separately relax and engage in post dinner activities.

However the most attractive feature of the house was that the bedrooms contained wooden bathtubs which the family appreciated having enjoyed that facility in India.

From the windows it could be seen that the house was set amidst many trees and medium sized bushes with little evidence of flower beds. A woodland path from the right of the driveway, bordered with rhododendron bushes, afforded a scenic walk to a medium sized cottage that Cymol, despite pleas to the contrary, insisted that he and his mother should use as their separate residence.

Father and Brother John after a brief walk around the grounds decided that they would rest awhile before dinner whilst Monnie and I, ever the adventurers, chose to explore the inviting woodland path together.

It was a mild and sunny October day with a gentle breeze that encouraged a controlled fall of leaves from the many trees as Monnie and I, agog with excitement, made our first entrance into what would become our woodland of destiny.

The path began its progress as a short yet steep incline that prompted me to hold out a helping hand to Moneysa who gratefully accepted my offer. For a few moments I just stood upon that incline, holding her hand and gazing down upon her as she in turn smiled up at me. I was still becoming accustomed to seeing Moneysa in different styles of English dress after all those Indian years, which had restricted her to a simple sari and Odhani, or sometimes without the latter having dispassionately cast it into a bush.

Her hair was now a picture of fashion which radiated the glow of a low sky autumn sun. Her maid and friend Ruth had arranged it as a mixture of curls and side ringlets and longer tresses at the back in sharp contrast to her white lace frilled fichu and black long sleeved jacket with white lace frills spilling out from the cuffs. Her small brown hands, with slender fingers, stood out in simple yet enchanting contrast to the white cuffs. The front of her coat had a low neckline that gave prominence to her favourite dark red pendant which, as I mentioned earlier, once belonged to her grandmother.

She slightly lifted her long, black skirt as she ascended the incline. This meant that because of my elevated position I was able to note her shoes were strikingly different from the canvas 'slip-ons' which were common in India.

Permit me to intrude briefly upon Charles's narrative so that you will know the shoes worn by Moneysa, on this occasion, were of stout black leather fastened with a single metal buckle with medium heels.

The path now took a downward slope and as we turned a corner Moneysa stopped as if transfixed. With her eyes wide open she clutched my arm and pointed to a whole line of bushes. In amazement, she said, "Look Charles, I cannot believe it. Those are rhodie bushes just like the ones at home." She ran over and held one of the rhododendron leaves then gently kissed it and thanked it for following her all the way to England.

Her happiness was contagious and soon my clouds of worry were dispersed as we walked along that woodland path laughing, and talking, whilst agreeing that we would call this our own secret little forest.

I led her up a small mound at the side of the path from which we had a view down the side of the wooded hill and, through gaps in the trees it was just possible to see part of what appeared to be a great expanse of water. Being much smaller than I, and in response to her demands to see the water, I knelt down and clasped both arms around her knees and carefully lifted her up until with delight she exclaimed, "There it is, I can see it now." I went on to explain that in this part of England the forests were as dense as those in India because very little development work had been done, other than in areas connected by a none too efficient roadway system.

When I look back upon our first walk together in an English wood I remain at a loss to remember just how and when a 'certain something' happened. Nevertheless it did happen because I suddenly became aware that we were walking hand in hand which did not seem improper but, rather, it would have been an affront to the bond between us had we failed to unite in this way. At that moment I briefly recalled Elizabeth's almost prophetic words which faded when we turned a corner and viewed a cottage before us.

Soon we were sitting inside drinking tea whilst talking with Cymol and his mother Lajila, who totally failed to recognise either Moneysa or myself. Additionally I had my suspicions that she was totally unaware of just where she was, or why she was there. In terms of content it was a tense conversation because Cymol was clearly unhappy with the dramatic change in his sister's appearance, together with her attitude towards the traditions in which they had been raised, and I have no doubt that the reason why Cymol held his tongue was due entirely to my presence. After a while and having established that they were well catered for in terms of food, water and fuel we set off on our return journey through our 'secret little forest' and back to the Hall.

In due course I noticed that Moneysa was limping slightly and, in response to my concern and much to my surprise, she replied in her musical accent, "It is these bloody shoes that are too tight for my feet."

Then horrified and wide eyed she said, "Sorry Charles but I keep forgetting that 'bloody' is a word that I should not use," which led to much needed laughter in the wake of our recent strained visit to her family.

She was quick to explain that although she felt confident with the English language, she was never quite certain which expressions were considered to be swearing words that should not be used by ladies.

With that she sat upon a wayside rock and slipped off both her shoes and announced, with a sigh of relief, that she was more comfortable with them off. I reminded her that there was much pre-Christmas dancing ahead so she must keep her feet in perfect condition and that I would be willing to carry her back if she wished me to do so.

Following her immediate, "Yes please," I lifted her into my arms as, in turn, she placed her arm firmly around the back of my neck and shoulder.

Looking me straight in the eyes, and with great sincerity, she quietly said, "Be it in India or England I am so very happy just to be with you Charles." In that position our faces were very close together and I was drawn to her expressive dark brown eyes, which radiated words unspoken that were in total harmony with my emotions towards her. I struggled to find the right words to say but they became disjointed, and of no value, until my desperation delivery of, "Are you comfortable?" was met with a smile and a whispered, "Yes, very much so."

I tried to turn my head away but the vision of her face, and the message within her eyes, when added to the compelling attraction of her presence in my arms, overtook my control as I leaned forward and, for the first time, I gently kissed Moneysa upon her lips.

Quickly I realised my impropriety as I apologised for taking such a liberty and that I would never again ...... but her request, "Please stop for a moment Charles," made me pause as I realised that she was not angry with me.

With a smile Moneysa then inclined her head and kissed me in exactly the same way.

"That makes it one kiss each which is a time for rejoicing rather than apologising. Surely a brother and sister can kiss once in a while?" she added as she snuggled her head into my shoulder.

"Let us make a pact Charles to walk in our secret little forest as often as possible and when we are apart, for whatever the reason, then we will walk its path alone yet locked together in our thoughts and dreams; do you agree?" I drew her closer to me as I readily agreed with what was 'our pact,' newly born, and sealed through my whispered words, "Which will endure throughout eternity."

So much was happening to my mind as I seemingly floated along the remainder of the path. Confirmation of the warmth between us gave me great joy only to fade into total confusion as to why Moneysa had introduced the sister and brother relationship; perhaps she meant it that way, or was it to cover inward guilt over the fact that she believed I was still engaged to Elizabeth?

I returned to reality when, as we reached the end of our journey, the first of the nightly owls announced its presence thus prompting Moneysa, without hesitation, to mimic it so expertly that other owls joined in the chorus.

"Fantastic, well imitated Monnie. You have learned well from your father way back in India."

Moneysa smiled at the mention of her beloved father and was going to say something further when she suddenly gasped, "Oh no, I have left my bloody tight shoes behind," as we laughingly walked up the entrance steps and into the house.

Intermezzo

You will also recall that when I am present within Charles Ganton, which is always at important or critical times of this narrative, then he concentrates upon matters of the heart but rarely comments, in depth, upon his surroundings.

In the next section I will, as it were, hand over the narrative to Charles Ganton but before that **I would like to spend a little time describing the nearby village, and its church, to which he will no doubt refer only in general terms.**

The Ganton house was accessed from a long and badly surfaced track flanked mainly with stone walls interspersed with bushes, and a prominent gap where decaying posts leant in memory of a long lost gate. Beyond the walls were dense areas of woodland that, in places, appeared to be impenetrable.

For quite a distance the track gradually descended downhill around a series of 'S' bends until, with a suddenness that took strangers by surprise, it turned sharply into a small yet attractive village.

On entry into the village and immediately to the left, there was a high banked wall topped with headstones and loose hanging foliage, suggesting that progressive strata levels of burials had unnaturally raised the height of the land surrounding an ancient church. Access was by six steps cut into a banked mound leading to a path through a lych-gate to the church porch. Several not too expertly carved slate and granite headstones were visible, together with trees and bushes. There was evidence that sheep had been used rather than a scythe to control the growth of grass.

The small Norman style church with its squat tower, probably dating from the 11th or 12th century, stood in a shallow valley formed by the elevated graveyard. The interior of the church would have been familiar to Brother John who had met its incumbent, during an earlier visit to England and it would soon be the regular place of worship for the Ganton family.

Those leaving the church were faced, when turning left, with a badly rutted but wide access road, bordered by grassed areas, which was the focal point for business and social activities. I add, purely as speculation, that the village design resembled that of a 'fortified village' prevalent before the union of the crowns of England and Scotland in 1603.

Adults, children, dogs, cattle and a range of poultry presented a picture of rural life where communal care and group help was the recipe for survival. Several, particularly the children, were dressed in smocks but many were in scant and ragged clothing that would be of little benefit to them when the fast approaching winter arrived.

On the right hand side of the road was a wide grass verge in front of a line of irregular sized houses and cottages some of which were almost derelict yet still inhabited. Wooden benches and produce stalls were on this grassed area suggesting that it was also the village green.

On the left hand side of the road was a narrow grass verge fronting several thatched cottages, a forge with a clearly visible anvil and other workshops. An abundance of *leather straps hung from a beam within the forge and, facing its wide entrance door, there was a cart with upturned shafts pointing skywards. Also outside the forge was a water filled horse trough, an age old attraction for village children to do battle with galleons made out of leaves and twigs.*

The village blacksmith was a gentle giant of a man who the children loved and the adults had great respect for, as judged by the number of people in happy conversation with him. Through the babble of voices I was able to make out that his name was Matthew who, as unofficial squire of the village, was kind and helpful to all those within his domain.

As far as I could see the main road appeared to lose width as it progressed into the distance, and there were three tracks leading off the road to what might be farms.

CHAPTER SEVENTEEN

Charles and Moneysa
meet Matthew the Blacksmith

My father had departed for a two day meeting with his old friend Derbie Salter, and Brother John had an appointment with his area bishop, leaving Moneysa and I with time to explore the neighbourhood and, in particular, the village which was about five miles distant.

Our one horse chaise was led to the front entrance and I took command of the reins whilst Ruth helped Moneysa into the twin seat, and tucked the travel rug around her knees. I scrambled alongside her and with a wave to Ruth, and a shake of the reins, our two wheels crunched along the gravelled driveway and slowly turned into the narrow lane leading to the village.

It was a dreadful road both below and above as we picked our way along almost at walking speed. Pot holes were many as were low tree branches that hung over the road from adjoining woodland that threatened, at any moment, to decapitate the unwary driver. Fortunately they did not present a problem for diminutive Moneysa, who

I referred to by that same title, only to be held to account for the meaning of the word. When satisfied with my definition she added that it was good that her hat had been left behind.

As we slowly made our way along I resolved to pay local rustics to fill in the larger holes which, apparently, presented a much reduced problem to their wide and heavy duty cart wheels.

Moneysa was aware that I had little opportunity to talk, as we picked our way along, so she spent her time plucking the overhead evergreen leaves whilst gently singing an Indian song that I was vaguely aware of. In response to my question, "Are you happy Monnie? She replied, "What do you think?" as she laid her head on my shoulder and tickled my chin with one of her captive leaves.

Carefully I guided the horse around a series of tight bends in the road until, to our surprise, an equally badly pitted village street appeared ahead of us, and an assortment of cows were drinking water from the rain filled pot holes.

"Please can we walk around and meet the people, Charles?" was a better option than trying to find a safe passage between craters, and unresponsive cattle, along the only road through the village.

With the horse safely fastened to a wooden post set in the grass verge I led the way over to the blacksmith's forge that we might see, first hand, the reason why the sound of metal striking metal was so loud in our ears.

The front of the building consisted of two ill fitting windows containing some panes in the bull's eye style and a main door, which was secured in a wide open position, presumably to let heat out of the forge. On the grass was a wooden bench with stools around it.

I remarked to Moneysa that the blacksmith was also the general grocer according to a faded notice in the window which advertised the following fare:

Gallon of flour 5d

lb bacon 4d

lb soap 6d

lb candles 5d

"Come along, it is time to meet a real life blacksmith," I said to Moneysa taking her hand as we moved over to the anvil inside the door frame.

The interior was as hot as India fuelled by a glowing furnace and a length of red hot metal being furiously beaten by a huge man wielding a large hammer. Through the smoke I could vaguely see a youth, mopping his brow, whilst pumping large air bellows which kept the furnace up to temperature.

Suddenly the blacksmith threw his hammer to the ground, wiped his forehead with his apron and, in a voice alive with local accent said to the boy, "Awez Ethan belay thy woruk and have some skemmy doon thee. Gow easy lest thou art kaylied."

On this occasion I recorded the exact words used by Charles Ganton in that they may guide a dialect expert as to the location of this conversation; hence the deviation from my declared policy to record my narrative in modern day English. For the record Matthew's words would sound today as, "Ethan stop pumping now and we will drink some ale. Not too much though for I do not want you drunk."

Perhaps it was the smoke and fumes or a desire to attract his attention that produced my gentle cough, which caused him to turn around and greet us with a big smile of welcome. Standing before us was truly a giant amongst men who must have approached seven feet in height which was proportionate to his massive chest, thick neck and muscular arms and legs.

My independent assessment of his height placed him close to seven feet which was remarkable considering that, in the 18th century, the average height for men was five feet and six inches whereas the value for women was five feet.

However his massive frame and awesome strength was tempered by a gentle and friendly disposition evident in his, "Good morning sir and miss welcome to our village. My name is Matthew. Are you the new tenants at the old hall down the road?"

My reply in the affirmative was cut short by his apology for allowing the anvil to act as a barrier between us, since it was there to keep straying animals out.

With that he respectfully asked us to stand back while he placed his large hands beneath the anvil and, without noticeable effort, he raised it level to his chest and walked several paces before lowering it to the grass whereupon, due to its weight, it immediately sank an inch or so into the soil.

Both Monnie and I were dumbfounded at such an amazing demonstration of strength and I broke the silence by introducing ourselves.

After wiping his hands upon his apron, he shook both our hands and invited us to sit down with him at the wooden bench.

Looking at Moneysa and begging her pardon Matthew asked if she came from India.

"Yes," Moneysa replied excitedly, "Have you been to India, Matthew?"With a wave of his arm Matthew dispersed several goats that had edged closer to us, driven perhaps, by a mixture of hunger and curiosity.

"May the Lord smile upon you Miss but I have only been there in my imagination, through working with two Indian jugglers in my last job." The urge to learn more about this interesting giant led me to ask him what his former work was all about. Feeling pleased with himself that two of the gentry class were genuinely interested in his life he warmed to his theme.

"Starting at the age of ten I trained as a blacksmith and began to develop into the size that I am now. When I reached eighteen a travelling circus set up camp, close to where I lived, and I became friendly with all the show people who, because of my build, urged me to become the circus strongman.

In a fit of drunken bravado the former strongman had boasted that he was as tough as the Biblical Samson and, by way of proof, immediately entered a lion's cage to grapple with the beast. Sadly he was wrong, and what was left of him was buried the next day, and that is how I came to get the job."

Our jovial giant laughed and, as if on cue, Ethan appeared with a liquid filled earthenware jug and three metal tankards which he placed upon the bench, bowed to us all, and without a word quickly disappeared.

Matthew apologised, with a grin, for his low stock of wines and spirits and, holding the jug aloft, asked it we would join him in what he called "liquid life."

Moneysa looked towards me for advice which prompted me to ask, "What kind of drink is it Matthew?"

By way of demonstration he filled his tankard with what was a dark liquid and, whilst in introductory mode, announced, "Meet Porter Joe which is cheaper than gin yet gets rid of your thirst and worries all at the same time."

For reference purposes the drink known as Porter, which was a strong dark sweet beer, became a popular drink in London in the early eighteenth century and quickly spread throughout most of the country.

"Would you like to try some?" Matthew asked of us both.

Moneysa looked a little perplexed and went on to explain that she had never tasted alcohol because she was brought up in the Muslim faith. Looking at me she asked, "Do you think that I should Charles?"

Thrilled with our new friendship within this intriguing little village I declared, "Why not, it is a joy to meet someone like Matthew so let us celebrate accordingly. Just quarter fill them please Matthew."

Immediately our tankards contained the requested amount with the rejoinder that anything left would be returned to the jug. Raising our tankards I proposed a toast to health and happiness to which Matthew immediately drained his tankard whilst I managed a few mouthfuls.

Moneysa, in trying to imitate Matthew and myself, swallowed a more than prudent mouthful then gasped and thrust her tankard into my hands. Clutching her throat and totally forgetting her previous faux pas with English swearing words she managed to wheeze out, "My bloody throat is on fire."

With a roar of laughter that echoed back from the church tower Matthew slapped his thigh and exclaimed, "Well said miss, it is a pleasure for me to be in such great company. Now what I suggest is that you take just a little sip, swill it around your mouth, and slowly swallow it after which your throat will be well."

Gently holding her hand I nodded my agreement for her to follow his instructions which, as viewed by the smile upon her previously contorted face, had immediately solved her throat burn problem.

"Thank you Matthew for introducing me to Porter Joe but I think, for the moment, I will return what is left to the jug," said Moneysa with a wry grin upon her face.

Moneysa, like me, was obviously interested in Matthew and we reminisced about travelling shows in India which mainly consisted of fire eaters, charmers and acrobats.

"Very much like the ones that travel around in this country Miss; jugglers are popular and so are strongmen showing off their various feats of strength and horses that are ridden around, in a circle, with a woman standing upon their back; then some shows have lions which spend their entire lives in a cage.

They are kept just for people to stare at or run away from in mock terror when they violently respond to prods from the keeper's sharp stick. It is of little wonder that out of hatred and frustration they attack anyone who strays within their reach.

That was one of the reasons why I gave up the circus because it was not right that such beautiful creatures should live out their lives being tormented in a small cage.

So one night, at the end of the show, I could stand no more of it.

As was his habit the sadistic keeper was tormenting a lion with his sharp pointed stick when I decided to intervene. I rushed at him, snatched his prodding stick out of his hand, and gave his arse a good thrashing until his blood ran.

Hearing the screams from his lion tamer and observing the look of anger upon my face the circus owner willingly handed over what he owed me and, within five minutes, I was striding down the road with my belongings hanging from a stick over my shoulder.

I found casual work on one or two farms then one day I found myself sitting on this very bench resting my feet and admiring the view.

Suddenly my solitude was broken when an elderly gentleman walked up to me, told me he was the estate manager, and asked if a 'fine looking man like me' was looking for work.

Jumping to my feet I tugged my forelock and said that I was and that I was a trained blacksmith and in no time I was working in this forge."

There can be no doubt that Matthew made a marked impression upon Charles and Moneysa and they upon him as they spent a happy time telling him about India as he, in turn told them all about life in the village and district.

"It is a fact that the poor folk here are just as imprisoned as the circus lions in their tiny cages only they do not get regular meals. Their husbands and sons are away on local farms, often for weeks at a time in between attending hiring fairs when new employment is sought. Their daughters are in domestic service so other than on St. Stephen's feast, they rarely get chance to come home and see their mothers, which means the village is home for mothers and young children, and those too old or ill to work.

In my work I have made lots of contacts, and through favours to them, I get basic household needs at cheap prices that I pass on to the villagers; hence the price list in my window which, in times of great difficulty becomes a free service.

Shall I introduce you both to some of my village friends?"

Leaping to our feet we both echoed, "Yes please," and soon we were picking our way across the rutted roadway with Moneysa arm in arm between us.

Laughingly Monnie declared that she would be the envy of all young girls having two fine and handsome men as her escorts.

Houses and hovels alike were visited and after villagers recovered from the initial shock of meeting a brown skinned woman numerous friendships were struck up and, as Moneysa lovingly cuddled babies and played with young children, it was agreed that she and Charles would organise a Christmas meal for all the villagers at Ganton Hall. My assessment of not more than 20 adult villagers meant that dining space at the hall would not present a problem.

On arrival at the village there was not a soul around to even notice the newcomers but it was very different when the time came for them to leave. The entire village, with Matthew in their midst, turned out to wave and cheer them on their way back to the Hall.

At this stage I can confirm that Moneysa and Charles became frequent visitors to the village and via the offices of Matthew brought food, clothing and love into the lives of the poor of the parish. They also helped resolve problems that beset several families they befriended and worked with.

I have not included these activities lest my narrative may lose direction of purpose, and pass into the realms of philanthropy rather than follow our path towards approaching tragedy.

CHAPTER EIGHTEEN

Charles opens his fears to John and his heart to Moneysa

Charles was looking forward to his meeting with Brother John.

It can, in truth, be said that Charles and John were brothers whose close bond of friendship remained with them throughout their lives. Like many others they had their differences but in their case, and unlike many others, these were restricted only to their respective appearance and nature. Charles had inherited his mother's fairness of hair yet he had his father's positive approach both to life and business activities. He was a born leader of men, and always confident when taking decisions and giving opinions. By contrast John was of medium stature and had inherited his mother's calm and patient nature yet, in appearance, he had his father's darker complexion.

It is because of his self-assured nature that Charles valued the product of his brother's analytical mind, in that he had the ability to sit back and study all aspects of problems put before him. John was very methodical and rarely, if ever, found himself to be in a fix. By contrast Charles was clearly in a corner and in urgent need of help from John more than ever before.

Soon it would be public knowledge that his much vaunted marriage to Elizabeth was dead, despite her insistence that her love for him would never fade. Conversely Charles dare not declare his feelings towards Moneysa because she looked upon their relationship in terms of sister and brother only; or so he believed.

Briefly that was the stage set for this meeting and future readers may look back at the transactions of this mid November evening, in the year 1780, and see within it the foundations of all that was to be.

We sat in facing armchairs beside a roaring log fire that was reflected in the brass and silverware displayed round the room. John with his finger ends lightly touching looked over my head at the room beyond whilst I arranged my thoughts as best I could.

Then in a burst of frustration, I threw away my mental notes and began in extempory fashion.

"Thank you for giving me your time, particularly when problems are rifer than answers available; but really it is difficult to know where to begin."

John leaned forward and fixed me with his keen and intelligent eyes then, after a smile of friendship, he surprised me with, "You are here to tell me that your engagement with Elizabeth is over because she will not live in India with you."

Initially I was taken aback by his understanding of the situation but rallied to ask the obvious question of, "How did you know?"

John replied with a shrug of his shoulders and referred to 'way markers' that followed our engagement in 1771.

Included within these were the observations that, in eight years, I managed but two visits to Elizabeth in England *(I was aware of only one visit in 1772)*, the fact that Elizabeth wrote five letters to my one and my total preoccupation with work inside the offices of the Honourable East India Company.

"There were other lesser issues but all point to my belief that, initially, both Elizabeth and you were 'in love with love' and cherished the idea that you were uniting the families. Then when reality dawned, in the form of where to live after marriage, your courtship fell apart."

I must have appeared downcast because John quickly added that he was certain Elizabeth would treasure her friendship with me, which would take on the form of a companionship vow rather than the marriage equivalent.

"Charles, when do Elizabeth and you plan to make the announcement official?" he asked.

I momentarily paused to take mental stock when I realised that John had deduced only part of the agenda I was to discuss with him, which restored my confidence a little.

"You will recall that Elizabeth and I had a meeting with both sets of parents over the problem of where to base the matrimonial home, which ended in deadlock. It was agreed that only Elizabeth and I could resolve this issue and we agreed to reconvene, after Christmas, when the future of our marriage would be finally decided.

I am certain that all present knew that the outcome was a foregone conclusion because Elizabeth was adamant that, in the interests of her health, she will never again visit India."

John quickly cut in with, "Then there is nothing more that can be said or done unless you change you mind Charles. Are you prepared to do that and settle for life in England?"

"Not at all," I replied as I warmed to my theme. "You above all others know that I am not a potential country squire because I yearn for a real challenge in life which, for me, can only be found in the India I love."

For a while we both sat staring into the fire until John broke the silence with an 'ahem' followed by "I admire the forthright way you and Elizabeth have dealt with this problem, rather than allowing capitulation to burden either of you with a lifetime of regrets. It goes without saying that you will have my help equally if required, and my prayers will always be with you. So what are our next moves Charles? You will return to India and I have been assured, by the bishop, that a comfortable living in this area will become mine. Those are the facts so far. What about Cymol and his mother? Presumably father will purchase a property and have them live with him? Moneysa has quickly adopted the ways of an attractive and highly eligible young woman, rich with Indian charisma, which has already caught favourable glances from many young and rich hopefuls who will compete to offer her marriage and status.

At all times father and I will be in the vicinity as her family base rock. Do you agree with my summary of the situation Charles?"

I remained with my eyes fixed upon the burning log before me until I broke the silence, and shattered his composure with my reply of, "Not entirely John for there is another feature that you need to know. You are the first person to hear this, but the fact is that I am deeply in love with Moneysa and I want her to become my wife and, before you ask, I am certain that she shares my feelings."

Almost as if attached to a spring Brother John leapt to his feet, cleared his throat, and announced, "It is fortunate that I am an ordained priest otherwise I might have said, "Bloody hell!"

His timing was perfect because it diffused the tension of my announcement and we both burst out into laughter, although I could detect just a little hysteria within my mirth.

John recovered his composure and explained that he was aware from earlier years of a strong bond between Monnie and me in that, whatever situation arose, it would not be long before we were side by side.

"You see Charles in my innocence I looked upon this as a brother and sister friendship, which indeed it was, but I failed to realise that it would not remain as such. Within the wine vat of time your friendship has matured into the love bond you have described to me."

I poked at the mass of burning wood in the grate and watched a myriad of sparks take flight up the chimney; then sat back and murmured, "But it does not make sense because it is devoid of all motives John. In terms of basic human reasoning my marriage to Elizabeth would bring much happiness through the unity of our two families, and the cherished prospect that it would continue through many generations to come. On the other hand what combination of justifications led to Moneysa and me falling in love, in the face of racial and cultural differences, that we have brushed to one side as if they do not exist? Also please do not allow a sense of the theatrical to cloud my sworn sincerity when I assure you that I would happily live in abject poverty, with Moneysa as my wife, than carry on with my present arrangement. I cannot offer you good reasons for what has happened but I pledge my future upon the outcome."

With that I slumped into silence feeling aggrieved that I could not translate my emotions in what, to me, would have been more suitable words.

Without a word John walked over to the window and silently studied the evening scene before him. Then he turned and thanked me for being frank, open and honest in all that I had said. John's reply then started with a series of questions, "Do we need a reason to fall in love?

Did God ever explain his motives for loving us, his fallen creation, with such fervour that he willingly died for us? Do you and Moneysa need to justify why you love one another?"

John paused and looked at me as if awaiting my reply which was restricted to the plea, "Please then give me your opinion on the bond between Moneysa and myself."

"Charles, my advice comes straight from my soul to yours. In truth I tell you that love born without reason is the surest love of all; and that is the love you share with Moneysa. Hold onto it, cherish it and grow stronger through it both in this life and throughout eternity."

I walked over to John and we threw our arms around each other as I thanked him for his support, which had both eased my mind and cast aside the many burdens that had threatened it. "Thank you for placing your confidence in me Charles which is best sealed with a well earned glass of port wine," John said as he led me to my armchair.

"Truly a vintage port," I remarked whilst confirming its clarity against the backlight of the mantle shelf candelabra. Nodding his head in agreement John commented that there was more of it to come starting with the first of the pre-Christmas balls at the Salter's tomorrow.

"I wonder how Monnie is getting along with her dancing lessons which have kept her in residence there for the last two nights."

John laughed as he surmised that by now she was probably teaching her instructor the rudiments of some obscure Indian folk dance.

In contrast to the light hearted flow of our conversation I startled Brother John when I announced that the next few weeks would be the most important and stressful period of my life, in that my love for Moneysa would be set aside to give her the opportunity to meet other men.

"Why is there a need for her to do that Charles?" asked a bemused Brother John.

"It is because she needs to be absolutely certain at this critical stage in her life.

So far I have never openly told Moneysa I love her and she still thinks that Elizabeth and I are engaged to be married. I know that many potential suitors will descend upon her, so she needs to be certain who she truly wants to spend her life with; for only then can she reap the fruits of the happiness she truly deserves."

"If that is the path you feel called to take Charles then I will support you," added John as we both paused at the sound of coach wheels on the gravel, announcing the fact that Moneysa had returned from Salter Hall

My brother and I were joined by father on the entrance steps, and I ran forward to open the carriage door for Moneysa and her maid Ruth to alight. Instantly Ruth was instructing the coachmen to take care as they lowered a large trunk and, with a wave of her hand, staff appeared to carry the trunk to Miss Moneysa's room.

Taking her hand I welcomed Monnie home and, in response to my question, I was told that the trunk contained all her new dresses for the Christmas season. In turn she was hugged by Papa and Brother John and hustled into the house with the promise of a meal that was about to be served.

During the meal an excited Moneysa regaled us with her adventures in what had turned out to be a dance class for relative newcomers to the ballroom. It was led by a professional instructor whose job it was to teach around 24 young ladies and men the rudiments of the more popular dances, in preparation for the Christmas season. Monnie admitted that the hardest dance to understand was one called the quadrille which was far more complicated than all the other dances put together.

As the clock struck 9.00pm we rose to leave the table and Moneysa asked leave to make a quick visit to her mother and Cymol, and requested that I walk through the woods with her.

Father instantly agreed and pulled the bell cord for a lantern to be lit and delivered to the entrance hall. In no time at all we were in our warm over garments and, with lantern held aloft, we entered our secret little forest.

Moneysa gripped my hand tightly and pressed closer to me when a disturbed creature made its rustling escape through the undergrowth, or an owl suddenly hooted in a tree above us. Quickly I put my arm around her waist and she followed suit and thanked me when I assured her there were no tigers in England, and only a few non-poisonous overgrown worms.

We spent around ten minutes talking with Cymol and his mother, who was clearly unaware just who her visitors were, and having established that all was well, and their provision cupboards were full, we began our return journey to Ganton Hall.

A break in the clouds allowed moonlight to filter through the trees and give a little light to the path ahead which drew into focus a wayside rock, later nicknamed 'Monnie's rock,' where she had sat previously to remove her tight shoes after which I had carried her home.

"Shall we stop for awhile Charles and enjoy the little time we have left together?"

As we sat down I put my arm around her because I could sense that all of a sudden sadness had replaced her outgoing nature.

"What is it Monnie? Please tell me."

She leant her head upon my shoulder and reminded me of the happiness we enjoyed together in India which had continued all the way over to England, but now the end was near.

"Soon you will marry my good friend Elizabeth and our woodland walks will be no more, and I will have to face life without you."

Moneysa tried to continue but emotions came to the fore and, despite her efforts, she burst into tears as I held her close.

Running my fingers through her hair I could feel tears trickling down my face, fuelled by the memory of my recent conversation, in which I declared it necessary to test Moneysa's response to other men before making my move. Was I searching for a reason to love Moneysa or had I already forgotten my brother's words that love born without reason is the surest love of all?

Monnie's voice broke into my thoughts as she apologised for being silly and for wetting my coat with her tears. "Thank you for listening to me Charles. Perhaps we should go home now?"

I helped her to her feet but held on to her hand rather than begin our walk.

Looking at me in the now clear light of the moon she was grieved at the sight of my visible tears, and began to apologise for upsetting me, until I raised her hand and gently kissed each finger in turn.

In those few seconds I realised that if I failed to speak now then this moment would never return; even the moonlight seemed to challenge me as it illuminated the sadness and resignation upon her face.

"Moneysa I have something very important I want to say to you, yet I struggle with fear that my words may cause you offence."

Moneysa slowly let her hand fall from mine as she almost whispered, "Now is the time I feared most; the time when you will tell me to walk alone because soon you will be a married man."

I felt my heart would break asunder at the sight of her standing dejected and abandoned yet trying to give me a smile of comfort.

Immediately I knew that if I wasted this moment then I may never again have such an opportunity. Even the moonlit woodland became very still as if awaiting the eternal union that was about to be sealed.

Human reasoning had once defied love but love finally won the day through my words, "Moneysa please look at me for I want you to know, that by mutual agreement, my engagement to Elizabeth came to an end some weeks ago, and our marriage plans will be publically cancelled after the Christmas period but, in the interim, we will still pretend to be engaged."

As I held her hands total shock replaced her sadness, she attempted to speak but fell silent as I continued, "Moneysa there is something far more important I must tell you and it is……….that I love you ….for being just as you are … for being my ever darling Moneysa…who captivated my heart all those years ago, with a love that has grown and blossomed awaiting this moment.

Monnie, having taken my confession this far may I add that I will be the happiest man, in all creation, if you will return my love and honour me by becoming my wife?"

I paused on realising that our hands were gripped tightly together as if they had independently begun their eternal union awaiting our intentions.

"There now I have said it, and to my last breath I will continue to rejoice over the truth within every word. What are your feelings towards me Monnie? Can you find a little space in your heart for me?"

Moneysa was transfixed as she stared at me with a look of almost total disbelief, which slowly turned to one of joy as she gasped out, "I am awake and it is not a dream. Charles, my love for you began when I gave you that battered old doll and yet I never imagined that you could ever love me. I am just a simple village girl from India with nothing more than ten rupees I have saved, but I have a heart overflowing with love for you."

Instantly we were in each others arms as we kissed over and over again in fervour of emotion that united our tears, as we wept and laughed together, and our secret little forest witnessed our love born without reason.

"Charles, I have not forgotten your marriage proposal and my answer is yes please," she added as hastily we wiped our tears away and, conscious of our long absence, hurried back to the Hall.

Both father and Brother John were waiting in the hall and father announced that he was about to send out a search party fearing an accident.

"Sorry we are late back father," and as I searched for an excuse Moneysa quickly said, "You must blame Cymol. Once he starts talking he never knows when to stop."

Father nodded and, out of the corner of my eye, I noticed that Brother John had suddenly become very interested in his fingernails.

With that they wished God's blessing upon each other and retired to their various rooms with the exception of Papa who, by tradition stretching back to India, went around the property checking that all doors and windows were locked and that fireguards were in place.

My warm and comfortable bed was secondary to my needs as I lived and relived all that had happened that evening. A strategy had to be thought through, plans had to be made and nothing must be left to the frailties of chance alone. From the distant hall I heard the large clock advise me that the new day was one hour old.

I was tired but sleep, as an act of veneration, would not tread ground sacred to resident thoughts of Moneysa and all that had happened between us but a few hours ago.

CHAPTER NINETEEN

The party season begins

At the breakfast table Moneysa apologised for her late entry which was due to her having to try on her new party dress whilst Ruth made a small, but urgent, alteration to the hem.

"You are always welcome and time waits upon you Monnie" replied my father as she wished a hearty 'Good morning' to all present.

As she sat down our eyes met and we gave each other a nod and a smile which, to me, was confirmation of our newly declared love in unspoken words.

Running her hands through the back of her hair, which hung in a series of tresses almost to her waist, Moneysa said, "Sorry about the state of my hair but Ruth has already begun the process of preparation for tonight."

"It is beautiful Moneysa, such that words can never express," replied my father.

"Although of a different colour it looks just like Molly's hair did when she let it down, it brings back such happy memories …" Here my father hesitated and looked down at the table clearly upset.

Immediately Moneysa held his hand saying, "Do not be upset Papa because making you happy makes me happy. I will always wear my hair like this just for you. When my father died I thought no one could replace him, but your kindness to me, and my family, means that I now love you as my father."

Much moved he put his arm around Moneysa and they held each other in the silent bond of father and daughter at peace.

For Edward Ganton and his two sons the early part of the day was one of relaxation in the form of chess, discussion and reading whereas Moneysa remained upstairs whilst Ruth slowly and painstakingly prepared her for the grand party ahead.

As evening drew near the men retired to their rooms and dressed accordingly; then assembled in the hall when they were advised that the coach had arrived. Charles was dressed in his best breeches and stockings complete with a high necked white shirt complimented by a drop front waistcoat, frock coat and buckled shoes.

Edward Ganton wore a tail coat with a velvet collar, breeches and plain black shoes and in honour of the occasion, he had decided to wear his little used wig.

As ever Brother John was in the traditional dress of his calling.

Suddenly there was a sound of voices and giggling as staff members, led by Ruth, entered the hall and, after token curtsies positioned themselves either side of the entrance door.

Addressing us Ruth asked our permission to invite a charming young lady to join the party.

Sensing there was an element of seasonal jollity father replied, "Of course you may Ruth, we are looking forward to greeting this particular lady, whoever she is."

With that Ruth rang a little hand bell and, on cue, Moneysa swept down the staircase and stood facing her audience enjoying their gasps of admiration. She wore a simple, high-waisted cream coloured satin gown. The low-cut round neck was trimmed with a white fichu, and the elbow-length sleeves were finished in white lace ruffles. Ruth had curled her beautiful hair so that her ringlets cascaded over her bare shoulders.

As everyone clapped their hands in appreciation of her beauty Moneysa, in turn, curtsied to those around her then rushed over and held Papa's hands, whilst thanking him for all the happiness he had given her.

"Thank you for making me the happiest father in the world," Papa replied gently kissing her cheek.

Going over to Brother John she thanked him for being a kind brother and, looking a shade uncomfortable, he kissed, nay quickly pecked, her proffered cheek.

When my turn came she said, "And thank you Charles for being my ever best friend." As I leaned forward to kiss her our hands briefly met in unspoken emotion.

Wrapped up in our cloaks against the cold of this early December evening that, according to Ruth's prediction, bore distinct signs of snow to come within the next two days, we moved towards the waiting coach. I helped Moneysa into her seat then stood back for Ruth who, as Lady's Companion, was to accompany Monnie.

Much to my surprise she began to climb aloft and join the driver.

"Where on earth are you going Ruth," exclaimed my father.

"To sit with the driver sir," replied Ruth in a tone suggesting that she knew her place.

"That will not do Ruth," he replied in mock reproach, "Your place is alongside your mistress who, at any moment, may require your services."

With that Moneysa popped her head out of the window and asked, "Did you bring my gloves Ruth?"

As Ruth climbed down she smiled at father and whispered, "I see what you mean sir."

Good conversation meant that time passed quickly and we were surprised to suddenly discover that our coach had stopped outside the now familiar Salter residence. Friendly oil lamps that lit up the driveway now cast their glow upon the Salter family, who were waiting to receive us at the open door.

Their words of welcome began with unrestrained compliments at the sight of Moneysa followed by warm embraces as the families were reunited. Grasping my arm Elizabeth whispered how much she had missed me, and was longing to hear from me words of hope that would give back purpose in her life.

However further conversation was stifled as a uniformed major domo, guest list in hand, ushered us to the reception room door.

Three raps upon the floor with his staff were followed by "Miss Elizabeth Salter and her fiancé Mr Charles Ganton."

In turn, my father and brother were formally announced and accepted with appropriate smiles and nods of the head.

Then the moment came when undertone talking ceased and a forest of eyeglasses, like rings upon a stick, were simultaneously lifted into place at the announcement of, "Miss Moneysa Ganton the adopted daughter of Mr Edward John Ganton."

The sight of a brown skinned and strikingly attractive dark haired young lady from India, dressed in the best of English fashion, was a sight that caught the breath, quickened the heart of young men and restored the fervour of those richer in passing years. Sharply applied elbow nudges, or whispered rejoinders from behind angled fans, brought to heel older men who had allowed maturity to briefly wear the fading mantle of youthful dreams.

However one man of presence, aged I would think around 30 years, approached Moneysa and bowed then announced that his name was Neville......

I must add at this stage that he appeared, from the deference paid to him, to be high in the social status of guests present and that, in phonetic terms, his named sounded like 'Nevilee.' My spelling of his name is the best attempt I can make under the circumstances.

.... "And I am honoured to meet you Moneysa," he continued.

With that he gently kissed the back of her hand which he did not release when he went on to say, "I have often read of the great beauty of the Queen of Sheba, but would never have believed that one day I would be honoured to hold her hand."

Kissing her hand again he added, "Dear queen, I am your most loyal and obedient servant." With that he bowed and backed away to his chair leaving Moneysa with a look of total bewilderment upon her face.

Elizabeth turned and whispered into my ear, "Remember my words Charles when I urged you to watch how young men will receive Moneysa, and then ask yourself if you still love her as your sister."

The fact that I already knew the answer would have to remain unsaid but, for the first time in my life, I felt what must be pangs of jealousy as I watched young men jostling one another in order to engage her attention.

The evening was one of dancing, drinking, eating and socialising from which I will pick out key points of era related interest. There were moments that were of deeper concern for Charles which he will introduce as and when they occur. The end wall of the dining room was set out with several tables filled with all manner of food including a range of meats, vegetables, bread rolls and cakes, sauces, various deserts and assorted fruit and many other delicacies which, on request, were served to parties as they sat at the many tables around the room.

The library doubled up as a relaxation room lit only by the cheerful glow of a log fire, with a commanding view over the sweeping moonlit rear lawn, already covered in a white blanket of frost. Staff members were discreetly positioned to serve drinks to guests at various tables tucked away in corners and recesses.

In a side room already thick with cigar smoke, which led from the library, several quartets of men were playing quadrille that was a popular card game in the 18th century, and was characterised by a distinctive pack containing 40 cards.

In the ballroom a string quartet had struck up, without intended coincidence, with the quadrille dance, a lively French square dance for four or more couples.

Already Charles and Elizabeth were dancing in sequence to Neville and Moneysa who had remembered all that had been taught her in earlier lessons.

With the dance underway it defied commentary as couples quickly advanced towards each other, changed places, alternately held and changed hands, danced back to back and then began all over again.

Again Charles was not slow to notice the intense look of adoration on Neville's face, as he advanced towards Moneysa, and held on to her hand far longer than rules of the dance required.

"I must be out of condition Elizabeth," I gasped as I relaxed in my chair. "Dancing is great until you stop and then the aching joints take over."

Elizabeth smiled as she gently rotated her glass of sherry only to suddenly push it aside and sit back in her chair.

"What is the matter Elizabeth?" I enquired as I placed my hand upon hers. "Is it the impasse in which we now find ourselves?" She nodded her head, paused and agreed with my thoughts.

Then her positive nature returned with, "We met and became very good friends and distance will never change that because I look upon our deep friendship, as an immovable bridge set between England and India that will last for all time."

I nodded in agreement and was about to speak when Elizabeth cut in with "It is my prophecy Charles that one day you will return to England and live again at my house which I have named Ganton Hall ...."

Here she paused and, with a look of sadness, gazed at the wall beyond me.

"There is something else on your mind Elizabeth, what is it?" I asked looking her fully in the face. After a pause she slowly said, "You will leave India sad and alone but I will be here to look after you." Further conversation was precluded when red faced and jovial well wishers descended upon our table.

The evening progressed with more dancing and intervals for eating and conversation including a chance face to face meeting between Charles and Neville:

"My dear Ganton I am so glad to be able to meet you amidst the throng, if only to briefly pass on my greetings before being swept away."

His hand shake was firm and genuine and I returned his theme of goodwill as, without a pause, he added, "One thing I must congratulate you over Ganton is that you are doubly blessed with my dear friend Elizabeth as your wife to be, yet you still manage to hold on to the devotion of Moneysa who never loses an opportunity to praise you, and I am damned if I know how you do it.

Nevertheless my friend I will not give in, so farewell for now as I seek to recover my Queen of Sheba from the hopefuls who have set up camp around her."

Finally the time came for departure as carriages arrived to transport the noisy revellers whence they came.

Despite appropriate dress it was doubly cold after exit from the warmth of the house and many hurried, albeit some were carried, into their carriages and the refuge of layers of travel rugs awaiting their pleasure.

The Salter and Ganton families exchanged embraces and best wishes as they sought to minimise time spent in the frost bound and bitterly searching cold, that embraced the night around them.

Moneysa, with teeth chattering despite her fur lined Pelisse, quickly climbed aboard and was immediately wrapped in carriage blankets by her ever attentive and loving companion Ruth.

Probably much to his displeasure Ganton senior was delayed in the cold by the sudden appearance of Neville who urgently sought a few moments of conversation away from the coach. I could not gain the gist of the conversation other than hearing Edward Ganton direct Neville to 'send his messenger the day after tomorrow.'

As the coach rumbled its way through the frost painted night a full ten minutes elapsed before warmth was sufficiently restored, to its occupants, so that shiver free conversation could resume.

Moneysa's head suddenly appeared from beneath her blanket and gave voice to the question, "Who was the Queen of Sheba?"

John awoke from his reverie and assured her that it was from the Bible, around the tenth chapter of the first book of Kings, and that he would explain her influence over King Solomon in their next scripture study, whilst correcting Neville's apparent problem with his geography.

Moneysa thanked Brother John and immediately disappeared beneath her blanket as the coach rattled on.

Despite the late hour of my retirement sleep was held at bay by recurring thoughts of Elizabeth and the imminent public cancellation of our engagement, and Moneysa who may have become vulnerable to less honourable elements within the many who sought to find favour with her.

Nevertheless I must have drifted away only to be stirred by the distant chiming of the fifth hour upon which I leapt out of bed and, as the clock struck the sixth hour, I began my daily walk around the grounds with my condensed breath forming a trail behind me.

I briefly called in to check the welfare of Cymol and his mother having forgotten that they would be in the midst of their first prayers of the day; and on the way back I paused to sit for a while upon 'Monnie's rock' and enjoyed reliving the happy memories which were born upon this spot. Then they were all wrecked when 'Neville' came to my mind and his obvious infatuation with Moneysa.

With that the demons of imagination started their prodding exercises with 'if Moneysa should fall in love with Neville what would you do Charles?'

"Enough of this," I muttered under my breath as I rapidly walked to the Hall and prepared to have breakfast at 8.00am prompt, a standard set and maintained by my father, who ran meal times with military precision.

Much to our surprise we had an additional place set at the table for Ruth who, in her new role of 'companion to Monesya' was there by invitation from father.

After grace led by Brother John we began what, by our standards, was a light breakfast of toast and preserves with tea or hot chocolate as the beverage. Fruit, although plentiful in India, was upon the table at high cost which led to some households keeping their fruit supplies under lock and key between meals – or so I was told at the Salter's house.

As the meal progressed father alerted us to what he called 'two affairs of immediate concern.'

He began by congratulating Ruth for the great work she had done, particularly yesterday, in helping Moneysa with her dress requirements and being discreetly close to her throughout the Salter's party. "Consequently, Ruth, you are welcome to eat with the family on all occasions," he concluded.

Clearly, Ruth had been taken by surprise and tearfully expressed assorted words of thanks. Sensitive to her distress Moneysa comforted her by putting her arm around her whilst adding her personal thanks for being a second mother and constant companion.

When she had recovered father concluded with, "It is needless for me to remind you Ruth that you must dress accordingly in styles suitable to all occasions, you will be at

Moneysa's side unless she decides to the contrary. So today please make the necessary arrangements and ask that the account is sent to me."

Ruth, now composed, thanked my father for his confidence in her and promised that she would look after Miss Moneysa, with the same love and care, as if she were her own daughter.

I briefly interrupt to give a little background to that of Ruth and her new appointment. Ruth was formerly a woman of lower middle class birth whose husband ran up massive gambling debts, committed suicide, and left her destitute.

Derbie Salter, out of pity, initially employed her as the family seamstress which meant she was a member of the servant's hall.

Her elevation to 'Lady's Companion' by Edward Ganton meant she was no longer a servant but the paid companion to Moneysa.

Her role was to spend her time with Moneysa providing company and conversation, accompanying her to social events, helping her with dress and hair styling and acting as Chaperone when so instructed by Edward Ganton.

The role of Lady's Companion was popular in the 18th century and later, and had similar responsibilities to that of a 'Lady in Waiting.'

"Thank you Ruth and now to my second point which deals with a request made by Neville as we left the Salter's early this morning.

Initially he asked for my permission to ask you, Moneysa, if you would agree to enter into a state of courtship with him. I immediately refused to give my consent on the grounds that he had barely progressed beyond the initial introduction stage.

His next request was for you to accompany him to a Christmas reception and concert at his parent's home in a place called 'Chevet' or something that sounded like that."

Looking over to Moneysa, and then to Ruth he concluded, "I told him that I will agree to this only if my daughter, Moneysa, wishes to attend and, if she does, then she will be chaperoned by her Lady's Companion. He concurred with my proposal and will send his messenger for my written answer in the morning.

Now Moneysa my response depends entirely upon your decision, so please advise me accordingly."

Taken by surprise, and conscious of every eye on her, Moneysa gave me a look of desperation as if to say 'tell me what I must do?' Soon she regained control of her mind and thanked father for granting her the right of decision.

"On the whole I believe that Neville is a genuine man with honourable intentions which is more than I can say about many of the men around me last night......."

I momentarily began to panic when Moneysa described Neville, in not unfavourable terms, which she may have sensed when she quickly looked my way and then qualified her remark with, "But he is not for me. So perhaps I should accept his invitation, and tell him gently that my feelings towards him are within the confines of social friendship only."

Father nodded and agreed to provide further details when the official invitation card arrived.

With that the breakfast gathering prepared to leave when Moneysa tapped the table with her spoon and asked if she could make a suggestion.

"Certainly my dear," replied father. With that Moneysa explained how we had both, through the village blacksmith Matthew, visited the homes of many of the villagers who lived very basic lives and would have little to show that the great feast of Christmas would soon be upon us.

"How nice it would be for those poor people, and their children, if we invited them here for a Christmas dinner followed by entertainment. It would be even better if the Salter family would join us in this venture of Christian charity and we could all put on aprons and serve at the tables."

Warming to her theme Moneysa suggested that extra tables could be set up in the hall if the dining room proved to be too small and, as a special treat we could hire a Punch and Judy show.

Suddenly she paused when she caught sight of Brother John who, strangely, was close to tears.

John held up his hand to indicate that all was well then, contrary to his nature, he walked over to Moneysa and gently kissed her on her cheek. "My sister in Christ you have depths of true compassion for which I yearn and it goes without saying that I fully support your suggestion. With your permission father may I ask for a show of hands as a measure of family agreement?"

Father responded by raising his arm followed by Brother John and myself.

Not to be outdone Moneysa nudged Ruth and they raised both of their arms which they held aloft and, in quadrille style, danced a little jig around the dining room.

When the applause ended they declared that they would dance for the party, and perform Indian tricks, whilst others could make up a singing group but they must not forget to hire musicians.

Before more ideas tumbled out it was agreed that we would all meet again in two days time, to set out a programme of events, and that Moneysa would be responsible for the entertainments.

As we left the dining room father took Moneysa by the hand and declared, "That her own father Drebar would never be dead whilst his daughter was still alive," and Brother John and I both with great sincerity said, "Long may we be blessed with her presence in our lives."

Momentarily Moneysa looked distant and sad, only for her to quickly return to the happy and outgoing person who had a place in each of our hearts.

CHAPTER TWENTY

Pre Christmas activities at Ganton Hall

In general it was a busy day for the household.

Father, Brother John and Ruth had taken the coach to a nearby town where father had business with his solicitor, Brother John had a deanery meeting and Ruth was going to order clothes in keeping with her new role of Lady's Companion.

At the same time Charles and Moneysa paid a visit to Matthew in the village then they distributed food and clothing to needy households.

According to Matthew, this charitable act was just in time because for the last seven days the village had enjoyed clear blue skies by day with severe frosts at night; but now heavy grey clouds moving in from the horizon heralded the coming of the first winter snow.

In his mind all Matthew saw were roads blocked in deep snow drifts whereas Moneysa, who had never seen real snow, was agog with excitement.

As I turned into the entrance drive and slowly manoeuvred the horse and trap, back to the stable area, Moneysa asked if I would walk with her to see her brother and mother; more so if they may be blocked in with the coming snow.

"Of course I will," I replied as I lifted her down and twirled her round in my arms, in the process of which Moneysa suddenly cried out that something cold and wet had landed upon her face.

Putting her down she pointed to some white flakes which were settling upon her black coat sleeve and, with her hands held high to the heavens she asked eagerly, "Is it snow?"

By now heavy white clouds filled the sky and it began snowing in earnest.

Watching thoughtfully Moneysa turned to me and said, "I prefer to think of it as those white clouds meeting again in the once empty blue sky. In the joy of their reunion they have cuddled each other so hard that bits of white cloud have broken off, and now float down on us, so that we can share their happiness with them."

"I must write that vivid description down Monnie," I declared, as hand in hand we ran for the shelter of our secret little forest. I congratulated her for the original and poetic description of a snowstorm, which I vowed to read out at our village Christmas party.

Soon we were sharing the view of the snow storm from the window of Cymol's cottage, which was warm and comfortable, courtesy of the Hall staff who had kept them well stocked up with every necessity.

He was fascinated with his first experience of real snow but his mother, locked in her own world, was oblivious to the white flakes building up on the window panes. After a while we said our goodbyes, almost unnoticed by Cymol, who was totally mesmerised by the winter scene outside his window.

Huddled together we walked our familiar woodland path although, in places, snow had found its way through the trees and had begun to settle in selected spots. One such exposed place was 'Monnie's rock' which was covered in a blanket of snow that I noticed in passing.

Unable to resist the temptation I quickly ran back to make a snowball from it and, with a careful lob, managed to hit a shocked Monnie in the middle of her back.

Gleefully accepting the challenge Moneysa ran and quickly scooped up some snow, squeezed it in her hands, then immediately dropped it with an anguished cry, "Its freezing my hands."

Almost in tears, she waved her hands around trying to warm them.

"Sorry Monnie it was my fault," I said as I took her cold hands in mine, rubbed and blew on them, then drew them beneath my coat on to my chest for added warmth.

In that position our faces were instantly drawn closely together and, silently, we enjoyed all that we saw and desired within our developing union. As a reflex response to my feelings I murmured, "I love you, Moneysa" then leaning forward I slowly kissed away the wet upon her eyebrows, as her body pressed closer to mine.

Her, "Thank you for loving me Charles" was barely said before our lips, by mutual yearning, repeatedly closed together oblivious to the snow that was building up around us.

Before we move on to the next scene I must express my intention to cease publishing further commentary upon the strengthening bond of love that was rapidly gaining momentum between Moneysa and Charles.

During the following weeks, particularly when Edward and his son John are away from the house, Charles and

Moneysa will spend considerable time together, ensconced in Charles room, when further dimensions of their love for each other will be enacted in ways that, I would imagine, are not strange to those who have shared similar desires of the heart.

Any moves upon my part to further publicise intimate details of their private emotions are unnecessary, and would be tantamount to gross intrusion upon their privacy, without adding further substance to my narrative. Sufficient to say they shared a depth of love which united them when alive and, in my view, will continue to uphold them throughout eternity; even if I prove to be alone in this belief.

"There is something about snow that makes me so very tired," remarked father as he sunk back into his armchair and enjoyed the warming glow from the log fire in the sitting room. Both Brother John and I agreed with father's feelings whilst adding that an abundance of parties, with resultant late retiring hours, may be a contributory factor towards our current lethargy.

The brother's hint of other house parties that have not featured in my report is not an oversight but, rather, one of expediency since most of these events followed a similar agenda and modus operandi that, if included, would lead my narrative into the realms of repetition rather than developing and advancing the Ganton story for your consideration.

Further reference to such events will occur only when, contained within them, are features relevant to the purpose of my presentation.

The approaching sound of singing directed our attention to the opening door as Moneysa and Ruth entered singing the closing bars of a song familiar to our ears.

"We have already begun practising our singing duet for the village Christmas party," announced Moneysa. "Ruth has started teaching me lines to a song that has captured my heart both in beauty of words and melody."

Turning to Ruth she asked her to sing it for the family and, after initial hesitation, she finally agreed to do so from her position in the centre of the room.

We were captivated by her surprisingly rich soprano voice as she sang unaccompanied a popular song which, by unanimous request, was repeated as an encore.

The song performed by Ruth, and copied below, was the popular English ballad 'Drink to Me Only with Thine Eyes' with lyrics from Ben Jonson's 1616 poem 'To Celia' to a tune composed around 1760 to 1770.

> *Drink to me only with thine eyes,*
> *and I will pledge with mine;*
> *Or leave a kiss within the cup and I'll not ask for wine.*
> *The thirst that from the soul doth*
> *rise doth ask a drink divine;*
> *But might I of Jove's nectar sup,*
> *I would not change for thine.*
> *(Jove is the Roman god Jupiter)*

"Upon my soul Ruth I declare that our gain is measured in terms of great loss to the stage," was my father's compliment shared by all.

Ruth curtsied and thanked everyone then moved over to a chair, in a far corner of the room, only for father to call her over to the fireside settee to be 'part of the family,' and close to Moneysa if needed.

After a period of conversation punctuated with the clink of wine glasses, and an occasional yawn, a general drowsiness was beginning to descend of the type in which voices echo along lengthy tunnels and faces take on a double appearance. However we were restored to maximum attention when Brother John suddenly announced that he had some important news for us all.

Standing with his back to the fire he remarked that it was one of the proudest moments of his career when the diocesan Bishop, who turned up unexpectedly at the deanery meeting, surprised everyone by announcing that he (John) was going to be installed as Rector of the village church just down the road in time for the Christmas services.

John basked in our congratulations that included a kiss on the cheek from Moneysa and, much to everyone's delight, was John's request to Ruth that she balance the act by kissing his other cheek.

Apparently the previous incumbent was apathetic and spent most of his time away from the parish and, when in residence, he made no effort to encourage the parishioners to attend services; nor did he ever venture out on pastoral visits. Consequently the church interior was mildewed and, along with the low spiritual morale of the villagers, was badly in need of restoration; particularly the tower which was beginning to part company from the nave.

Brother John had been given the task of recovering the congregation and restoring the church as the focal point of village life which, according to John, was endemic of apathy among many Church of England priests.

Immediately I told John about Matthew the blacksmith and his unofficial role of village squire cum whatever else was needed, and promised to introduce them in the morning to enlist his help.

With that father rose and solemnly proposed a toast to Brother John in his new appointment as village Rector. John responded with a moving little address in which he described gratitude, as the half brother of love, to be the basis of our ministry in this life.

He sat down as we applauded with the exception of Ruth who could not move her arms because Moneysa had fallen asleep with her head firmly upon her shoulder. The onset of sleep was always instantaneous as far as Moneysa was concerned and on many occasions, in India, I had carried her home for her mother to put her to bed. Walking over to Moneysa I gently lifted her into my arms as she transferred her head to my shoulder and with a weary smile; her arm went around the back of my neck.

"Please lead the way Ruth and I will carry her to the bedroom and leave the rest to you."

CHAPTER TWENTY ONE

Moneysa and Neville part company

Without doubt the Ganton household was very busy as Christmas approached and the hectic, and event filled year of 1780, slowly drew to its close.

Forgive me for my condensed account which, sadly, does little to reflect the enormous detail and effort that was planned and led by Brother John, and the tireless Matthew, wherein local volunteers transformed the interior of the church to pristine condition in time for the Christmas celebrations.

Services began on the penultimate Sunday before Christmas with Elizabeth Salter and the Ganton family assembled in a front row box pew, reserved for them. The remaining box pews and benches were filled to capacity with locals who, impressed with the humility and charity of their new and hard working Rector, literally flocked to the church.

Also, because of his hard work and dedication, Matthew was invited to sit with the Ganton family which, by his facial appearance, certainly enhanced his Christmas. Through some of Matthew's contacts Brother John enlisted the help of two violinists, supported by an oboist and a bassoon player, who formed the beginning of a church orchestra; with Ruth acting as the lead singer in a newly formed choir.

The now warm and cosy church was a blaze of light from numerous candles obtained by Matthew at minimum cost, and there was an abundance of holly sprigs on the window ledges to remind all that Christmas was near.

To my mind the most appealing feature of this pretty church was an attractively carved rood screen which, when viewed through its ornate trellis holes, gave prominence to the Ten Commandments printed in scroll form, and set at the back of the altar.

However, betwixt now and the joy of Christmas was, to quote Charles, 'Neville's party,'

It was two days before Christmas and, in many ways, I dreaded the onset of this day and more so the next few minutes which was the appointed time for the Neville coach to collect Moneysa and her companion cum chaperone Ruth.

Neville worried me because of his suave yet apparently genuine manner inherited from family tradition and training, foreign to one weaned on the heat, smell and life style of a turbulent India. I could not match him for his vast vocabulary always available to match any occasion and, more so, I was afraid of his obviously strong feelings towards Moneysa fondly known as his 'Queen of Sheba.'

"**His** Queen of Sheba indeed," I mused, as I paced across my bedroom chiding myself for allowing jealousy to tarnish my reason. Was it not a fact, which would soon be publically declared, that Moneysa and I were in love and intended to become husband and wife? There could be no doubt that Moneysa and I were in love and in several ways we behaved as if we were already married, more so within this very room.

Fortunately, Moneysa and I had time to ourselves daily when I escorted her through our 'secret little forest' to see her mother and brother and, earlier this day, she had assured me her intentions were to divert the flow of Neville's emotions, away from her, for the prime reason that she was already committed to another; whilst leaving him to ponder upon who that person was?

"Damn his eyes," I muttered to myself as I walked incessantly up and down over to the window then back to the fireplace. But there it was; the unmistakable sound of a post horn as the carriage wheels ground to a halt on the drive.

In no time I had joined father and Brother John in the hall as Moneysa, looking radiant in yet another fashionable dress, swept down the staircase closely followed by Ruth. She paused to hug father and kiss him on his cheek then smiling at John and myself she was gone.

In the half light I saw a resplendent coach complete with a family crest emblazoned on the door and seated aloft were two uniformed coachmen who controlled the four horses. Following the coach was a mounted outrider whose presence confirmed the upper class status of the Neville household.

Each member of the entourage wore identical light blue coats with gold coloured cuffs, collar tassels and pocket flaps. This style of uniform was typically worn by 'gentry class' coachmen in the 18th century.

However the mood of Charles Ganton was applicable to every age, old or modern, when he muttered his apologies in advance for missing dinner on account of not feeling the least hungry, as he continued to stare from the window until the fast moving coach disappeared from his view.

"Upon my soul, what is the matter with Charles?" asked Ganton senior in a hushed voice.

"He has a lot on his mind," replied Brother John without enlarging upon the nature of his problems.

"No doubt he is worrying about Elizabeth and their forthcoming marriage?" concluded his father.

Perhaps Charles heard what was said but I believe it to be unlikely because his entire life was with one person only; and she was on her way to meet Neville. With that he turned and rushed upstairs, two treads at a time, and the sound of his bedroom door closing was clear to even the most impaired ear.

The sound of my repeater watch announcing the midnight hour awakened me from an uneasy sleep and prompted me to leap off the bed where, fully dressed, I had spent the last hour or so. For a moment I was puzzled by the sound of joyful activity going on, throughout the house, until I remembered that household volunteers were decorating the place with winter greenery to greet Christmas 1780, which was almost upon us.

Although only a minute had passed I again looked at my watch as I fretted about the late hour and the possibility of there having been an accident; or had Neville captivated Moneysa with his charms and persuasive talk? Then through my concerns I heard the sound I had so long rehearsed within my mind; a short and discreet blast on a post horn followed by wheels upon gravel grinding to a halt.

Feeling rather guilty, as one prying upon matters not of my business, I rushed to the window and peeped down at the stationary coach. Opening the carriage door the coachman stood aside to allow Ruth to step down and walk slowly into the house. Next Neville climbed out and assisted Moneysa as she alighted.

They both walked up the entrance steps and stood just outside the entrance porch. After two or three minutes of seemingly intense conversation Neville gave Moneysa's hand a farewell kiss and, as she turned to walk towards the door, he suddenly reached out, grabbed her round the waist and pulled her close to him as his other hand held her head in a frenzied kiss he could no longer retain.

Immediately Moneysa fought him, with all the fury of an Indian tigress, with both her fists frantically punching at his shoulder and the side of his face.

Realising his impropriety Neville quickly broke away and held out his hands symbolising an apology; which was rebuffed by Moneysa as she wiped the back of her hand over her mouth, thus demonstrating that she wanted no further part of him or his actions upon her person. With that she turned and ran into the house and a despondent Neville slowly climbed into his coach and, with head in hands, began his journey home.

My feet hardly touched the stair treads as I hastened towards the sound of frantic voices and crying as I entered the hall. Father, Brother John and Ruth were trying to comfort Moneysa and two shocked house maids remained in the distance wondering what they could do to help.

I felt almost a spectator to the sound of my own voice as my heart cry of, "Moneysa, I am here," immediately silenced all but Moneysa's cry of "Charles" as she ran into my outstretched arms and threw hers around my neck.

In close embrace we shed tears together and she held me even tighter as I whispered, "You are safe now Monnie for I will never again let you out of my sight." A smile broke through her tear stained face as she said, "Thank you, my ever best friend" and kissed me lightly on the lips.

For reasons I know not I suddenly became aware of that lovely melody I first heard played in India, which added a type of spiritual essence to the bond between us.

During this pause I must add that the above scene of tenderness, between Moneysa and Charles, occurred as if they were totally oblivious to the fact that others were present; and I truly believe that to be the case.

Every face, with the exception of Brother John, wore an expression of stunned amazement as they, in robot fashion, immediately obeyed John as he ushered them out of the hall and along the corridor into the living room.

After a short time during which I helped Moneysa dry her eyes and regain her composure we walked hand in hand along the corridor and into the living room.

Father, John and Ruth stood up as I led Moneysa to the sofa and sat alongside her as three pairs of eyes looked our way in anticipation of further revelations to come.

I made the obvious point that the morning of Christmas Eve was already one hour old, and Moneysa was tired after her distressing experience. I suggested we all drink a cup of hot chocolate before retiring and, after about twenty minutes of general conversation, I felt Moneysa's head gently fall on my shoulder signalling that 'instant sleep' had once again claimed her.

Tenderly scooping her into my arms she quickly adopted her now routine sleeping position as Ruth led the way to her bedroom.

Previously I stressed that I can never act independently of Charles Ganton and when he leaves a room then I am automatically drawn with him. On a number of occasions this has caused me to miss important conversations and this was no exception.

As I passed through the door into the corridor I heard Brother John begin the say, "Father, I would be grateful to spend time with you….." which then faded out of hearing distance. I surmised that John intended to update his father with all that had happened between Charles and Moneysa prior to their meeting with the Salter family on Christmas Day.

For me sleep was sporadic thus allowing me to mentally replay, many times, all that had happened during the previous 24 hours.

I eagerly anticipated the moment when everyone would know the truth; but the way it suddenly happened had taken me totally by surprise. Rather than being offended with Neville over his ill behaviour perhaps I should thank him because the entire household now knew that Moneysa and I were in love and, starting tomorrow, I would not relax until my immediate world knew of this glorious fact.

I was late starting my morning walk and duly returned after less than one hour; having decided that I was ill dressed to accommodate the inclement weather. As I walked towards the house I became aware of holly sprigs placed against all lower storey windows and, inside the portico, was a small tree top hanging upside down as a triangular symbol of the protective nature of the Holy Trinity. I was impressed by the way the staff had used their artistic skills to add an attractive seasonal dimension to Ganton Hall, which appeared to encourage the falling snow to swell with pride into larger flakes in keeping with the occasion.

Rather than dirty the recently cleaned steps and entrance foyer I walked in via the rear stable yard and through the steam filled wash house, having first removed retained snow from my over-boots. Within two minutes, before the summons of the attendance gong, I entered the breakfast room with a hearty 'Good morning' to all present.

Brother John was standing with his back to the log fire whilst Moneysa and Ruth sat in the window recess admiring the snow. Moving over to Moneysa I knelt alongside her and holding her hand enquired if she had begun to recover from her adverse experience of a few hours ago.

"Perfectly," she replied as she raised and kissed the back of my hand. "All thanks to your love combined with the love of my wonderful family."

I stood up at the sound of the breakfast gong.

By tradition, father entered as the last vibration from the gong faded away. Immediately Moneysa rushed towards him and kissed the side of his face, he hugged her and asked, "Have you fully recovered from your ordeal my dear?" Moneysa smiled at him and gripping his hand replied, "Having a Papa as kind as you erases my brief moments of sadness."

In turn Brother John and I echoed our greetings to father whilst Ruth followed with a symbolic half curtsey.

During breakfast father enquired from Moneysa how, apart from Neville's inexcusable conduct outside the house, the general pattern of the evening had gone and had she otherwise enjoyed her visit?

"I was very well received and immediately felt at ease. His parents, younger sister, and many other gentlemen and lady guests were all experienced hosts and, with but a few exceptions, made me feel very welcome.

On entering a big entrance hall with uniformed footmen at either side of the door, I was initially shocked by two large men dressed in iron suits with long pointed masks over their faces, standing on each side of a huge fireplace. As soon as I was not the centre of their conversation I nudged Ruth and asked who the 'iron men' were?

My knowledge of English took another step forward when I learned they were suits of **amour.**"

Moneysa looked surprised at our good natured laughter until Ruth whispered in her ear that they were 'suits of armour' quickly followed by Brother John's quip, "That their passions would weigh heavily upon them."

Light hearted banter dominated the breakfast of Christmas Eve and, as the table was cleared, the sound of a horse trotting towards the stable yard aroused looks and murmurs of curiosity.

"Sounds as if a messenger has arrived," remarked father.

A few minutes later his prediction was confirmed when a maid appeared, with a tray holding an ornately sealed envelope, which she offered to him saying, "If you please sir the messenger begs permission to await your reply."

Father nodded and said he would summon her in due course.

Examining the envelope he moved over to the window, where he broke the seal, and sat to read its content. Clearing his throat he announced that it was from Neville and, considering that he had offended both Moneysa and her family, he would read it out aloud if Moneysa was happy that he should do so. Her nod of approval was followed by
....

"Dear Mr. Ganton, I thank you for reading my words that come from the depth of a soul struggling in the pit of deepest remorse. The fact that I behaved in a most unbecoming manner, particularly to the one who is my cherished vision of all that I could ever wish for, is totally beyond my comprehension. In desperation I would go to any lengths to turn back the clock upon my ill behaviour but, sadly, this cannot be done and leaves me trying to undo that which cannot be undone. Mr Ganton please believe me when I declare to you my deepest sorrow for the offence that I caused to Moneysa and her family and, through your compassion, I implore you to pass my apologies to

Moneysa in the hope that one day she may find it within her heart to forgive me.

I beg to remain sir, your most obedient servant. Neville."

Looking around at all present, and finally at Moneysa, father commented that courtesy demanded that he should reply to Neville and what should he say?

Instantly, Moneysa replied, "Papa please say to Neville that I have forgiven him for his actions, and that I never hold ill feelings against anyone. Also ask him to reflect upon all that I said to him and realise that it is no longer prudent for us to meet again, other than in a social gathering, and that I wish him well for a happy and successful future."

Nodding his agreement father rose and asked to be excused so that he could write his reply and delay the messenger no longer than necessary.

CHAPTER TWENTY TWO

Edward Ganton reveals the situation between Elizabeth, Charles and Moneysa

Filled with the spirit of Christmas Eve we quickly changed into suitable clothing and helped load a cart, with food items and warm clothing, to help villagers through the Christmas period. On completion we paid homage to the hall fire before venturing forth.

Father came down the stairs in order to wish us well and, as I expected, to request our presence with Cymol and his mother at a family meeting in the living room immediately after dinner. The single item on the agenda was to assess the situation prior to our meeting with the Salter family who were joining us for Christmas celebrations at Ganton Hall. I grinned as Moneysa's glance caught my eye when she realised that I had correctly predicted the family meeting when, during our recent visit, I had insisted that Cymol and his mother dine with us in courtesy to the season.

The snow had given way to sunshine from a cloudless sky that added reflected brilliance to the snow scene around us. Our horse drawn cart produced deep ruts on the snow covered road, as we slowly headed towards the village. Moneysa and I were on the driving seat and Brother John and Ruth sat among piles of clothing and provisions in the body of the cart. Occasionally we passed rustics huddled up in leggings with sacking over their smocks who, regardless of their discomfort, returned our waves and goodwill greetings. As we entered the village Matthew strode out of his smithy with a huge smile upon his genial face, and dressed as if it was a summer's day, he met us by the side of the road.

Our joint "Good morning Matthew," was returned with a wave and a response that, once again, seemed to echo from the nearby church tower. He thanked us for coming and assured us that the villagers were looking forward to a much better Christmas than they had experienced in many a year due to our generosity.

"It is our pleasure that we can do God's work, more so at this season of the year," replied Brother John.

"Now the snow is soft and slippery, let me help you from the cart," warned Matthew as he placed two enormous hands around Moneysa's waist and, without effort, lifted her from the driving seat and placed her on the verge. He immediately repeated the procedure with Ruth who, patting his hands, thanked him for, 'making an ageing widow happy.'

Then to everyone's amazement he did exactly the same with Brother John whilst I, trying to be independent, leaped off the cart and promptly slipped upon my back into a pile of drifted snow.

"Bravo Mr. Charles," roared Matthew, as he enquired what I did for an encore.

The party spent several hours during which they visited every house in the village leaving provisions and clothing, according to need, and Brother John left a blessing on each household with an invitation to attend church on Christmas Day.

Moneysa was particularly welcomed by the children, who literally queued to be picked up, cuddled and danced around with by the one they addressed in words meaning 'that lovely lady from another land.'

Ruth, who once had children of her own, excelled in telling them Christmas and winter time stories whilst Charles, feeling just a little out of his depth, spent most of the time talking with Matthew except when the latter was busy entertaining young and old alike with his feats of strength.

When the shadows were seen to lengthen it was agreed that the time had arrived for them to return to Ganton Hall and, when safely aboard their horse drawn cart, Matthew assured them that he would light the church heating stove in good time for the place to be cheerfully warm for the Christmas service, and he promised to clear the snow away from the church path.

The return journey was noisier due to the contact of wheels with now frozen snow, as John and Ruth carefully controlled the horse so that the wheels would, as far as possible, seek sanctuary within the tracks left earlier in the day. It was the turn of Charles and Moneysa to huddle together in the now empty rear of the cart as a cold cross wind set teeth chattering, and increased the longing to be within the warm walls of the slowly approaching Ganton Hall.

On arrival they quickly abandoned the cart and horse to the stable lad and rushed into the kitchen seeking the warmth of the large cooking range. Huddled in front of it they were soon sipping hot tea provided by the kitchen maid who, together with the rest of the staff, continued in the preparation of dinner as if they were not there.

Pre-dinner conversation and the dinner with its many culinary attractions did well for the family spirit around what only can be described as a 'table of delight.'

Initially there was a minor problem when Lajila arrived and promptly lost her confidence when seated at the table. Fortunately she caught sight of and remembered one of the serving maids, who made regular deliveries of provisions to the woodland cottage, and had become accepted by her as a friend. Consequently a combination of Cymol and the friendly maid restored some semblance of reassurance which enabled Lajila to partake of, and indeed enjoy, the meal before her. Although Moneysa often spoke to her mother across the table, Lajila's response was as if to a total stranger rather than her daughter, despite repeated prompting from Cymol.

When the dinner had formally ended Edward Ganton invited the family to adjourn to the living room and, by name, he requested that Ruth must also attend in support of her responsibilities towards Moneysa.

After the post meal benediction Moneysa went over to Papa and whispered an obvious request into his ear to which he nodded his approval. With that Moneysa indicated to Ruth that her presence was requested and they both ascended the stairs in the direction of her room.

In due course the family settled down in a wide semi circle before a roaring log fire and, to further retain the warmth on such a bitterly cold night, heavy curtains had been drawn across the orangery windows.

"Has everyone who wants brandy been attended to?" asked father as he viewed nods of agreement from the male heads around the room.

"Before we left the dining room Moneysa asked my leave to try out a little experiment in advance or our family meeting and, unless I am mistaken, I can hear them coming along the corridor."

With that there was a knock on the door as Ruth entered and stood aside to admit Moneysa wearing her sari and Odhani. Immediately she walked over and knelt before Lajila and holding her hands cheerfully said, "Hello mother, do you remember me?"

Immediately Lajila's face lit up and throwing her arms around her daughter she cried *(in hesitant English which I have translated)* "My little Monnie has come home. You have been away for such a long time." With this she began to cry as Moneysa wiped away her tears, gently kissed her face, and told her that she had never been far away.

Addressing us all she confirmed our thoughts that her mother could only recognise her when she was dressed according to Indian custom and, for the sake of her mother, she would remain in her sari but not the Odhani which she had already removed and given to Ruth. She stressed that her Odhani wearing days were over and, for the purpose of this experiment, she had to borrow back her last Odhani which she had previously donated to Ruth. "One fact is that I have grown accustomed to the English dress and undergarments, hence I feel very cold wearing just a thin sari on a bitterly cold night like this," she said as she wriggled a seating space between me, and the arm of the large easy chair, which happened to be closest to the fire.

Moneysa's antics brought laughter from everyone, including her mother, thus adding a touch of light relief to what was a serious meeting.

Smiling at all present father opened the meeting with, "In truth I am blessed and honoured to have children that continue to work hard and bring happiness into many lives, not least of which is my own. Brother John, who is revitalising the parish church and village community, has found the time to counsel and support Elizabeth Salter by showing her that there is more to life than books and the clavichord. In parallel to these works he helps Moneysa with her Christian studies and is introducing her to an understanding of the many oddities of life in England. Also I am blessed in the knowledge that Charles and Moneysa dedicate many hours working with the poor of the parish assisted, with his strength and enthusiasm, by our beloved village blacksmith, Matthew.

We must not forget our very loyal Ruth, who works tirelessly helping, counselling and mothering dear Moneysa, to whom I owe my sincere gratitude. Finally there is Cymol and his mother Lajila. In between caring for his mother Cymol volunteered to look after the gardens which are a tribute to his efforts. All in all I am truly blessed by my immediate and extended family which, within the spirit of the season, I offer each of you my humble yet sincere gratitude."

During the following spontaneous applause father had a sip of brandy to, using his words, 'clear his throat' after which he rose to his feet.

"I now have some very important items for you that will become public knowledge following our meeting with the Salter family tomorrow. For obvious reasons some of you are familiar with what I will say, whilst others have little or no idea of the dramatic happenings of the last few weeks.

We are a united family and I am determined that we meet the Salter's with the agenda clearly in our minds and free from hidden surprises.

My first announcement is that the engagement to be married bond, between Charles and Elizabeth Salter, has been cancelled, by mutual consent, due to logistic rather than compatibility problems." Father paused as if awaiting questions during which Moneysa's hand slid into mine.

"I must stress that the long standing friendship between our two families appears to have survived mainly because responsibility for the breakdown lies equally between Charles and Elizabeth; thus cancelling out individual blame. Nonetheless I will leave that issue because Mr Salter may have more to say upon that topic tomorrow.

However, now is a good opportunity for me to alert you to what is both planned and hoped for in 1781.

The owner of this house, who gave it the name 'Ganton Hall,' is Miss Elizabeth Salter who will later reside here but allow my son, the Rev. John Ganton, to both live in and use the Hall as the centre for his parish work. Additionally, she has agreed to finance the building of a meeting house for the use of the village community, and it is hoped that the work will be completed in the New Year. In addition to his ministry Brother John will remain in close contact with the Salter family both as their chaplain and family friend.

This brings me to my second announcement concerning Charles and Moneysa which, thanks to the tact and diplomacy of Brother John, I first became aware of after Moneysa became the victim of an assault whilst being escorted home at midnight on the 22nd December. I need not comment upon the unjustified action of a misguided yet zealous suitor, who has since apologised for his adverse conduct, other than to say the matter is now closed.

I am now aware that the passing years have seen the filial affection, between Charles and Moneysa, rapidly develop into a love bond that has the sole objective of them living together as man and wife."

With that a suppressed gasp was heard both from Ruth and Cymol as Moneysa gripped my hand even tighter.

"After the initial shock I willingly accepted Brother John's assurance that their latent love for each other had never been discussed, and would certainly have remained locked within their individual hearts, had not Charles, in confidence, assured Moneysa that his engagement to Elizabeth was over. Prior to this declaration was the fact that Charles, in a recent meeting with his brother, had given his word that his now open courtship with Moneysa had not been preceded by clandestine and dishonourable actions."

Father allowed a short period of silence to allow minds, new to the changed situation, to come to terms with what was to happen. Very briefly I met Moneysa's side glance and wondered if she like me was classifying our moments of emotion, behind my locked bedroom door, within the context of expected family honour.

After a further sip from his brandy glass father sat down and continued, "It is well known that I am the legal guardian of Moneysa and, following a formal application for her hand in marriage from Charles, I will give my considered decision at a later date. I will not pre-empt my judgment other than to advise all other interested male parties to look elsewhere for a wife.

As you know Charles has been offered the post of senior area manager with the Honourable East India Company which will be held in abeyance for him until the 1st January 1782. The date was calculated to allow sufficient time for his marriage to Elizabeth and all necessary legalities and other arrangements to be finalised prior to their departure. With the changed situation there is nothing to stop Charles and Moneysa leaving for India around March when the seas are kinder to land based travellers. Subsequently they will marry in India and take up residence in the former Ganton home in which he was born."

Father paused in silence for a few moments as if reflecting upon all he had said so far before continuing following his familiar introductory cough.

"Without a doubt my critics would challenge me to explain why all this could not have been achieved, with less hassle and expense, if the Ganton family had simply remained in India?

Those closest to me are aware that the reason I returned to England, following my retirement, was based on the premise that Charles and Elizabeth were to marry and that the Reverend John Ganton would gain, which indeed he has, a ministry in this country. Naturally I wanted to be close to my family, and potential grandchildren, in order to light up my declining years. Now that the hand of destiny has redrawn life's scene it is my hope that Charles and Moneysa will permit me, together with Cymol and his mother, to return to India with them until the time arrives for me to rest within the same grave as my dear wife Molly."

Immediately Monnie and I gladly accepted his request and insisted that he came to live with us in the former family house. "Thank you for being the delight you are and I gratefully accept your invitation," father replied with a hint of a break in his voice.

"Finally I would like to thank you all for giving me your attention and I feel sure that you will share with me in giving our love and congratulations to Charles and Moneysa for a long and happy married life together. From this union I will have the added blessing of being able to address Moneysa as my 'daughter through law' which, if my darling Molly had survived, would have given her infinite joy."

Close to tears he sat down and relied upon his upturned brandy glass to hide his facial emotions as family members spoke quietly together as custodians of what was to be.

Suddenly Moneysa leapt up and held her arms aloft to gain attention for what she termed as her 'speech of thanks' to her beloved Papa who she would always love as if he were her natural father. Then with pretend seriousness she asked permission to make her first request as the 'future Mrs Charles Ganton' by inviting Ruth to live with them in India as her companion and advisor.

In total shock Ruth held both hands to her face, burst into tears, and blurted out, "Yes please Miss Moneysa" at which she rushed into Moneysa's arms in a profusion of gratitude. Back in their seats Moneysa reminded Ruth that she would be kept busy helping to raise little Chamon's as and when they arrived to which Ruth, amidst further laughter, agreed, "Only if there are not more than ten."

This was the second occasion on which the expression 'Chamon' was used in my presence and I can only surmise that it was a play upon CHARles and MONeysa as a pseudonym for children of their marriage?

Throughout all that had been said during that historic evening Cymol sat stern faced in total silence yet, inwardly, he was fast approaching bursting point which happened during the laughter described above. White faced and shaking he leapt to his feet as every head turned towards him and total silence fell on the room. As a prelude to what is to follow please remember that Cymol's spoken English was not brilliant, because it was little used, hence I will decipher what he said and record it free from word error. You will, I feel sure, appreciate it is vital to know what he said rather than the way he said it.

Edward Ganton observed to Cymol that he was obviously worried and that he must feel free to share with us whatever his concerns were and if he felt the need to sit down then he was free to do so.

"Thank you sir," replied Cymol as he drew from his pocket some notes to which he frequently referred. He reminded everyone that the village Muslim council had asked that he accompany Moneysa to England so that he could minister to

her Islamic needs yet, despite his endeavours, he had failed to dissuade his sister from leaving Islam and converting to the Christian faith.

Although he was saddened by what she had done there was nothing he could do about it, more so as he had been given to understand that she intended to spend her life in England.

When to his horror he heard that Moneysa and Charles were to return to India he had realised that everyone was unaware of the dangers facing them. He then went on to strongly advise against a former Muslim, who had converted to Christianity, returning to a part of India that was strong in Islamic traditions and to go on offending them by marrying a Christian man. He begged to bring before them the fact that a Muslim has no permission to ever leave Islam and any Muslim who left the faith would be given three opportunities to revert to Islam. If the one who left Islam refused all three opportunities then that person must be killed.

If a Muslim woman married a non-Muslim man then she would be guilty of adultery, a grave offence punishable by one hundred lashes or by stoning to death depending upon judgement. Sentence of death would be pronounced on the discovery of a sexual relationship between a Muslim woman and a man outside of permitted marriage.

Almost in tears, and to the astonishment of all present, he rushed over and fell upon his knees before Edward Ganton stressing that there was a large element of his Islamic community that would hate Moneysa for deliberately offending Allah 'Azza wa Jal' (which means 'Mighty and Majestic is he') by what she had done, and would not rest until they had punished her for bringing disgrace to Islam. Also, he stressed, it was accepted teaching that anyone who dies as a disgrace to Islam would be eternally tormented in hell. Still upon his knees and now openly weeping he pleaded..............

"Please Mr Ganton, please ...please stop Moneysa from returning to certain death in India and make her remain in England. I love my sister and I don't to want her to die .... please help"

He was overcome by his emotions as both Moneysa and Ruth put their arms around him and tried to console his obvious grief.

When Cymol had eventually recovered, and returned to his seat, my father stood up and thanked him for his frank and honest advice, together with his graphic description of the heartless and savage conduct of a minority of fanatics, within the Muslim faith, then went on to ask him the following question ....

"Through my experience in India I am very aware of both good and evil aspects within Islamic traditions, as indeed with Christianity and all religions, but **what matters most is what YOU believe, Cymol**. Please tell us if you accept these extremist views or are you a man of compassion and Godly peace?"

There was a long pause during which Cymol looked down at the floor in silence. Eventually, and without lifting his head, he murmured, "I don't know...I just don't know."

Following this scene the meeting drifted to its close and Charles and Moneysa, now dressed in warmer clothing, escorted Cymol and his mother back to their cottage.

On our way back to the hall it had rapidly become our tradition to use 'Monnie's rock' as a table for our lantern while we tarried awhile, with our arms around each other, bathed in the shadows of our beloved 'rhodie' bushes.

With her declared cold left ear against my chest I gently ran my hand through her hair as I murmured, "It is good that our future is now beginning to be generally known and, after tomorrow, the entire district will soon learn of our love for one another. We will no longer have to be careful over what we say, or how we respond to each other when in general company and have to rely upon dark places, however pleasant they are, to conceal our moments of emotion.

Monnie, we defied convention and our day has now arrived. We have won."

Breathing a sigh of mutual happiness Moneysa agreed, "The events of this evening have opened wide the doors of our future together, and I have loved every moment, until Cymol drew a cloud over it with his silly remarks."

Looking down at her serious face I asked, "Don't let him make you unhappy Monnie, so come on now where is your smile?"

"Gone to bed," she replied. "Shall I wake it up for you?" – "You can't," she muttered playfully as we rose to our feet.

She leant back upon me as my hand began to gently caress her neck whilst my other hand surreptitiously hovered above a very sensitive 'tickle' spot I had discovered upon her waist. When in position I announced a confident, "But I can make you smile," and launched an immediate attack upon her sensitive zone with full gusto. Her shriek of laughter awoke several slumbering birds as she leapt into my arms to escape my fingers upon her responsive point. What then followed clearly demonstrated that her cold ear was not matched by the warm fervour of her lips upon mine.

As hand in hand we later walked back to the Hall I did stress that if she was concerned about potential dangers in India, then I would willingly seek employment in England and a place for us to live.

Pulling me to a halt Moneysa said, "Charles Ganton, I just do not understand you. Why was it that you refused to marry Elizabeth because she wanted you to live in England rather than India; and now you are offering me a home in England?

Explain that if you can."

With suppressed confidence I replied, "The reason is obvious, it is because you are Moneysa and not Elizabeth Salter. I am fond of Elizabeth but desperately in love with Moneysa. It is as simple as that."

For a few moments we stood together in silence then hand in hand we continued our walk home until Moneysa, filled with emotion, whispered, "Thank you my ever best friend and, for the record, I am desperately in love with you."

Back at the Hall father and Brother John were seated in front of the entrance hall fire awaiting our return. "We were getting a little worried," remarked John with a half smile upon his face. "More so when we heard a shriek but we concluded that it came from screech owls which are active at this time of the year – or so I am told."

CHAPTER TWENTY THREE

Christmas Day 1780.
Presents and problems

Although I am an early riser I was, by comparison with the household staff, a convicted sluggard when I found that all fires had been reset and lit and kitchen and cleaning activities were in full flow by the time my feet touched the floor at 6.00am.

At 7.30 am father invited Brother John and myself to accompany him to the servant's hall where after a short address of thanks he presented them with a wicker basket filled with sweetmeats, bottles of wine, what looked like confectionery and assorted items of fruit.

It is worth noting that in the 18th century fruit was rare and more so in December and it may have been that Edward Ganton came by it through the East India Company. However received it would have been a welcome gift to the servant's hall.

Finally we assembled in the stable tack room where father dispensed Christmas greetings and 'Porter Joe' to stable hands dressed in their smocks and coachmen in their aprons, with traditional cleaning rags in their belts *(see opening comments about my earliest recollections)*. Then, after seasonal conversation we joined the ladies in the breakfast room and, later, began preparing for the arrival of the Salter family.

At the appointed time the Salter coach rumbled into the drive and stopped outside the steps leading to the main door and a welcome party consisting of Edward Ganton, Moneysa and Charles with apologies from Brother John who had set off earlier to prepare the church for the forthcoming service.

Thereby followed scenes of hugs and handshakes as Derbie and his wife Elizabeth, with their daughter Elizabeth were led into the house amidst constant chatter and words of joviality consistent with it being Christmas Day. One such quip came from Miss Elizabeth when she asked, "Does my house uphold the true spirit of Christmas from cellar to attic?"

After personal refreshment both families set off, in two coaches, for the Christmas morning service at the village church with Ganton senior and Charles joining the Salter family whilst Elizabeth, Moneysa and Ruth shared the second coach in 'order to catch up on the news.'

A third hired coach carried such members of staff who could be spared from their household duties.

The sun shone from a cloudless sky adding brilliance to the snow covered churchyard as both families approached the church entrance where Rev. John Ganton was waiting to receive them. Such was the energetic warmth of Derbie Salter's greeting that I would wager John's hand bore some evidence of his sincerity, long after the event, although he did not betray any discomfort during the many handshakes that followed. Perhaps it came as a relief when his hand was rested in favour of kissing the hands of mother and daughter Salter quickly followed by Moneysa who, not to be outdone, held out her hand whilst mischievously adding, "I did not recognise you dressed in your preaching robes, white tabs and wig."

Standing behind Brother John was Matthew, resplendent in his best clothing befitting his role of verger, which was one of various positions he occupied within the parish system. His face lit up at the honour of being introduced to the Salter family, of whom he had heard, but never thought he would one day meet.

As I entered the church my attention was immediately drawn to a wide range of dress styles ranging from rustic Sunday best to ornate and expensive clothing worn by ladies of fashion. Although the occupants of these dresses represented the extremities of a broad social stratum they appeared to be at ease with one another, and were even generous with their smiles and kind words. From snippets of conversation I was aware that in certain urban parish churches, in 18th century England, there was a mandatory seating plan that meant the rich were allocated the front box pews and the remainder worshipped from benches at the back of the church.

This was not the case in this church because Brother John would have none of it and his words, "We all have sins to confess so it matters little were we sit to confess them" brought unity of purpose to the congregation.

In the packed church shafts of sunlight through the leaded plain glass windows, and winter greenery in abundance around this hallowed place inspired the congregation, accompanied by the violin, oboe and bassoon players to lustily sing their praises in celebration of the birth of Jesus. I did not recognise any of the melodies but one set of words was familiar. They were those to the carol, 'Joy to the world the Lord has come' although the tune was not the well known present day version.

Between hymns there were appropriate lessons given by readers who, although displaying varying degrees of reading ability, had a uniform desire to retell the Nativity story with all the pride of having been invited to stand at the lectern for that purpose. Brother John gave a short yet evangelically inspired address that was punctuated with two or three cries of "Thank the Lord" and "Amen" from spiritually inspired members of his congregation.

All too soon the service came to an end and the Reverend John Ganton shook hands with each as they left and wished them a "Holy and happy Christmas Day." The villagers walked in groups back to their cottages no doubt looking forward to the special provisions delivered by the Ganton family during the afternoon of Christmas Eve; whilst the better dressed climbed into their carriages and proceeded in the direction of an awaiting dinner of gargantuan proportions.

Finally Brother John shook hands with Matthew and thanked him heartily for all he had done and that he was looking forward to a long working partnership with him. On occasions such as this Matthew suffered from deep discomfiture as he searched for words that, perhaps, he never knew although his honest face, and broad smile, said enough as he strode out and caught up with his village friends.

Derbie took hold of John's arm and they joined father and me in the lead coach. As we were about to depart we were rather bemused when Ruth popped her head through the door, and asked if we would all mind waiting in the entrance hall when we arrived back at the house. I noticed that she then went to the other coaches presumably to make the same request.

Puzzled looks and shrugs of the shoulder followed her entreaty except for Brother John who closed his eyes and settled back in his seat. However, his reverie was soon disturbed by Derbie Salter who spoke highly of the transformation of the once near derelict church, and the splendid service we had just enjoyed, and that it heralded a rebirth of the village community spirit.

Back at the house we all, as requested, assembled in the hall and gazed curiously at 'a something' that, in our absence, had been hung upon the panelled wall to the left of the staircase. Whatever was beneath had been covered over which, presumably, was why we were there to witness its unveiling.

Without further ado Brother John positioned himself beneath the covered object and invited my mystified father to step forward and stand alongside him. He began with, "It is common knowledge that Moneysa and I often go off together in the trap for Christian instruction, but there are occasions when we go elsewhere and that is far from common knowledge; and the fact that I encouraged her to pose for a local artist is known only to the artist, his model and me."

I was equally carried along by Brother John's story as was everyone else because, even in jest, the average person enjoys the mental stage set of a juicy scandal. This was evident by good-natured gasps of surprise and pretend nods of 'well I never' that quickly passed through the group to a background of laughter, until John held up his hand and Moneysa walked over and stood by his side. With a smile she began to address my totally bemused father.

"Dear Papa I have always wanted to give you a present just to begin to say thank you for all that you have done for me. You have made me feel that I really am your daughter and, on this special Christmas Day, I want to give the Papa

I love this present for you to remember me by." After pausing for effect Moneysa slowly pulled a silk cord, and the cover floated gently to the floor.

There for all to see was a life-like oil painting of Moneysa, who appeared to be completely at home against a background of rhododendron and other woodland bushes. She was portrayed wearing a black double breasted coat with pale blue lace cuffs, and the coat was cut away at the front revealing a cornflower blue dress beneath. The high neckline of her dress was trimmed with a frilled collar and her soft ringlets fell on to her shoulders. The artist had done justice to her small shapely hands as he had to Moneysa in entirety, as she formed a picture of total harmony with her beloved 'rhodie' bushes around her. She had been portrayed in 'left profile' and appeared to be staring thoughtfully at something in the distance.

Varying sounds of approval could be heard as father silently gazed at Moneysa's portrait. Moneysa took hold of his hand and with a gentle smile asked him if he liked his present?

After a few moments he turned and threw his arms around her visibly sobbing, unable to speak other than to say, over and over again, "Thank you…thank you …"

Throughout the years I have known Moneysa she has never been slow to share her tears with others be they shed in the name of sorrow or, as in this case, total happiness. To the sound of applause father and daughter faced one another, with tears streaming down their faces, earnestly thanking each other for their respective kindnesses that had led to this moment.

Finally this gathering of friendship began to slowly disperse at the sound of the dinner gong.

As an observer from present times I was a little surprised that table conversation, and the selection of food served, suggested little difference between Christmas Day and any other day of the year. A very large goose was the central attraction and sprigs of holly upon the table gave some indication of the day which was, generally, looked upon as a day for church service and attending to the needs of the poor.

Both ends of the table were reserved for the respective fathers with Mrs Salter sitting to the left of her husband. Facing her was Ruth who by special invitation, and looking a shade uncomfortable on what was a family occasion, had been invited by way of thanking her for her loyalty and support of Moneysa. The table was completed with John and Charles sitting side by side facing Elizabeth and Moneysa.

Pleasant and general conversation passed smoothly around the table but I was aware of a 'subdued almost strained atmosphere,' which probably reflected the long promised family meeting to follow, after which private knowledge would take a large and irreversible leap into the public domain.

Perhaps many around the table realised that matters would never be quite the same again, as long held dreams of family unification would not immediately be realised, and the placid mill stream of local upper class society would soon become a torrent of prejudice and self generated scandal.

Nevertheless the meal was enjoyed and completed in an atmosphere of family love and loyalty that would prove to be invaluable in the face of all that was to follow; beginning with the long arranged family meeting which was about to begin.

The living room had been prepared for the family meeting since the first light of dawn.

A traditional log fire was burning in the grate, complimented by winter evergreen boughs displayed around

the room. The background of snow reflecting the setting
sun did much to bring cheer into a room soon to become a
chamber of sad words.

Ruth called in the maids with trays of drinks to be set out
on a side table, and was about to depart with them, when
Edward Ganton called her back and requested that she sat
with Moneysa in the event she may be required. With a nod
of the head to Edward Ganton, Derbie Salter rose to his feet
and began..........

"First I would like to thank my friend Edward Ganton
for his hospitality towards me and my family together
with the excellent meal we have just enjoyed, preceded by
the joyfully moving service led by the Reverend John in
the newly refurbished village church. Then there was the
highly professional painting of Moneysa, that took all of
us by surprise, and I know that Edward will treasure this
spontaneous gift from one who truly loves him, perhaps
more than a blood daughter ever could."

His sentiments were endorsed by a gentle applause from
all present.

In a more restrained tone of voice he said "I would have
dearly loved to share Christmas with you but, much to my
regret, my wife and I will have to leave you this evening so
that I may prepare myself to chair the final 1780 meeting
of the all important County management committee in
the morning. The good news for you is that Elizabeth, as
agreed earlier, will be remaining with you over Christmas
and will return with you for New Year celebrations on the
31st December."

Following this announcement Elizabeth became the
focal point for a ring of smiling faces and discreet waves of
many hands.

But Derbie regained full attention when he declared "Within this season of gladness I feel sad over what lies ahead of me and I do not, for one moment, enjoy the prospect of what I have to say but, in advance, I must stress that every word that passes my lips carries with them the spirit of friendship that family difficulties will never obliterate.

I am going to speak severely; but within the context that nothing will ever wreck the bond of solidarity that has grown between the Ganton and Salter families, as the years have advanced.

We are faced with what promised to be a story book romance and a marriage that is now in tatters, mainly because of lack of attention to essential detail. To me it is almost unbelievable that Elizabeth and Charles, despite the length of their engagement, had not found the time to seriously discuss where they intended to live after their marriage.

I even tried to resolve the matter for them by purchasing and signing over the ownership of this residence to Elizabeth, as their base for married life.

Imagine my shock and disappointment when, only a few weeks ago, I was informed they had belatedly discussed this matter and had reached a total deadlock. Charles wished to further his business life in India with Elizabeth as his wife; whereas Elizabeth found the Indian weather incompatible with her health and required Charles to remain with her in England.

It is beyond my comprehension that they went ahead with their engagement without first agreeing where their matrimonial home would be. Perhaps they hoped, through gentle persuasion, to create a compromise as time went by. Alternatively they may have been influenced by the long held desire of the Ganton and Salter families to seal their deep friendship through the union of marriage which, if so, must reflect some blame upon their parents?

But the fact remains that as their marriage drew closer they realised that the situation was hopeless so they agreed to end their engagement, remain very good friends, and commit the much vaunted 'society wedding of 1781' to the pages of forgotten dreams. Few would change places with me tomorrow when I attend the final County meeting of the year, and advise them to change the social diary because the 'wedding of the year' is dead and buried."

At this stage Elizabeth was visibly distressed and began to sob gently when her mother put her arm around her, whilst Charles clenched his hands tightly together and fixed his gaze upon the Yule log burning in the grate. At this stage Derbie Salter paused and looked to his wife for assurance that his daughter had recovered and, following her nod to the affirmative, continued with his address.

"Then there is the further development which my friend Edward shared with me earlier today. The fact that Charles and Moneysa are unofficially engaged, and that they plan to marry when they return to India in early 1781, is the subject of my best wishes for their future happiness together. Naturally it has no part within the proceedings of the County meeting tomorrow since it is a matter for the Ganton family only.

But, with great respect, I must counsel you all, as my dearest friends, that rumours will travel the district with the speed of a forest fire. A breeding ground of distasteful gossip will be opened up and so delight those born of evil tongues. Please permit me to leave this scenario to your imagination, lest the benevolence of Christmas and the joy of our gathering become stained by agencies of ill will.

Under normal circumstances I would have mentally capitulated beneath the shock and strain, of much I have described, had it not been for the support and strength received from one person alone. Consequently I would like to openly thank the Reverend John Ganton for his support as chaplain to my household, in that he has counselled and raised Elizabeth from severe depression, and has never been short of effective words of encouragement to my wife and myself. Without his God given strength I would have found it impossible to continue both as a Magistrate and Squire within this district. Thank you sir and know that you are a credit to your faith."

With that Derbie Salter sat down to a silence broken only by muffled sobs from his daughter and the sighs of escaping steam from the burning Yule log.

After pausing to collect his thoughts, father thanked Derbie Salter for his long friendship, and echoed his belief that nothing would ever erode the strong bond between the two families.

He went on to stress that he was prayerfully confident that 1781 would bring new opportunities for each family to share and reflect upon with joy ....yet I sensed that deep within he was troubled, as I was, with lingering yet distressing thoughts that lacked clear definition.

For example why did Moneysa when presenting father with the oil painting say ".......And on this special Christmas Day I want to give the Papa I love this present for him to **remember me by**......." Where was she going or was she unwittingly being prophetic? Inwardly I was beginning to panic when my mind was refocused as father completed his address to gentle applause.

Essentially that marked the end of the family meeting as the party slowly walked and talked their way to the entrance hall and, in line, shook hands with Mr and Mrs Salter and exchanged good wishes for the season before they embarked in their coach.

To a flurry of waving hands, and smiles from faces shrouded in vaporised breath, the coach rumbled away from Ganton Hall as the family rushed into the house to escape the attentions of the seasonal yet bitterly cold weather as they duly huddled in front of the hall fire.

Father took a long and loving look at his newly presented oil painting of Moneysa which had raised his spirits, and restored his relaxed and positive nature, more so in the knowledge that recent family problems appeared to have been resolved.

He rubbed his hands and announced that Ruth and he would have a seasonal drink in the servant's hall prior to their traditional departure, early the next day, to visit their families on the feast of Saint Stephen. Father, with pride, declared that his was not like other households that expected their servants to walk many miles to their homes, particularly through the depth of snow that currently covered this district. Hence a number of hired carriages would be available to take servants to their family homes in and around the nearby villages.

As a final goodwill gesture he intended to invite the entire staff, if they so wished, to spend this evening with the Ganton family as a token of gratitude for a year of hard work.

We stood as father and Ruth left for the servant's hall after which I hurriedly closed the door they had inadvertently left open. "Cold draughts are a problem in houses of this age," I muttered as I sat on my hands in an attempt to warm my frozen fingers.

"It has been an interesting if not an historic day," remarked Brother John as he added another log to the fire. "We are certainly living in changing times which, although challenging, will never undermine the bonds of deep friendship that we, the valiant four, have enjoyed seemingly since our lives began. It feels as if an eternity has passed us by since those happy days, when fully dressed, we sat together in a mountain stream happily throwing water at each other. It may well be that in the months ahead we will be severely tested but let us never lose sight of our declared friendship, which I suggest we now renew in the sight of God."

With that they sat in a circle and held hands whilst John led them in a few minutes of family devotions after which they said the Lord's Prayer together. Then they stood up and embraced one another knowing that soon they would be distant in body but ever as one in spirit.

With that they filed out of the hall and down the passage way to the living room.

However as I turned I again caught sight of Moneysa's portrait looking at some distant object and once more wondered why she used the expression, "To remember me by." If I were to ask her for an explanation I know she would reply with something akin to, "I don't know" or, "Did I really say that?"

Suddenly Elizabeth's voice broke into my thoughts when she said, "It is such a lovely painting and so much like her." I nodded and began to turn for the door when Elizabeth caught my hand and asked for a few moments of my time.

"I just wanted to tell you something Charles because we may never be alone like this again. I need you to know that I will never stop loving you and we would have been happy together, had not events conspired to change our lives. Please Charles let us keep our deep friendship alive as a bond between us until we meet again."

Gently holding her hand as I reassured her that I would always honour our friendship and that one day I would return to this house and recall memories dear to us both.

With that Elizabeth slid her hand out of mine as we entered the living room and joined Moneysa and Brother John around the fire.

What followed later was a happy impromptu party in which the family and staff joined in and gave unabated enthusiasm to seasonal joys; such as passing the parcel, eating mince pies or dipping into the bowl of punch.

Obviously 'mince pies' were new to Charles and, after his first bite, he expressed his delight with the taste and asked 'who made them and what are they?' Emboldened after several dips into the punch bowl and duly red in the face as a result, a young kitchen maid proudly announced to Charles that she had made them for this party.

"Well done," cried Charles as he led a round of applause, "Please tell me how you made them." By now the wench was overcome with embarrassment and her muddled reply took quite a time to understand, despite some help from Ruth.

The essence of her answer was consistent with my research into the topic which confirmed that mince pies had been eaten at Christmas since the 16th century, and were actually made from minced meat. Those celebrating Christmas in the 19th century would find that meat had been replaced with dried fruit and spices.

Let me add that if I had been writing a general novel for your attention then I could have made great score out of the fun and enjoyment at the heart of this much loved Christmas night party. I have little doubt that it would be remembered by family and staff alike when, as if by the wave of a wand, social position became second to the true spirit of Christmas which shone in the lives of all present.

Towards the end of the evening, when fatigue and over indulgence was beginning to take its toll, the revellers sat around the clavichord and sang seasonal and popular songs, mostly unknown to me, from Elizabeth's never ending repertoire of sing along melodies.

Due to their close attention to the music no one noticed Charles and Moneysa move into the orangery to view the frozen snow scene illuminated by moonlight.

"Happy Christmas to my ever best friend," were the words that accompanied my arm around Moneysa's waist as she rested her head upon my shoulder. "Just think Charles, next Christmas we will be husband and wife sharing the same greeting but standing on our house veranda in India."

Trying to sound serious I said, "Well one cannot be too sure about that."

Turning to me with a look of deep concern upon her face she asked what I meant by that remark?

"The answer is above your head Monnie."

A glance upwards led to the equally quick reply of, "A ball of Christmas evergreens is all I can see."

"Correct," I swiftly replied, "But they are special leaves with special properties. It is called a mistletoe ball and tradition has it that if a young lady is caught beneath it, as you have indeed been caught, then she has to agree to be kissed otherwise she will never marry. So the choice is yours Miss Moneysa."

Surveying me with one of her whimsical looks she agreed that tradition must never be put to the test, as our arms went round each other and our lips repeatedly paid tribute to the requirements of mistletoe and the depth of our love.

Suddenly, we became aware that the playing and singing had stopped, and silence reigned within the sitting room, which led us to turn our heads in that direction. That was the immediate cue for the hushed witnesses, to our seasonal romance, to burst into laughter followed by hearty cheers and applause.

I bowed and Moneysa curtsied as they continued to cry out for an encore.

CHAPTER TWENTY FOUR

Feast of St. Stephen followed by New Year at Salter Grange

A sudden attack of cramp caused me to leap out of bed and repeatedly bang my foot upon the floor which, on reflection, was not the best way to begin a day regardless of the season of the year. Neither was the pain in my head that reminded me of the excesses of last night from which I vowed never again to treat a communal bowl of punch as if it was my private cup. After some minutes sitting on the edge of the bed, with my head in my hands and my foot pounding the floor I decided that enough was enough.

Remembering the house staff had gone home for the day I managed to restore the fire from its low level of smouldering ash and soon had two logs in full blaze in the grate; which gave me time to consider my next question of the day. If the staff were not here then why was the house alive with the sound of cleaning and kitchen activities?

Charles together with his father and brother were totally unaware that Elizabeth, Moneysa and Ruth had decided to become servants for the day and, under Ruth's experienced direction had been hard at work since 4.00am. When Charles became alert to the plot he immediately offered his services but was politely refused and advised to either go on his morning walk or clean his room and make up his bed.

It was many years later that Elizabeth announced that she regularly looked back in her diary and relived all the fun and hard work the trio had shared upon that memorable 26th December 1780. Immediately after breakfast they had taken provisions to Cymol and his mother and established that all was well with them. Then logs had been carried into the house, essential washing completed and hung out to dry in the hot kitchen, and the living room put back to rights after the events of Christmas night.

However, it must be recorded that the three men did make themselves responsible for their own bedrooms.

While the ladies were scattered around the house, occupied with their appointed tasks, father invited Brother John and me to join him in his visit to the two ostlers, who had volunteered to remain behind to look after the horses. We met up with them in the immaculately laid out tack room where, attired in their long aprons, they were busy cleaning the many horse brasses of different sizes and designs hung upon the walls. They were taken by surprise at this our second visit, within two days, and after furiously wiping their hands on their aprons they shook our proffered hands; as we exchanged seasonal greetings as equals in the name of He who the season represented.

Prior to our walk to the tack room I had been given charge of a jug of porter, and Brother John had been entrusted with tankards, which father filled and handed around so that, in the words of one of the ostlers, "We could wet the head of the newly born babe."

Following a light tea the family, and in particular the exhausted ladies, relaxed until Charles broke the silence with a stark reminder that they had not paid their end of day visit to the Cymol household.

I pretended to cover my ears at the groans of dismay and volunteered to undertake the journey on my own which, I believe, inspired Elizabeth, Brother John and Moneysa to be upstanding, whilst Ruth announced that she would get the bedrooms ready and prepare hot chocolate for our return. For his part father announced that he would look after the settee and ensure that it did not move away from the fire.

Although warmly clad we were not fully protected against the bitter cold as the shadows lengthened and the first stars became visible in the darkening sky. We walked closely together to keep warm and Moneysa thrust her gloved hand into my pocket for added protection.

It was too cold for anything other than chattered noises that resembled nothing of real purpose but, nevertheless, kept spirits high particularly when we compared this woodland walk with the hot and humid ones we enjoyed in India.

As we walked on I thought it was a trick of the fading light until a second and third discreet glance confirmed my observation that Elizabeth and Brother John were not only walking closely together but were, in fact, walking hand in hand.

Perhaps it was the magic of what Moneysa and I called 'our secret little forest' that had again cast its spell upon lonely hearts searching for unity.

We did not have to tarry too long at the cottage for all appeared well in that Cymol was in the midst of his prayers and his mother had gone to bed. Thus after a wave of our hands we began the return journey with the bitter cold biting at our tired feet. John and Elizabeth announced they would stride out to beat the cold whereas Moneysa sat down upon 'Monnie's rock' and announced that she was too tired to take another step. This was a time honoured cue for me to sweep her up into my arms whilst she arranged her right arm around my shoulder and pressed her face close to mine. By now we were several steps behind Elizabeth and John which prompted a tired voice to slowly whisper in my ear, "Did you notice that Elizabeth and John were walking hand in hand?" after which Moneysa fell into one of her instant sleeps.

On this occasion Monnie's fatigue proved to be contagious and was quick to spread to everyone which meant that, within the hour, the last light had been extinguished and Ganton Hall stood alone in the moonlight, whilst its tenants slept peacefully within.

It is a fact that the Gantons were exceptions to the rule because at this time of the year most families of social status would be engaged in endless rounds of parties, some of which lasted for two or three days at great expense and to the detriment of bodily health. Sadly the society that promoted such costly contact was of no real substance and quickly fell apart when its paper strength rules were broken, as Derbie Salter believed would happen, when the circumstances of the cancelled 'wedding of the year' were made public.

As it was impossible to predict just how society would react to news of this nature it was deemed prudent that Elizabeth, Moneysa and Charles should avoid social gatherings, other than the family get-together at Salter Grange on New Year's evening. It was also agreed that Charles would test out reactions when he attended, by long standing invitation, the traditional hunt on the 1st January 1781.

The agreed period of social absence covered the period 26th to the 30th December 1780 which, in particular, gave Edward Ganton the opportunity to rest, read and write of his career within the Honourable East India Company; whilst the 'valiant four,' together with Ruth, spent much of their time in the village discussing the planned 6th January parish party with Matthew.

Also they visited most of the houses, particularly those where need was much to the fore, and distributed food and other necessities together with prayer and goodwill in return for God's blessings being showered upon them as they left each humble dwelling.

Immediately following the day of Saint Stephen the weather became milder and rain cum drizzle quickly washed away the standing snow that, according to Charles, augured heavy going for the hunt on New Year's Day.

Finally the last day of 1780 arrived and after much early bustle and staff activity the family, including Elizabeth and Ruth, were finally on the road as their coach headed towards the Salter residence and New Year celebrations that lay ahead. However within the coach I gained the impression those planned festivities were not high upon the agenda, because during the last few days the 'valiant four' had thoroughly enjoyed each other's company and had, in fact, lived and relived those earlier days of pleasure gained from their adventures in the forests of India.

At this stage of my written account I am aware that house parties have previously been described in detail and, within the format of a general novel, such events offer an abundance of material for creative writing. My task is different and prudence will not allow my pen to become over active in these areas lest the impact of my narrative is diminished, or even lost, if I were to lose direction.

In broad details I can confirm that the cordiality, meals, music, dancing and fashions were identical reflections of those that I have earlier described to you. Several strangers of good will were present and conversation, although polite and relaxed, remained far away from the now defunct 'society wedding of 1781.'

One of the first faces I recognised belonged to Derbie Salter's cousin, Captain Brentwood, who instantly remembered meeting and conversing with Charles at the house party in 1772. During their conversation it transpired that Brentwood had also been invited to ride in tomorrow's hunt, and they agreed to travel down together and give one another moral support.

As the evening progressed I was not aware of any special attention being paid to several clocks chiming midnight. In fact it would be perfectly fair to say that in 18th century England the period 24th December to the 6th January was, in wealthy circles, one of sustained eating and drinking with scant regard to any deeper meaning attached to this period of the year. The passing of the year 1780 played no part in lives that were dedicated to self indulgence; and less so for 1781 as, without the clink of a glass, it stealthily set foot on what would become a stage of destiny for several within this room.

CHAPTER TWENTY FIVE

Trouble after the New Year's Day hunt

Derbie Salter prided himself on his horses and also the efficiency of his stable staff, and in particular the head man of the stables, who was tempted into employment in the face of competition from other affluent households. As a result of his expertise Captain Brentwood and I were each given a carefully selected horse, which was securely reined to the rear of our coach, as we headed for the venue of the traditional New Year hunt.

On arrival I was courteously received by the assembled horsemen who, perhaps from embarrassment at my presence, were not over keen to extend conversation beyond the usual outflow of 'comfortable' words demanded by politeness.

As for the hunt itself the outcome went into their record books as one of the least productive events ever held. Twice the hounds were favoured with the scent of a fox, and twice they duly lost their quarry, to the disgust of the master of the hunt and his regular riders.

After the ride I was so very grateful that Captain Brentwood had come along with me, otherwise my only human contact would have been the occasional nod of the head, from men who immediately strode away and joined colleagues distant from me.

Having realised that we were an embarrassment to the majority we decided to rest awhile in one of the club drawing rooms in which four elderly non-hunting men were sitting in front of the fire, and in the corner of the room three younger men were playing cards. One of the card players was an odd looking fellow who appeared to be the dominant member of the group, despite the fact that he was wearing an absurd wig which was too big for his head and in need of regular adjustment.

Our request to join the group at the fire was met in the affirmative and, for the first time this day, we were engaged in polite and general conversation. Sipping our glasses of claret Captain Brentwood and I were beginning to enjoy both the company, and atmosphere of this room, when suddenly I heard one of the men in the corner distinctly remark to his colleagues, "So help me it is my view that this club should not allow coolie lovers under its roof."

My companion looked at me and gently shook his head as if saying 'Ignore him Charles' whilst one of our fireside companions spoke out in a deep rich voice, "That is enough Elliott, please have respect for our guests."

Those words of advice brought immediate laughter from Elliott and rising to his feet he faced us across the room.

"Respect sir is truly an odd word to use in this context," he remarked glaring at the elderly gentleman. "You may have better served truth if you had waved the respect banner at Ganton rather than me sir. God's teeth man don't you realise that Ganton here is a total stranger to even the most basic elements of respect."

For me that was enough and the time for action had arrived. I leapt to my feet, brushed aside Brentwood's attempt to hold on to my sleeve, and in four strides I was face to face with Elliott.

Immediately the elderly gentlemen vacated their armchairs to seek safety away from the confrontation zone as Elliott's two friends stood up to offer their support. This prompted Captain Brentwood to quickly join me and, with arms folded, he showed his obvious contempt for them, as if viewing enemy ships from his quarterdeck.

Feeling contained and in full control of myself I offered Elliott the opportunity to apologise, after which we could shake hands and start afresh. Sadly my offer achieved nothing more than a snort of contempt from Elliott as he continued his tirade against me.

"Are you so bloody naive Ganton that you cannot see what is happening? There was the time when your Indian bed mate, of name I cannot recall but sounds like Monsoon *(which generated laughter from his supporters only to quickly fade when Brentwood moved closer to them)*, sat with her arse firmly in the dust of India and planned how she could better herself.

I concede that she is a clever schemer and if fate had given her a brothel she would have made a fortune.

But she turned her attentions to you in the process of which she destroyed the dreams of that lovely young heiress Elizabeth Salter, thus leaving you the sole victim of her wiles to manipulate at will. Notwithstanding her success with you, and the defeat of Elizabeth Salter, she went on to weave her witchcraft upon my good friend Neville who fell hopelessly in love with her and threw a lavish party at Chevet in her honour. I was present at that event and noted how well she interacted with and was quickly accepted by his parents; whilst he made no secret of the fact that he loved her and wanted her to be his wife.

Then your 'little joy of India' suddenly became bored with him and walked away in the company of others; no doubt laughing within whilst notching up yet another victory. You may care to know that Neville still sits alone in his room yearning for and bemoaning the loss of your Indian girl, who has become like a plague upon this area.

Do your betters a favour Ganton and take your native whore back to India before she wrecks the lives of other men, far above her class and, by return, allow us to try and heal the wounds you have left upon our cherished society."

Still in control of myself I explained to Elliott that, if he felt called to do so, he could criticise me at will which would generate nothing more than my utter contempt for his ignorance and stupidity. "But your cardinal error has been to slander the name and actions of Moneysa, who will soon become my wife, and that I will not tolerate." Coolly staring him full in the face I continued, "Elliott you will immediately apologise for the evil and unjustified lies that, in the presence of witnesses, you have levelled against my future wife."

From my manner he knew that I meant business and that I was not afraid of him and all he represented. Clearly he was used to imposing his will upon others but, perhaps for the first time, his bluff had been called. This was evident in his face that had become distinctly paler yet, with a side look of desperation towards his colleagues, he managed to stammer out the words, "Go to hell Ganton and take your coolie with you."

I half turned as if to walk away only to suddenly swing back, and with clenched right hand, I caught him full in the face with the back of my fist which sent his wig flying in one direction and its owner spread eagled into a nearby armchair. In one bound I was over to him and felt my left hand tear through his pleated collar as I pulled him up, punched him again, and with great effort, managed to contain my desire to carry on punching those hated features before me. Full of fury I snarled into his now terrified face that until he apologised for insulting my fiancée, then every time I met him I would again give him a thrashing. With that I threw him back into the chair and left him trying to stem the flow of blood from his nose and mouth with his ornate handkerchief.

In contempt I glared at Elliott's two companions who remained motionless, transfixed at the sight of Captain Brentwood and his non-compromising glower of warning.

Suddenly I was both amazed and startled when, through his handkerchief, Elliott broke into a high pitched wail, in the manner of a hurt child, 'that I had hit him and made him bleed.' Ordinarily his juvenile action would have caused amusement but these circumstances were far from normal.

Nearby servants had become aware of the confrontation and had alerted the master of the hunt who burst into the room followed by his immediate aides. The stage set was obvious to the newcomers and the offer of statements from the elderly gentlemen who had witnessed all that had happened, together with Captain Brentwood and I, quickly had the hunt master seated with us around a table, where he carefully recorded all that had led up to the final confrontation within that room. After detailed questioning he thanked us and confirmed that he would hold a full enquiry into the incident after he had interviewed Elliott and his colleagues, who had been escorted into a side room, and were to be next on his agenda.

Following the hunt master's advice we both, after pausing to thank the elderly gentlemen for their testimonies on my behalf, immediately left and within the hour were back at the Salter residence and in conference with Derbie Salter, my father and Brother John.

They listened first to my account and then to Captain Brentwood who confirmed my evidence in terms of what happened and the level of provocation to which I had been exposed. Additionally Derbie Salter was pleased that four independent witnesses had also given corroborative evidence to the hunt master.

"I dare say that I will be invited to sit upon the board of enquiry and I am grateful that you have forewarned me of what is to come," remarked Derbie as he walked over to the window and gazed at the distant woodland scene. "It is a damned bad business nevertheless" he muttered. "In truth I would rather be at odds with a swamp alligator than with that no good fellow Elliott.

He trades on the fact that his father is a major general and his older brother is a staff captain in the same regiment; albeit they cannot stand the sight of him. Once in my presence his father described him as an 'evil jackass' who would end his conniving life on the gallows. His mother refuses to have him in the house so, as a compromise, his father provided him with a rented property, and a monthly allowance, which he augments by despicable means.

I firmly believe he is mad in the head but he is not a fool and, believe me, he is a very vindictive and dangerous person who through lesser associates controls a gang of cut throat thugs who are indirectly in his pay. Early last year I led an investigation into the murder of a local household servant who had been savagely beaten and left for dead. Yet before he died he gasped out that he had disturbed a group of men trying to break into his master's house, and one of them fitted the description of the leader of a group known as the 'gang of six' who I am convinced are in Elliott's pay.

Then there was the tragic suicide of a lady I will not name who, on the evidence of her husband, was being blackmailed and Elliott was the prime suspect. I am convinced that he is behind most of the serious crime that exists in this area but, as ever, I lack solid evidence with which to take him to the Assize court and then to the gallows where he truly belongs."

Then turning to me he said, "Be very careful Charles for it would appear that both Moneysa and yourself have made a lethal enemy who will never give up until one or both of you are in your graves. I beg you to understand that I am not being melodramatic but very factual; and it would serve you both well if you returned to India just as soon as possible."

Nodding his head in agreement father stressed that in the interim we must both remain within the safety of the house and grounds, and restrict our journeys to no further than the village where Matthew would willingly add his protection.

"It would appear that Elliott has condemned us both to a term of house imprisonment awaiting deportation to India which, to my mind, rather flatters the strength of a so called man who cried like a baby when I hit him," I said with a hint of disgust in my voice.

"Quite so," replied Derbie. "You are the first person to openly confront him which means he has lost credibility that must be regained, before others emulate your stance against him. I firmly believe there is a real danger so much so that I will immediately send, under the guise of gardeners, six experienced and armed men to discreetly patrol Ganton Hall grounds, night and day, until such time as you both leave for India."

Eventually the incident packed first day of 1781 ended with the 'valiant four' sitting around the living room fire, quietly discussing all that had happened, as heavy rain beat down upon the orangery and the sound of leaking water, falling from the glass roof into an awaiting bucket, resembled a metronome beating time to their voices around it.

In the days that followed Charles and Moneysa spent most of their time in the house, with Elizabeth and Ruth, during which they planned the bill of fare and agenda for the 6th January village party. In the interest of security their twice daily visit to Cymol and his mother was made with two armed escorts discreetly placed in the surrounding woodland.

Perhaps it was on the 4th January that Derbie Salter arrived at Ganton Hall, and gave the family an account of the official enquiry into the incident at the hunt club house on the first of January. The evidence from Captain Brentwood and the four elderly gentlemen who had witnessed the happenings, plus several others who had earlier heard Elliott openly slandering both Charles and Moneysa, was sufficient to uphold the fact that Charles had been sorely provoked and that Elliott had become a victim of his own arrogance and offensive behaviour.

On hearing that he was to be banned from the club for two years he reportedly stormed out of the room muttering, "They have not heard the last of this matter."

These, as Derbie warned, were not empty words but a sinister fact.

Although Elliott's mercenary 'gang of six' had not been noticeably active during the last few months he (that is Derbie Salter) was certain that their services would be called upon to wreak his vicious revenge upon all who had offended him; starting with Charles and Moneysa. He thus stressed that vigilance must remain a top priority until they left England;

whilst the authorities would wait for Elliott to make a fatal mistake that would guarantee him a place on the gallows.

On hearing that report Moneysa burst into tears and rushed into my arms as, between sobs, she asked, "Surely we are not an evil couple – what have we done to deserve all this ill will? Cymol declares that hatred awaits me in India and now our lives are in danger in this country; and all we want is for people to love us as we love them …."

Cradled in each other's arms emotion reduced them both to tears and their grief was openly shared by Elizabeth and Ruth; whereas the remaining men became very quiet as they sat in silence as nature, as if in support, shed its tears down the surrounding windows.

Ruth was a very practical woman of the type that was indispensible in every household and, through her love and encouragement, some happiness returned to the beleaguered Charles and Moneysa. In parallel she was the driving force behind the forthcoming 6th January village party and her organising abilities were legion.

When the great day arrived rumour had it that many village families were ready and waiting long before the owls had ceased their activities, and the proverbial 'early birds' were still hard asleep in some frost covered bush.

Back at Ganton Hall, and after a hectic start in which family and servants had also been at work since long before dawn, the place was finally ready. Tables, stocked with all kinds of food and drink stretched from the hall and though into the dining room; and the centre for entertainment and relaxation was down the corridor and into the living room. I have no idea how the villagers got to Ganton Hall but suddenly, to the sound of horse hooves and cart wheels, they all arrived led by Matthew.

For my part I tried very hard to enter into the spirit of what was, particularly for the villagers and more so their children, a joyous and first in a life time experience for them all. They were in the 'Big Hall' in sight of more food than they had ever known not to mention the warmth, the luxury of comfortable chairs and, as some of the younger ones said, " With Miss Moneysa" smiling down at them from the wall; which was their way of referring to the new oil painting in the reception hall.

As the festivities got underway I watched, from my vantage point on the staircase, a veritable panorama of happiness, in its many forms, that had cost us so little in monetary terms but was giving priceless joy to many families of poverty. The good humour was deafening as children chased one another until brought to heel by a judicial clip around the ear from their overawed mother.

Fortunately, and on the instructions of my father, large fireguards were in place and the main staircase was 'out of bounds' to all guests.

When Ruth, Elizabeth and Moneysa tried to call the company to order from what was the main table, they had limited success until Matthew bellowed, "Quiet," which instantly had the desired effect.

Drawing her breath Ruth went on to explain the reason why a large, ornately decorated cake occupied the central position which, happily, captured my interest and distracted my mind from Derbie Salter's security concerns for Moneysa and myself. Ruth called it a 'Twelfth Night cake' which would be cut and shared between the guests. However, they were cautioned to eat it carefully because within the cake was a coin and the finder would be crowned king or queen of the Twelfth Night.

After much careful munching the 'monarch elect' announced himself, with a resounding shout of delight. He was a young boy with a crop of bright red hair and facial spots of a similar colour. A paper crown was carefully placed upon his head and he was paraded around, in state, on Matthew's shoulder.

Another centre piece which Charles did not mention was a large pewter bowl filled with something I heard referred to as 'Wassail' which, from research, was a Twelfth Night drink composed of ale seasoned with spice and honey. As the guests drank it they would toast each other using the greeting 'Wassail' which is derived from the old English term 'waes hael' meaning "be well."

Under normal circumstances I would have been fully involved in the fun being enjoyed by so many who little knew what eating and laughter, in a relaxed atmosphere, was all about. I watched them excitedly paying their forfeits when they failed to complete a verse from "The twelve days of Christmas" as Elizabeth accompanied them on the clavichord; and how they screamed and begged for more when Matthew lifted them up with six children hanging on each arm.

Then momentarily the happy scene before me became dim as the unwelcome vision of Elliott's evil face suddenly filled my mind, and caused me to rush to my bedroom in order to study the garden; just in case anyone was lurking about intent on violence.

"You are becoming obsessed Ganton," I muttered to the view upon realising I was allowing Elliott to dominate my mind. "Just get downstairs and enjoy the company," was my personal command as a familiar voice at the door said, "And I agree with you Charles. Come on because we all need you."

It was Moneysa and instantly we were in each other's arms in a long embrace which ended as we both sat together on the edge of the bed, regretting that we did not have the time to climb within it.

Pulling me to my feet Monnie said that she was going to change into her sari in order to sing an Indian song with Ruth, who was already dressed in one she had made for herself. "Would you like to help me change my clothes, Charles?" invited Moneysa as hand in hand we quickly left for her room.

One by one several of the children, with full tummies and contentment written all over their faces, slowly drifted off to sleep and as 11.00pm struck throughout the house the great exodus began.

The Ganton men stood in line with Moneysa, Elizabeth and Ruth to hug and wave farewell to their guests, who left amidst laughter and tears as they poured down upon the household the blessings of heaven for evermore.

Matthew made certain that everyone was accounted for and aboard, then with a wave of his arm, the convoy slowly lumbered away towards the village as the sound of singing and hilarity gradually faded away leaving owls to serenade the moonlit night.

CHAPTER TWENTY SIX

Slaughter on the village green

It was now the 10th of January and I began to seriously reproach myself for behaving like a scared rabbit.

Perhaps Elliott had thought better of creating further trouble for himself and had called off his hirelings who had not been seen in these parts for several weeks. Even our security guards were visibly relaxed and took more notice of the state of the garden, than potential villains lurking in the grounds. Thus with increased confidence Moneysa, Ruth and I declared that we would take some provisions and clothing down to the village and call in on Matthew.

Reluctantly father agreed but declared that if we were not back within two hours then he would send the security guards on horseback to escort us back to the house. I nodded my head in agreement whilst thinking that, although with good intent, father was over reacting to dangers that were just not there.

I had to drive steadily along the road in order to avoid more snow and ice induced potholes lest some of our load be lost which, more by God's grace than my skill, was achieved as we slowly drove into the village and on to the village green. Instantly we were hailed by Matthew as he strode over from his smithy and several villagers as they hurried from their houses at the sound of his voice. Matthew reminded us that the 6th January party at the Hall was still hot conversation between villagers as they relived their individual moments of absolute bliss, which led some to think ahead to a repeat party in 1782. "Then be sure to remind the Reverend John in early December and I am sure that he will be delighted to arrange another event," I replied knowing that Monnie and I would then be in India.

Already some villagers, including the red headed boy who was 'king of the twelfth night,' were looking with anticipation at the load on our cart as Matthew set out in the direction of a cluster of stone roofed cottages, from which the rich aroma of wood burning fires added rustic character to the village scene. "I'm just going to collect a few more worthy cases," Matthew added as he disappeared around a corner.

Already Ruth and Moneysa were busy sorting through a pile of clothing, trying to find a dress and coat of suitable size for a poorly dressed woman before them, whilst I managed to fit an elderly man with a pair of boots which, he declared, "Were the best he had ever owned."

Absorbed in the chatter, and with scant regard for a burst of sustained dog barking, pleasure suddenly froze as my heart 'missed a beat' to the sound of a menacing voice shouting, "We are in luck lads; we have caught Ganton and the brown coolie together."

Quickly turning around I saw to my horror six men with cudgels in their hands walking towards Moneysa and myself.

Despite my fear I was in command of my mind as I told Ruth to take Moneysa and join the villagers at the cart, as

I turned to confront what must be the notorious 'gang of six'. In such circumstances it is surprising how relatively small details remain in the mind, like the sight of the red-headed boy running towards the houses, as the villagers began a chorus of verbal abuse towards the thugs standing before me.

"Did you think we had forgotten about you and your Indian witch, eh Ganton?" snarled the obvious leader of the gang. "We are experts in punishing those who have offended against their betters and when we have finished with you both, along with any others who try to help you, there will be plenty of broken bones for these yapping dogs to feast on."

"I am the one responsible for all that has happened so leave the others alone and, if you have the nerve, come at me one at a time with your fists and not cudgels," I shouted at them, aware that anger was overcoming my initial fear.

"We fight as a team Ganton," shouted their leader, as they slowly advanced towards me in an ever widening half circle, with the obvious intention of attacking me from all sides.

To this day I remain convinced that the Lord had heard, what I thought would be my last prayer in this life, when a familiar voice thundered, "Stand still or those cudgels will be so far up your arse that they'll tickle your throat."

Matthew had returned followed by the boy with red hair and several other villagers.

Immediately he was by my side as I implored him not to get involved as it was my fight….only for him to mutter at me, "Mr Charles, you are my master when it comes to brain work, but when it comes to fist work there are few in England who can match me. These heaps of rotting dog shite will never give you a fair fight, so please stand back and look after the ladies."

With anger building up in him by the second Matthew was in no mood to be argued with, so I stood back as he faced the 'gang of six' who, despite their numerical advantage, were clearly uneasy at the sight of seven feet of towering and angry muscle that clearly meant business at their expense.

"Do not forget 'big man' that there are six of us and we are armed and are well known for never losing a fight," said a hesitant voice from the gang.

"Here are my weapons," roared Matthew as he held up two enormous clenched fists. "If someone sent you to hurt my friends then they forgot to tell you that I am both their protector and your executioner."

At this stage Charles directed several villagers to the rear of the cart away from the combat zone thus giving me a clear view of what was to follow.

*Please imagine the gang of six, facing Matthew in an ever decreasing semi-circle, advancing hesitantly towards him. In order to fully describe what followed I will identify the attackers as **numbers one to six** starting from the left hand side of Matthew and working around to his right.*

With meaning Matthew growled at them that if their numbers were only six then fate had done them great ill, for they were far too few in number to deal with the task before them. The undertone within these words of caution caused the gang to feel even less confident, thus causing their uneasy advance to almost come to a halt.

*That was their undoing because it gave immediate advantage to Matthew who, despite his size, was extremely fast on his feet and literally in the blink of an eye his left fist crashed into the face of **number one** who, to the crunch of breaking bones, hit the ground with his face a mask of blood.*

As a joint action the blacksmith's right fist thudded into the throat of **number three** who was reduced to a writhing and gasping mass alongside his colleague.

This was the signal for the rest of the gang to rush at Matthew with the exception of number five, who thought better of it, and literally got in the way of number six causing him, with a loud curse, to stumble and drop his cudgel.

As **number two** with raised cudgel closed in he received a massive kick in the groin which literally lifted him off the ground and left him rolling about, screaming in pain, as he clutched what was left of his 'private quarters.'

By now **number four** was close enough to lash out towards Matthew's head with his weapon whilst I looked on in dismay wondering what might happen next. As it turned out I had nothing to fear because Matthew's reflex actions were as fast as his fist and feet, as his head dodged swiftly out of the way and the cudgel inflicted only a glancing blow to his shoulder.

That made him even angrier as he caught his attacker with a thunderous uppercut that lifted him off the ground to the sharp crack of either his jaw or neck breaking, from which he crashed down and lay still with arms outstretched and mouth wide open.

The still diffident **number five** surveyed the carnage, and then saw an enraged Matthew bearing down upon him. That was enough. With a shriek he dropped his cudgel and ran off pursued by a baying crowd; as Matthew yelled for them to bring him back alive.

Number six, the leader of the gang, rushed forward with his cudgel raised only for Matthew to snatch it out of his hand and quickly snap it across his knee as if it were a twig. In an instant Matthews's right arm shot out to grasp the gang leader by the throat and, lifting him up, he held him kicking and gasping at arms length as he fought in vain to loosen Matthew's hold upon his neck.

"Now is the time for me to save the hangman a job," growled Matthew.

His mighty arm muscles stood out as he shook the once leader until his face turned blue, and his eyes appeared ready to pop out of their sockets. I could see blood oozing between Matthew's fingers as his grip tightened on his opponent's throat until his flailing arms and legs became still; which was Matthew's cue to hurl the lifeless body to the ground.

Probably to liberate the strength of violence that still dominated his mind and body Matthew raised his arms aloft and, with head back, gave vent to a mighty roar after which he washed his hands in the horse trough and reverted to the gentle and jovial Matthew, who was the guardian and friend of all people of good will.

I stood transfixed by the side of the cart as the memory of what had just happened replayed, in vivid detail, over and over in my mind. Never had I seen such a clinical yet devastating example of skill and power delivered by one who, with total indifference, now walked slowly around the arena inspecting what remained of the once feared 'gang of six.'

The entire encounter was totally mind boggling.

Through an incredible display of speed and strength an enraged Matthew had, within less than a minute, destroyed a gang who had plagued the region for many months. Four were motionless and appeared to be dead whilst one body *(number two)* moaned slightly and, from the appearance of his shattered pelvic area, would not live for much longer.

Suddenly Moneysa, supported by Ruth, appeared from the back of the cart and ran weeping into my arms. "All I could hear was shouting and the sound of fighting and then screaming and I thought they had killed you," sobbed Moneysa and she started to tremble violently as I held her close.

Ruth moved closer and spoke to her like a mother to her grieving daughter. "All is safe and well Monnie because Charles is holding you and Matthew's loyalty has saved all our lives."

With that Ruth ran over to Matthew and did a running leap up at him in order to throw her arms around his neck, and reward him with a big kiss on his cheek, which left him red faced and grinning sheepishly at the ground.

The sound of rapidly approaching horse hooves caught our attention as several armed riders came to a halt on the village green. They were the guards from Ganton Hall and the leading horseman hurriedly dismounted and rushed over to Moneysa and myself. His, "Are you and Miss Moneysa alright sir?" was answered in the affirmative.

Apparently my father, as a sentry at his bedroom window, had witnessed a horse drawn cart, containing six men, pause at the house gate then drive on. With that he had summoned the guard leader. "Immediately he feared the worst, called us together and sent us in hot pursuit; only to miss out on the fun by the look of the battle field," remarked the lead rider. "Did you and all the villagers overcome the gang sir?"

Smiling at the thought of it I pointed to Matthew and declared that he alone had wiped out the mob thus saving our lives, and that only he deserved the credit for this brave act.

"I am glad that he is on our side," he replied with a grin as he walked over and shook hands with Matthew. "You are a rich man sir," he said. "You will not know but there is a 100 guinea (*worth around £20,000 today*) reward out for the capture, dead or alive, of this gang."

While Matthew was mentally digesting the prospect of being rich the sound of loud and mainly female voices burst on the scene, as about 30 villagers prodded, pushed and kicked the missing gang member (*number 5*) into the centre of the green.

Times were hard and quality clothing was scarce, meaning he had been relieved of his heavy duty coat, knee length boots and every item of clothing other than his shirt which was torn beyond further use. Any embarrassment he might have felt, over his exposed nakedness, became secondary to him when he caught sight of Matthew rapidly approaching with clenched fists.

Immediately he fell to his knees and, in tears, begged Matthew to show pity on him.

This brought howls of coarse laughter from many of the village women as, if in contest with Matthew and the Hall guards, they sought to outdo each other with bawdy and ribald comments aimed at this naked wretch, who believing he was about to be lynched, cowered and screamed for mercy on the ground before Matthew.

Emboldened village children, armed with stones and sticks and spurred on by their families, laid into him with gusto as he tried to fend off a pack of snarling resident dogs. As the blood lust gained momentum one villager, fuelled with primitive hatred, snatched a dropped cudgel and began to beat him with it encouraged by loud cheers of approval.

As a spectator I had little sympathy for the remaining gang member knowing that, if they had succeeded, then the two of us and perhaps even Ruth would have been beaten to death. I was totally indifferent to his suffering until Moneysa gave a cry and threw herself into my arms. "Please Charles; please stop them from torturing that man. There has been enough killing today….please stop them …." Then, clutching her stomach she was violently sick and Ruth ran to her aid. Immediately I called the guard leader and ordered him to stop what was happening and to take the prisoner and bodies away.

He instantly responded by prodding the dazed and bleeding gang member, with his boot, whilst ordering him to his feet. "Come on my beauty for we have seen enough of your bare arse and it is off you go to Squire Salter, who will be delighted to meet the sole surviving member of the six gang. But remember well that if you fail to answer his questions honestly, then you will soon be the late sole member." Quickly they had his arms and feet securely tied and thus trussed he joined the bodies of his companions, in the back of their former cart, which was driven by two of the Ganton guards with two more riding escort.

It was agreed that we would travel with them as far as Ganton Hall and then summon medical assistance for Moneysa who remained in a state of deep shock. Without a doubt the screams and sounds of violence as the gang were defeated had left its mark upon her, which had been compounded by the savage and merciless torture of the surviving gang member who, in the eyes of the majority, was justifiably punished and publically humiliated as befitting one held in the lowest contempt.

Waving to the ecstatic villagers the party set off for the Salter residence, and we followed with Matthew driving and the remaining two escorts in close attendance, whilst Ruth and I comforted a distressed and shaking Moneysa in the back of the cart.

Ruth whispered in my ear, "Moneysa was sick on at least four occasions during the trouble. She was terrified that you had been killed. Whilst the battle raged I cuddled her to keep her warm and reassured, but with every thud of what I now know to be Matthew's fists and cries of pain from his attackers, she feared that you were the victim." I thanked Ruth for being such a good and loyal friend to both Moneysa and the entire family, which was concurred with a smile and a nod from Moneysa as she snuggled even closer to me as her bouts of shivering became more intense. In an attempt to give her further warmth I held out my right arm for Ruth to join me so that she would benefit from the combined heat from our bodies. Suddenly joy leapt back into our lives when, between bouts of shivering, we heard her faint voice murmur the words, "You are my ever best friends."

CHAPTER TWENTY SEVEN

Surprising news for the Ganton family

Father anxiously ran to meet us as we drew to a halt outside the main entrance and, seemingly within a few minutes, he had a rider galloping away with a signed request for the local doctor to attend the Hall as a matter of extreme urgency.

Not wanting to disturb Moneysa, who had slipped into a restless sleep punctuated with short cries and sudden hand movements, I carefully handed her down into the arms of Matthew who, at Ruth's command, followed her into the house.

As I watched them I was suddenly overcome with fatigue as I realised that the immediate danger was over, and I was surrounded by family and friends within a loving home. Father had obviously noticed me relying on the cart wheel for support so he came over quickly and put his arm around me as he whispered, "Welcome home Charles, truly the Lord has been with you today. Let us retire indoors and thank him for delivering you both."

After prayers, hot drinks and some food around the hall fire, I felt far more relaxed and echoed my agreement as father repeatedly thanked Matthew for risking his life to save Moneysa and myself. Prior to this I had given my account of what had happened and Matthew followed up with his contribution which, true to his nature, he tried to minimise yet failed to do so because I was an eye witness to all that had happened. In order to spare himself further embarrassment, at being the centre of goodwill, he got up and placed new logs on the hall fireplace and carefully wiped his hands down his trousers before he sat down again.

Looking at Matthew father continued with, "I believe you have been told you will receive a one hundred guinea reward for destroying this gang of thugs? Well it is my intention to double the amount paid to you in gratitude for saving the lives of my son and my ward for which I will be eternally grateful to you." Having said this father smiled at him and Matthew bowed his head, as if in prayerful mode, in order to hide the strong feelings that I had already read upon his face and confirmed by a slight catching of his breath.

We returned to our daily concerns when a servant answered the door to the local doctor who entered, complete with his large medical bag, and was immediately ushered upstairs to Moneysa's room and handed over to Ruth who had remained at the bedside.

Father, after a brief absence, returned with a bottle of brandy which he presented to Matthew as a small token of our thanks, and also to help him sleep after the activities of this day.

It was evident to me that Matthew found it far easier to handle six vicious thugs than to deal with the kindness and gratitude that was showered upon him in the Ganton household. Nevertheless he thanked us and hoped that Miss Moneysa would soon be fully recovered, more so because the villagers looked forward to her visits. With that he shook hands with us both, thanked us once more, and took his seat alongside one of the coachmen who was to take him back to the village.

Father and I sat gazing at the antics of sparks and how, when freed from burning logs, they hovered awhile before gracefully pirouetting their way up the welcoming chimney. It was a pleasant and therapeutic scene which took some of the sting away from all that had happened during this eventful day, but did little to abate our worries over Moneysa who had been traumatised by the sights and sounds of violence so recently around her.

My comment, "The doctor appears to be taking his time…….." was cut short when we heard him coming down the stairs and coughing as if to clear his throat.

"Come and sit down with us doctor," invited my father pointing to a vacant seat.

"Thank you sir, but with your leave I would prefer to stand to give my report which may come as a shock to you both."

Immediately, I feared the worst and began to speak, only for the doctor to hold up his hand and beg my pardon for a few moments.

"The fact is gentlemen that Miss Moneysa has endured a terrible experience, as confirmed by Ruth her attendant, and she is in a typical state of shock which I have treated with a sedative and, after a few days in bed, all will be well with her but………"

Here, much to our alarm the doctor paused and briefly stared at the floor only to quickly lift his head and continue with "…… only for the moment," which caused us no small amount of trepidation.

In fact the impact of that four word addendum to his report caused us both to leap to our feet as, fearing the worst, I gasped out, "Why only for the moment?"

The doctor was clearly searching for the best combination of words but, aware of the alarm on our faces, he just blurted out the news that, "Miss Moneysa is two months with child and, thank God, her pregnancy has not been harmed by the events of this day; but it does explain repeated bouts of sickness that Ruth told me about."

My father was dumbfounded and stared at the doctor for a full half minute before sinking back into his chair with his head buried in his hands; which was my cue to thank the doctor and lead him to the door.

His departing words were, "Do not worry Mr Ganton because all is going well and she will be up and about the house in no time. I will call again at the same time tomorrow."

I stood in silence surveying the panelling of the closed door and musing over the doctor's assurance that, "All is going well," before I walked back and sat facing father across the fireplace.

Sensing my gaze upon him he raised his head and addressed me with, "Please advise me Charles if I am to accept as factual what the doctor has just told us. Do you believe that Moneysa is having a baby?"

Looking my father full in the face I was grateful that my nature was one of giving straight answers to straight questions, and this occasion was no exception. "The doctor is accurate in his diagnosis and I can confirm that Moneysa is pregnant and that I am honoured to be the father of our child, whose conception reflects the love that will always hold us as one."

My father did not speak but, suddenly, I saw not his familiar face but, rather, one of a man who had suddenly aged and relied more upon emotion than words. Despite the slight turn of his head I did not miss the tremble of his bottom lip, together with tears just contained within his eyes, as he slowly and firmly delivered the words, "It is the Lord's will, blessed be the name of the Lord."

His eyes moved away from me and rested awhile upon the oil painting of Moneysa before returning to the antics of the sparks in the grate.

Two days passed by during which my father recovered his composure and we had several positive conversations, from which I was delighted to learn that the news had made him a happy man. He was already elated that Moneysa would be his daughter through marriage and that now she would bear him a grandchild sired by his own son.

His major regret was that we were not officially engaged meaning that it would be born illegitimate unless corrective action was taken. Intermingled with this was the fact that even if we set sail today then our developing baby would be very obvious when we arrived at our goal, and a heavily pregnant bride would be a much talked about sight in East India Company circles.

"The answer is obvious," he declared. "You must marry here, in the village church, and considering that Brother John is the parish priest the event can be given special licence urgency after which we can return to India."

As one present but unable to ask questions I must admit to being rather bemused over the relaxed way that Edward Ganton readily accepted the fact that a baby had been sired out of wedlock; more so since his son and pseudo adopted daughter were to be the parents.

This led me to research 18th century attitudes towards the occurrence of such events within 'gentry class' households.

To avoid a lengthy essay on this topic I have extracted from the archives such facts that will alleviate my concerns, and can be summarised as pre and post 1753 Marriage Act also known as Lord Hardwicke's Marriage Act. Therefore let us consider:

1. Pre 1753 Marriage Act

By the early eighteenth century although church marriage had become in many ways the general social ideal the cost of a church wedding was prohibitive for many. A less costly alternative was a legally binding oral declaration of intent to marry in front of witnesses.

A marriage could be established by verba de praesenti, that is, the statement of consent by both parties, or by verba de futuro, a promise of marriage in the future better known as' Engagement to be Married.' It was not unusual for babies to be born within the engagement period and such children were deemed to be legitimate within the spirit of the Act.

2. Post 1753 Marriage Act

The act required that if both parties to a marriage were less than 21 years of age then consent to the marriage had to be given by the parents or guardians. Even with consent, parties were not allowed to be married unless the male was at least 14 years old and the female was at least 12.

*When the Act was passed it required, under pain of nullity, that **banns** should be published on three Sundays preceding the marriage and that the marriage should be solemnized in an Anglican church.*

It was interesting to note that the need for a witnessed declaration was built into the 1753 Act, in the form of the mandatory banns mentioned above.

*Thus it can be seen that the attitude of Edward Ganton, and indeed others of his age group, was established within the **pre 1753 Marriage Act**, whilst conceding that Charles and Moneysa were nominally, rather than formally, engaged to be married. I can only surmise that he (Edward Ganton) was happy that their 'intention to marry' was genuine, considering they readily fell in with his plan to bring forward their marriage as a matter of urgency.*

In this respect he would have no hesitation, as Moneysa's guardian, to give his consent without challenge from her mother whose mental stability was in rapid decline.

Perhaps my earlier concern regarding Edward Ganton's 'liberal' approach to the situation was influenced by the later Victorian condemnation of premarital relationships; which was a notable and prominent feature of the nineteenth rather than the eighteenth centuries.

CHAPTER TWENTY EIGHT

Update from Derbie Salter and the future of Charles and Moneysa

During the next three weeks Elizabeth arrived and was alarmed to find that, for our own safety, Moneysa and I were 'prisoners' within the house following the recent assassination attempt upon us. Elizabeth was soon followed by Brother John, fresh from a five day meeting at Bishop's House, which reunited the 'Valiant Four' that did much to raise our spirits despite the presence of ten armed guards within the grounds. Much to their chagrin Elizabeth and John declared they would have arrived earlier had not heavy snow falls marooned Ganton Hall from outside contact; however a steady thaw gave hope that the roads would soon be totally accessible.

Our concern for the villagers had been eased when father allowed a delivery of essential supplies to leave, in the care of stable staff, in deference to his ruling that Moneysa and I would remain within the safety of the house for the time being. Despite my arguments to the contrary father was not prepared to take any further risks until Derbie Salter arrived to advise us of the present status of the Elliott crisis and he, in turn, could be advised of the reasons why Moneysa and I were to be married here rather than in India.

Notwithstanding recent events we had a further catastrophe, in the form of a collapsed orangery roof that had put the sitting room out of action until repairs could be put in place. The weight of thawing snow had proved too much for a weakened section of the roof through which heavy rain was a regular intruder. Necessity now meant that the library would be the venue for our meeting with Derbie Salter who, according to a mounted messenger, would be with us early the next day.

By a unanimous decision we spent a quiet and lethargic evening around the hall fireplace, enjoying past journeys and adventures, until Moneysa's head upon my shoulder was the signal for us to retire for the night. At times my sleep, and probably that of others, was disturbed by the sound of footsteps and the clanking of metal containers as the rate of water ingress, from the damaged orangery roof, had increased due to the onset of a rapid thaw.

True to his word Derbie Salter arrived in time for a short pre meeting with father in which he would learn why my marriage had been brought forward.

When he joined us for a late breakfast he appeared to be in good spirits and, in due course, we retired to the library for our information exchange meeting which, due to its agenda, required that Matthew must also be present. He had been honoured to receive the invitation to attend but had, with the greatest respect, asked if he could have his breakfast in the servant's hall. His reasons for this were given in words that meant he was a 'stranger to the requirements of societal eating.'

It must be said that the library had been impressively set out with an ornately carved table on the far wall, behind which sat Derbie Salter and my father. Facing them in a 'U' formation were four double teak and leather chairs with side tables, and servants were discretely nearby to meet requests for drinks or any other needs. Seated within the double chairs were Charles and Moneysa, Brother John and Elizabeth, Cymol and his mother Lajila and Matthew and Ruth.

Derbie Salter brought the meeting to order and expressed his delight at seeing Moneysa looking happy and well again after her recent ordeal.

"Before I update you all I must put first matters first," remarked Derbie smiling and looking towards Matthew.

"Without our brave friend we would be mourning the tragic loss of at least three members of the Ganton household whose lives were saved through his loyalty and strength. In the process of protecting our loved ones he also successfully rid the county of a vile and murderous gang of cut throats, who for far too long have created havoc in our community."

Matthew stood up as Derbie walked over to him and presented him with a sealed envelope. "Matthew, please accept this small token of our appreciation for all you have done for our families and community. Your reward money has been doubled, by Mr Edward Ganton, meaning that I now present you with two hundred guineas in the form of a bank deposit that has been opened in your name. All the documents are within this envelope and the Reverend John Ganton has agreed to help you manage your affairs." Matthew struggled valiantly with his rehearsed speech of thanks which he delivered with a level of sincerity that both moistened our eyes, and gave vigour to our applause, as he sat down awash with embarrassment.

After taking a judicial sip at his brandy glass, Derbie skilfully summarised the route of his investigations, starting with his interrogation of the remaining gang member (*number five*).

"I began by flattering him and even told him 'as gentleman to gentleman' that if he was open and honest with me then his life would be spared. In no time he confessed to the fact that the gang was paid by a person called James Reed who I promptly had arrested and identified, by Captain Brentwood, as one of the two men in the club with Elliott.

Then I had a great breakthrough with Reed's wife who had been the victim of beatings and ill use by her husband and, when told that he would be charged with being party to several local murders and other serious crimes, which undoubtedly would put him on the gallows, she literally sang and danced with delight. The prospect of owning the property, and inheriting all Reed's money, led her to his desk which had a concealed compartment. From this she produced Reed's diary which she gave to me in the hope it would help confirm his place in the hangman's cart.

I was breathless with excitement when I studied the contents of the diary which turned out to be a comprehensive record of all crimes committed by the gang and the amount of money that Reed had paid to them.

The coup de grace caused me to shout out with joy.

Reed had even recorded the dates he received orders for the gang to punish debt defaulters, deliver loot from burgled houses and to murder someone who had fallen out of favour; and the penultimate entry was for Charles and Moneysa Ganton to be severely beaten and finally killed.

The last entry was acknowledging receipt of a sum of money described as the monthly payment to Reed and the gang he managed, on behalf of ……..."

Here Derbie paused for effect and looked around at the expectant faces before thundering out the name, "Thomas

Elliott; which appeared no less than twenty four times within this record.

Immediately I sent two constables to arrest Elliott but the bird had flown, having probably heard that the only living member of his once feared gang was in custody and that his game was up. Also missing, and presumably with him, was the third man who made up the trio that confronted Charles in the hunt club on the first of January last.

In conclusion the remaining gang member, and his foreman James Reed, are in irons awaiting trial at the Spring Assizes where, undoubtedly, they will be found guilty and sentenced to hang.

Should any of you wonder why I told the gang member as 'gentleman to gentleman' that if he was open and honest with me then his life would be spared, only to later renege on my word when his usefulness was over, then the answer is simple. Earlier I used the term 'gentleman' which on no account could ever apply to him."

This was met with hearty laughter followed by a vote of thanks proposed by my father.

"Nevertheless," Derbie said, "Elliott is still at liberty. He is an evil vindictive man and we all know who is at the centre of his hatred. Thus I propose to leave with you the ten armed men until such time as Charles and Moneysa have left the country; which is my cue to hand over to my friend, Edward, who will advise us when the departure date will be."

Instantly father was on his feet and began with, "You will recall that the plan was for Charles and Moneysa to return to India, early in February, where they would marry and set up home under the auspices of the East India Company wherein Charles will be a senior manager."

Looking slowly along the faces before him father continued with, "Well there has been a dramatic turn in events following the discovery that Moneysa is expecting a baby, of which, as far as I know, everyone here is fully aware."

"No sir, that is not the case," cried Cymol as he leapt to his feet. "Please let me explain the situation ...." With that my father cut in and asked Cymol to sit down until he had finished, when he would have an opportunity to state his case.

"So there is every incentive for Charles and Moneysa to marry here, in our village church, and I am grateful to my son the Reverend John Ganton who will add to the occasion by officiating at the ceremony."

This news was followed by hearty applause from all present with the exception of Cymol and his mother whose eyes never rose from the section of floor within her vision.

"So on each of the next three Sundays the marriage banns will be read, and on the following Saturday, the 10th March 1781, the wedding will take place to which everyone, including the entire village, is cordially invited. Afterwards we will have a marriage feast on the lawn if the weather permits; or indoors if otherwise.

Whilst Brother John was arranging all this I have been busy with the shipping company and have secured berths for Charles and Moneysa, Ruth, Cymol, Lajila and myself in an Indiaman. On March 22nd the vessel will raise anchor and sail in convoy from London to India.

This means that after an appropriate farewell party we will sadly say goodbye to our dear friends on the 17th March 1781, in the knowledge that we will never be able to fully repay our many 'comrades in life' for their love, care and compassion combined with laughter which carried us successfully through several unscheduled difficulties. Thank you my friends."

With that my father sat down and asked if anyone had questions either for Derbie or himself.

Realising that all eyes were upon him Cymol rose to his feet and asked for permission to share the grave concerns he had over his sister's welfare on her return to India.

"Previously I explained to you that Islamic tradition does not permit Moneysa, as a born Muslim, to convert to any other religion, and that she is also guilty of adultery if she marries a non-Muslim man. The signs are clear for all to see; have you forgotten that my sister, as a final warning, was almost killed on the Foxton Road? Allah '*Azza wa Jal*' will not be mocked."

…. "Cymol, that is enough," were the stern words from my father that left Cymol silent and open mouthed. "I will not permit this meeting to walk your biased and boring path for a second time; do I make myself clear?"

Cymol's, "but it is unlawful …." was curtailed when father, with rising anger, ordered Cymol to change his attitude or sit down, which he promptly did whilst muttering that the death of his sister would be upon our heads.

With a murmured, "Quite so," father looked around the room whilst inviting further comments which came, surprisingly, from Moneysa whose eyes blazed with rage as she leapt to her feet and faced her brother.

"Cymol, unless you are blind and deaf to reality you have deliberately chosen to ignore the dangers that face me here in England which, unlike yours, are not speculation.

But for the love and bravery of Matthew both your sister and her future husband would have been brutally murdered less than four weeks ago and, because of prevailing danger, we cannot leave the house unless armed guards are with us. Do you call that living in a safe country?

Yet according to your reasoning my life will be in serious danger if I return to India.

So just where the hell would you have Charles and myself live?"

Pausing for breath Moneysa continued to glare at Cymol as, in a voice full of meaning, she slowly concluded with, "India is where we belong and India is where we are going to go, regardless of your veiled threats which stem from fears for your own neck.

You were ordered to come to England with me and ensure I remained within Islam. They will hold you responsible for the fact I chose to go my own way and their judgement awaits you and not me."

The tensions and fears of recent happenings came to the fore as Moneysa almost screamed at him, "You can stay in England if you so wish, but we are returning to India."

With that Moneysa, trembling with rage, sat down and pressed her head on to my shoulder as my arm went around her. For his part Cymol raised his hands in a gesture of resignation and set to work on his prayer beads.

CHAPTER TWENTY NINE

Marriage of Charles and Moneysa on the 10th March 1781

For three Sundays we listened, hand in hand in the family pew, to Brother John reading out the public banns for our forthcoming marriage; but now the great day had arrived. To say that the house was active from an early hour would be an understatement because I firmly believe that large sections of it never went to bed that night; but it had all worked out well thanks to the dedication of Ruth and Elizabeth as the church awaited the fruits of their labours.

The church interior was not large and for normal services it easily catered for the needs of the district.

Today was an exception with all seats full, except for the reserved Ganton pew at the front, with an overspill of male villagers standing up at the back. Some had the foresight to stand upon the raised base of the font to gain a better view, whereas smaller people relied upon a whispered commentary from those tall enough to see what was happening.

There were no recognisable faces from previous county events, and the general congregation consisted mainly of local people in the form of agricultural and trade workers, their wives and families. However Matthew was easily recognised, sitting head and shoulders above others, in his place of honour in the Ganton pew.

Two flower entwined archways spanned the aisle which led into the sanctuary and the raised yet plain altar. The ornately carved rood screen had been decorated with early spring flowers and evergreens and, within its portals, four church musicians, aided by their tuning fork, skilfully converted ear rending discord into celestial harmony in keeping with the occasion.

Charles Ganton stood alone facing the altar awaiting the arrival of Moneysa and showed possible signs of nervousness by frequently 'tweaking' his short pigtail. His wedding suit consisted of an embroidered silk grey jacket, with double patterned bands above the cuffs, and trousers of similar texture.

Suddenly I heard the sound of carriage wheels stopping on the lane outside the church and the sound of hand clapping, and cheering, as the party alighted to begin their walk to the church door.

It was then that I thought my heart would burst as, to the sound of footsteps approaching the church, the two violins hauntingly struck up with my favourite tune, (*the same that was later used for the previously mentioned popular song 'Those Endearing Young Charms'*). I later discovered that Elizabeth had arranged this surprise as, to quote her words, "Her gift of love to us both."

To the strains of that lovely melody the party, led by the Reverend John Ganton, slowly entered the church and began walking up the aisle and immediately behind Brother John was Moneysa holding the arm of her guardian, Edward Ganton.

She wore an off the shoulder full length deep blue dress with elbow length lace frilled sleeves. On her head was a silver bandeau which secured a pale blue demi-veil at the back. Her hair was styled in a way that allowed an emphasis of side ringlets to fall more upon her right shoulder than the left.

Behind them in dresses of the same colour were Ruth and Elizabeth who smiled and waved to the many who knew them.

The congregation listened to the violins playing 'my tune' and even Brother John, resplendent in his formal Church of England service robes, was visibly moved as he stood before us, with book open, as he waited for the violins to play their final chords.

When Moneysa reached my side our hands immediately closed together, and she smiled as I whispered how beautiful she looked. Indeed she was a vision of beauty and happiness and, as she looked up at me, the sight of her black hair, brown skin and dark eyes quickly replaced my anxieties over our future safety.

"We are Charles and Moneysa happily sharing a love that the passing of eternity will not erode, and what could be better than that," I whispered to myself as the violins stopped and the wedding service began.

Stages of the service that remain at the front of my mind are when I received the blessed ring from the Reverend John and lovingly placed it on the third finger of her left hand. Our marriage was sealed and both our faces proclaimed that glorious fact with smiles awash with tears of happiness.

I was favoured to catch sight of the gold and diamond set wedding ring referred to, which was in the form of two ornate hearts, slightly raised from the body of the ring.

It was during the singing of the final hymn that I heard the words 'Love divine all loves excelling ...' but to a tune I was not familiar with. However the lyrics were consistent with Charles Wesley's hymn, written in 1747, and bearing the same name.

When I thought back to the wedding my mind was repeatedly drawn to the dresses worn by Moneysa and her two 'ladies in waiting' which were attractive and colourful, yet lacked the expensive and flamboyant style of dress designs that dominated the many social events I attended in the presence of Charles Ganton.

A brief literature search on this topic confirmed that throughout the 18th century most brides and their attendants, regardless of their status in society, just wore their Sunday best at their wedding.

With great pride I can now announce that a radiantly happy Mr and Mrs Charles Ganton emerged from the church to face a flood of congratulations, cheers, hand clapping and waving from our devoted village friends as we trod carefully over a carpet of rushes, and shielded ourselves from an avalanche of hurled rice.

Never before have I been hugged and kissed by so many women, and Matthew hastily stepped in to protect Moneysa, who was fast disappearing beneath the growing throng of women around her. Several were keen to see her wedding ring and kiss it for 'good luck,' particularly those hopeful young spinsters who hoped to tread the same path before the year was out.

Finally we managed to gain the sanctuary of our waiting coach, which may have given our discreetly concealed security guards cause for relief, and then we slowly drove to the Hall leaving a group of children playing knights and dragons using the reeds as swords.

On arrival we were greeted by staff members who had volunteered to remain behind and set out the food and drink for the many guests who were fast following us down the road.

In the relative calm of the recently repaired sitting room we were congratulated in turn by my father, who hugged Moneysa and declared that when he last felt this happy was when he married his beloved late wife, Molly.

Brother John, who had travelled ahead of us, was far less reserved than normal and embraced Moneysa with such sincerity and vigour that I jokingly expressed concern for the well being of my wife. Then it was Ruth's turn to almost wring the breath out of us in declaring that she would be a second mother to us both; after which Elizabeth and Moneysa gently held each other and shed tears in the process.

Later I felt the need for a few moments of solitude so I moved away from the happy clamour and sought sanctuary in the orangery, only to find Elizabeth staring out of the window at the wedding guests on the lawn enjoying the early spring sunshine. I had a strange inner feeling that she had 'willed' me to come and what she said seemed to support my conjecture, "Charles, I am so happy that you came because I fear that many years will slip by before I can be alone with you again."

Holding hands we looked at each other, perhaps wondering who would speak first, until Elizabeth whispered, "Thank you Charles for the happiness you brought into my life and I hope that in some small way I brought pleasure to you.

Before we go our separate ways ...." Here she paused for a few moments and then continued with ..... "I cannot say any more Charles other than to assure you that I will always love you." I began to speak but Elizabeth gently placed her hand over my mouth and whispered, "Our day has ended but after the darkness a new day will begin."

With that Elizabeth quickly broke away and ran through the orangery door to join the crowds on the lawn leaving me strangely disturbed as to what she meant.

When I arrived here from India my forthcoming wedding had already been described as the 'prominent social event of 1781' which would engage the interest of the entire county, and be attended by all leading dignitaries and people of note. I smiled to myself as I looked around at our guests composed almost entirely of village peasants and local tradesmen with their families. Yet their presence radiated love, sincerity and loyalty as, in return, they were being feasted and entertained in ways that they had never previously dreamed of.

The sight of Moneysa, a picture of complete happiness and the centre of attention in her blue wedding dress, convinced me that I was witnessing a wedding reception rich in real friendship that, thankfully, broke every rule in the social etiquette book.

Where they came from I will never know but, to the delight of the children, there was a Punch and Judy Show, jugglers and even a clown wearing enormous shoes.

The highlight of the wedding party was when Moneysa and I cut the wedding cake that was displayed for all to admire on a central table in the main hall. The large single tier circular fruit cake was covered in what looked like marzipan which readily accepted our joint cutting action to the cheers of all present. It was then whisked away to be divided up into smaller sections to the joy of young ladies, who had already asked for residual crumbs, so that they could carry home the cherished fragments to the safety of their straw pillows. With their heads at rest upon those precious crumbs they hoped to dream of their future husband, and that he would become a reality before the leaves left the trees.

At this stage Moneysa asked Matthew to use his loudest and most commanding voice to summon all guests into the reception hall, where we both stood alongside a table holding a central large candle, with two smaller ones placed diagonally in front of the larger one.

When curiosity had gained everyone's attention, Moneysa explained that she was going to complete her marriage to me through a simple wedding tradition that was popular in India. With tapers from the fire we lit the smaller candles that represented us both before our marriage. Then with a nod of the head from Moneysa we simultaneously lit the large candle from our smaller ones, extinguished the small candles, and then threw them to our guests.

Moneysa described that the act of jointly lighting the large candle, with our smaller ones, meant that our once separate inner light was now united as a solitary flame that would burn throughout eternity. "Together with being husband and wife we are now soul friends," Moneysa declared. "It also means that when we are parted in this life the spirit of the absent spouse will hold aloft the light, to guide their loved one home, along the path leading from this world to the next."

The beauty of this simple yet highly moving little service brought emotion to several throats, and free flowing tears from a multitude of eyes, as 'our love that was born without reason' became a living reality to all those who knew us as friends.

I too found Moneysa's spontaneous little ceremony to be very moving and, out of respect for its honest simplicity, I chose not to make it the subject of detailed research.

Eventually the time came for our guests to depart and following much kissing, cuddling and tears of joy the convoy of assorted modes of transport disappeared down the road as the singing and laughter gradually faded into the night which was left to the owls and us.

Despite feeling very tired we stood in the bedroom window recess looking out at the moonlit scene. Turning to Monnie I smiled and remarked that with all the excitement of the day I had been denied the presence of my wife in my arms, which must be corrected as a matter of urgency.

"Then what are you waiting for?" was her immediate reply ……………..

…which was the start to their night of bliss wherein imagination must replace written commentary.

CHAPTER THIRTY

The final scene

The remaining few days were hectic for the staff, who in addition to their daily duties, had the arduous task of packing several large sea chests under the watchful eyes of Ruth, which led my father to ruefully remark, "We are returning to India with far more than when we arrived."

Security within the grounds of Ganton Hall remained at a high level of vigilance ever mindful of the fact that, despite an intensive and ongoing manhunt, no sightings of Elliott had been reported meaning that further revenge attempts had not been ruled out. However the presence of a large number of armed men did not intrude upon our privacy because they had been positioned at key points, along the perimeter of the estate, thus preventing any unauthorised entry. This meant that Moneysa and I could still walk within our 'secret little forest' but were denied the pleasure of our regular excursions to the village or indeed to anywhere outside the grounds of Ganton Hall.

It was pleasing to know that our friends in the village, including the inimitable life saving Matthew, were regularly visited by Brother John in his role of parish priest with his companion Elizabeth, who jointly had gained the love and trust of their new parishioners. During the final Sunday service, prior to our departure, Brother John had arranged for the entire village to be present at Ganton Hall when, accompanied by father, Ruth, Cymol and Lajila, we would set off on our long journey to India and the real beginning of our married life together.

Although there was a general air of sadness, particularly among the staff who had become as 'family' to us, the next few days passed by very well other than when, due to her condition, my wife (I like using her new title) developed bouts of sickness which confined her to bed. In attempting to adopt a suitable bedside manner I managed to make matters worse through my faux pas that went along the lines, 'I hope the sea will not be too rough for us.'

By the time our departure day arrived Moneysa had made a full recovery from her bouts of sickness and, with no small amount of pride, announced to me that her clothes were a shade tighter around her middle meaning that our little 'Chamon' was beginning to grow. Nevertheless we rose early and went on our last walk together in our 'secret little forest' and sat awhile, with our arms around each other on Monnie's rock, reliving our many happy times in this wood, wherein the first seeds of our destiny came into fruition.

"Do you think that one day we will return to this place of happiness Charles?"

"Yes, I really do. Perhaps, when we are old and grey, we will sit again on this rock plotting what little jokes we can play upon each other." Lightly rubbing my nose with hers she whispered, "Thank you dear husband" and following my, "Thank you Mrs Ganton" our lips closed together as if to symbolically unite us in our love for each other, and the life we had planned together.

"Only two hours left," I murmured as we slowly walked along the last stretch of the path, as it dipped towards the entrance. Our progress became slower and slower until we eventually stopped and, perhaps for the last time, we looked back upon our woodland of dreams that, for us, had become a reality. With hands held tight we waved an emotional goodbye to the gently moving bushes and trees, and then we returned to the house via the tack room, and on through the kitchen, in order to see as many staff members as possible.

During our progress the young maid who made the mince pies happened to come face to face with us at which she promptly burst into tears and, with her pinafore covering her face, ran as if to escape the sorrow of our impending departure.

Throughout the course of the next two hours we slowly went around and said our farewells as Ganton Hall became a hive of activity. First, Derbie Salter arrived to head our farewell party, followed by Matthew and many of the local villagers in quick succession.

Fortunately it was an early spring day and there was even a hint of warmth in the sun that favoured us, from a clear blue sky, thus allowing the staff to set out tables of assorted food and drink, which became the first port of call for hungry children and parents when they arrived in the grounds. They were not quiet eaters as, on a scale of rising volume, they noisily extolled the culinary glories of whatever they were eating, whilst thanking staff for keeping their plates well topped up.

Aware that the time for departure was getting near, and farewell addresses were next on the agenda, Edward Ganton asked Matthew to bring the meeting to order.

Happy and honoured to oblige Matthew drew in his breath and gave voice to a mighty, "Quiet," which was concurred by several mothers, who did their bit by soundly clipping the ears of their children; whether they deserved it or not. Following further bellows from Matthew some semblance of quiet and order was achieved thus giving Derbie an opportunity to publically wish us well as husband and wife in India.

There followed an emotional embrace and handshake between Derbie and my father who, after a lifetime of friendship, perhaps knew that this was the end and they would not meet again in this world.

In turn my father thanked the Salter family for all their valuable support and particularly singled out Elizabeth by saying how much the Gantons appreciated her kindness in allowing them to live rent free in her house.

From the sight of several arms held up in the air it appeared that many people wanted to mark this special day with their verbal blessings; and one contribution, that brought great delight, was from the red headed boy better known as the 'King of the Twelfth Night' who thanked us for our kind work in the village.

Many verbal tributes were expressed during the course of which I remained at a table, which supported an excellent bowl of punch, in the company of a party consisting of Matthew, Elizabeth, Ruth and a group of village women. Conversation was not a problem. In fact a stream of abstract matters were discussed which, in all honesty, was an attempt to disguise the sadness of separation, deep within us all on this day of happy sadness (if indeed such a state is possible).

Ruth, who was to accompany us to India, rapidly interchanged between laughter and tears then back to laughter again as she held tightly on to Elizabeth's supporting hand, fearing that hysteria may win the day.

Moneysa, wearing her favourite white blouse and black skirt and coat with long sleeves, was talking to father and Derbie Salter and appeared to be saying farewell to Derbie as he kissed her on her cheek and then held both her hands.

The pace was visibly accelerating as our time to leave came nearer.

Looking around I saw that two large coaches had arrived and our sea chests, and other luggage, were already being loaded under the supervision of stable staff which, although well meant, was not to Ruth's liking. Intending to personally supervise the operation she began to walk to the coaches until, overcome with rising emotions, she ran back into Elizabeth's arms in floods of tears; brought on by our imminent departure.

Moneysa had also seen the activity around the coaches that prompted her to hurry over to me with the news that Cymol and her mother were late.

Just a little agitated she said, "It probably means that mother is having one of her mental attacks and is refusing to leave the house and Cymol cannot handle the situation. I will go and add my voice to the proceedings, at least I can be firm with her and she can still recognise the sound of my voice."

"Let me come with you, Monnie," I offered.

"Better not Charles too many of us would make her worse."

Leaning over she kissed me gently, smiled and said, "I will be back very soon," and with that she turned and ran into the woods.

"Monnie should not rush around like that in her condition," I fretted out loud, only for Ruth, through her tears, to remind me that women were stronger than most men would ever know.

All guests were now slowly drifting in the direction of the coaches led by Ruth and Elizabeth who, with an unconvincing show of relaxed happiness, promised to frequently write to each other. Father and Derbie Salter showed all the characteristics of two elderly schoolboys as they walked, with their arms around each other's shoulders, totally engrossed in friendship conversation; whilst Brother John was already alongside the coaches ready to deliver his prayers of blessing as we departed.

Now that the time for separation had arrived all conversation became much quieter, and the sound of birds and the light wind in the trees brought a timely peace upon hearts afire with love and companionship which, within minutes, would fade into the realms of happy memories.

Then in an instant that tranquil picture changed as, without warning, the denizens of hell descended upon Ganton Hall and its grounds.

Faces that had glowed serenely through a veil of love born tears were immediately turned into masks of horror, and gentle weeping became cries of fear when a loud noise, like the sharp crack made by wood being broken, was followed by a scream of short duration that stilled all voices and set a chill of fear in every heart.

Even nature responded adversely when many birds fluttered and cried their protest along with an owl that had been roused prematurely from its sleep.

I hurtled down the woodland path as if running over a bed of fire, all the time shouting, "Moneysa I am coming," on and on until I turned a bend and there I saw her.

Moneysa was lying on her right side beneath a rhododendron bush overhanging the path and, as if in slow motion, I watched a rapidly increasing pool of blood spread from beneath her body.

In despair I knelt beside her and cried out her name over and over again; but to no avail for all was silence. I felt totally alone as if even the bushes and trees around me had turned away from this scene of untimely death which, in an instant, had become my eternal legacy.

I gently held her left shoulder, carefully rolled her over onto her back and moved her hair from her face. The front of her blouse was saturated with blood and, as one abstractly observes in times of deep shock, her dark red pendant was hardly discernable against the crimson background of her fading life.

"NO," I cried aloud. "Moneysa you will live; I will not let you die."

In stillness she lay in the shadow of the rhododendron bush she loved so much totally dependant upon me to restore her to life; as I did all that time ago when she almost drowned beneath the Indian torrent.

Tenderly I held her head in my hands and whispered, "Moneysa, I love you and I will never let you go."

She stared back at me and it appeared that in her eyes she was trying to ask a question, literally a question devoid of words but, nevertheless the intensity of her gaze transmitted to my mind what she laboured with; it was the question "Why?"

Then her eyes became a lifeless stare as, with a gentle cough, a trickle of blood came from the corner of her mouth. "There now Monnie, you have cleared your throat, and I will soon have you better again."

With that Charles, in a kneeling position, lovingly gathered Moneysa up into his arms and, with his hand at the back of her head, held her close to his chest as he gently hummed his favourite tune to her.

Moneysa's arms hung limply by her side as many around sobbed, held their hands to their faces in horror or moved forward to coax Charles away from this scene of death.

Immediately Matthew stepped forward and held out his arms as a barrier protecting Charles and Moneysa from those who, in good will, would end that which if truth be generally known was just the beginning.

"Are you feeling better now Monnie," I whispered as I gently kissed the side of her face.

"Don't worry because your Charles is still here holding you and will love you better again, just like I did after the Foxton Road accident and we celebrated by playing a duet on our hair. It was so funny darling…..do you remember….. I imagine that the doctor still talks about it.

You feel very cold now but, as ever, I will soon have you warm again. You wait and see."

I ran my fingers through her hair and told her that she had to get well because her husband and baby and everyone around us loved her so very much.

I briefly looked at those aghast faces about me and, trying to smile, I said, "Do not worry because Monnie is only asleep….she suddenly becomes tired …and falls asleep …she has done all her life ……..after which wakes up feeling fine….."

Stroking her hair I said, "We know don't we my darling wife ….my darling..please say something to me ….."

Suddenly my breath became a series of painful gulps and there was a surge in my head and a shimmering white cloud gathered around me, as I felt myself falling forward.

Screams and cries quickly faded from my ears as peaceful oblivion intervened and gave me rest.

Charles suddenly slumped forward, seemingly unconscious, and the body of Moneysa lay on her back with Charles alongside her with his arm across and protecting her as he always did.

Close by them Matthew stood with tears running freely down his face and his mighty hands opening and closing, as if searching for a tangible enemy from whom to reclaim the life of Moneysa.

Brother John stepped forward from the crowd and knelt down beside Charles and Moneysa, laid his hands upon their heads, and led all present in a few minutes of prayer. He then nodded towards Matthew who reached down and gently scooped Charles into his arms and, with his face radiating protective loyalty, began his slow walk towards the house.

Figures melted out of his way and just stood with heads bowed; then Elizabeth ran forward and placed her cloak over the body of Moneysa after which, lost within her tears, she threw herself into John's open arms as the watchers wept with her.

Interlude

A sudden gust of chilling autumnal wind swept through the trees and brought down a shower of golden leaves both upon and around me; as if a curtain of intermission had been lowered upon my stage of eternity. My mind slowly returned to the present time and the fact that I was sitting upon 'Monnie's rock' and for reasons unknown a well-timed pause in my narration, and a return to the year 1811 had come about.

Perhaps it is as well because it is not easy to document all that happened after the death of my wife. I admit there were times of grief and anxiety within the account I have put before you so far but, prior to her death, I was upheld by Moneysa who was my pillar of strength. Together we overcame all that stood between us and we became, albeit for only seven wonderful days, man and wife with our first child already being formed within.

As I turn my head to my left I can clearly see the spot where Moneysa died in my arms which, despite the passing of thirty years, has retained visual clarity in a woodland setting that has changed little.

Inspired by Moneysa I found that memories became the key to my happiness which, in turn, has motivated my narrative to this stage; whereas what must follow has, for me, the hollow finality of life without reason, supported by words reminiscent of a verbal memorial. Out of your charity please do as I did and view the rhododendron bush in whose overhang my Moneysa died, for upon that hallowed ground I too gave up my life.

I am but a wraith of the Charles Ganton than began this narrative.

In truth I have been a highly successful business man because I worked hard in order to forget; I eat only because without food I would die, and I smile to delude others into thinking that I am in control of my life. That is why it so funny, to me, to talk about being in control of my life.

In God's name – what life?

Forgive me my friends for burdening you with my sorrows which is not what this narrative is about and, within your compassion, please remain with me as I commit my concluding words to the care of what Monnie and I called 'our secret little forest.'

CHAPTER THIRTY ONE

Life without Moneysa

The shimmering white cloud increased in intensity then began to slowly disperse allowing an opulent ceiling gradually to come into focus.

Slowly turning my head I recognised that I was in my bed, and my now familiar bedroom was all around me, yet bright morning sunshine was streaming into the room. Why was I still in bed? I felt around but could not find Moneysa then, much to my surprise, I saw the figure of Matthew seated alongside with a look of deep concern on his face.

"Hello Mr. Charles. Can I get you a drink?" I tried to speak but dryness within my mouth permitted the merest wheeze, prompting Matthew to carefully raise my head and hold a glass of water to my lips.

"Thank you Matthew," was the reply from my now refreshed mouth.

I lay back and gazed at the ceiling and then, as if mentally stung, I suddenly sat bolt upright and stared at Matthew, who immediately avoided my eyes by looking down at the carpet. Some terrible memory was forcing its way back into my conscious mind. I fought against it and longed for a new sleep from which I could awake and find that all was well. Immediately realising that my inner terror, whatever it was, must be faced I, with no small effort, forced myself to slowly look around the room until I saw a certain something loosely hanging upon the corner of my wash stand; it was my bloodstained shirt.

My heart felt as if it would burst. Suddenly it all rushed back into my mind as I remembered that it was Moneysa's blood, the same blood that had baptised both me and the woodland path as life flowed out of her body. In disbelief I gazed at Matthew and, in desperation, said to him, "I will never again see my ever best friend. We needed each other and lived only for the moments when we were together. I cannot......" Words fled from me as my throat refused to respond and the vibration from my pounding heart became unbearable.

Sensing my rising emotions Matthew knelt by the bedside and enclosed both my hands in his. "I wish I was good with words Mr. Charles but I want you know that I will do anything to help you."From the caring look upon his face I knew he meant it. It is probably semi hysteria, but I have previously noted that in times of stress totally unrelated items can take over ones mind. I remembered that a few weeks ago the hands that now so gently held mine had, with single blows, despatched several villains straight to hell; yet now they were as gentle and caring as those of a father comforting his child.

In response to Matthew's pull of the bell cord he was quickly joined by father and Brother John, who were able to calm me down with their words of love and condolences. Then, in response to my questions, they gently broke the current news to me.

With a tremble in his voice John told me that Moneysa was now in the care of the undertaker, and she would be returned to Ganton Hall the day before her funeral which, with my permission, he would conduct. Overfilled with grief at the thought of burying my wife I nodded my head by way of approval.

Next my father explained how Derbie Salter's security guards, who were stationed around the perimeter of the estate, had advanced from all sides to the scene of the crime and apprehended the person responsible.

"For my guess it was that damned Elliott or one of his paid henchmen."

Father paused and looking a shade uncomfortable replied, "No Charles. As much as I would desire to hang Elliott he cannot be charged with Moneysa's murder. It would appear the culprit was Cymol who committed the deed after suffocating his mother and, from all accounts, he failed in an attempt to take his own life prior to his arrest. Soon he will be questioned under caution by magistrate Derbie Salter. In the short term, he is sharing the same dungeon as the two cohorts of Elliott and, no doubt, will go to the gallows with them."

Holding my hands to my head I slowly shouted, "Please God tell me that all this is a nightmare acting out its script from hell within me."

Father took my hand and those around me stood with heads bowed; aware that words could not, for the moment, have any impact upon me. I was vaguely aware of a great pressure in my head, and in desperation I began to shout….. "You don't understand ……….not one of you bloody understands ……..I need oblivion …I need brandy ……… get me it …get me it ….get.."

Charles had finally succumbed to the pressure of his inner emotions and he finally lost control of his words and actions. **In a loud voice that echoed through most of the house he repeatedly cried, "Don't take Monnie away .....she needs to be in my arms ....she will wake up soon ......and I need to be there with her.......Monnie needs her husband and not a bloody undertaker .....!"**

His bouts of loud and uncontrollable crying and sobbing was fast developing into a severe fit of violent grief, during which he hurled a bedside goblet at the opposite wall and began to beat his head with his own fists. Immediately father and brother rushed forward and held him tightly in their arms to both console and prevent him from harming himself, whilst nodding to Matthew who quickly withdrew in search of the brandy so earnestly requested.

Fearing that his condition was worsening Edward Ganton sent the family coach under the command of the indomitable Ruth, with instructions to bring back the local doctor with all urgency. True to her ability, and within the hour, Ruth arrived with the somewhat dishevelled doctor who had surrendered his appearance in the face of Ruth's forceful demands.

Following a detailed examination his diagnosis was one of 'high emotional shock' that required Charles to move away from the area with its attendant memories, as a matter of urgency.

In the interim, and to promote relaxed sleep, laudanum (alcoholic solution of opium) was prescribed and supplied and he promised to call again, in two days, with more of the sedative should it be required.

After two complete days confined to my bed I was pleased to soak in my tub and dress in casual clothing after which, and by his suggestion, I walked around the grounds with

Brother John enjoying the fresh air of early spring. For obvious reasons we deliberately missed out the woodland walk, but I forced myself to return to Ganton Hall via the front entrance in order to pause at the oil painting of Moneysa hanging to the side of the fireplace.

John held my arm as I stared longingly at her and recalled her facial expression which the artist had captured so well.

The real me wanted to burst into tears, and curse God and Cymol over the loss of Moneysa, but the laudanum had done its work as it held my mind in a fog of 'peaceful confusion' in which state I allowed John to lead me by the hand, into the dining room, and to a place prepared for me.

Father, Elizabeth and Ruth sat in silence but rose to their feet as I entered then resumed their seats when I sat down.

"When will the undertaker bring Moneysa home father?"

"At two hours past noon, and I have arranged for her to rest in the living room close to the large windows overlooking the lawn. She loved that view...." he replied as the proximity of tears foreclosed on his words, causing him to look down at the table.

We each sat quiet and still, until a timid female voice broke into my mind with the words, "If you please sir, I have brought you some soup." With that she scurried away as I stared at the steaming liquid that matched a pleasant odour to the promise of favourable taste; yet it found no favour within me.

"Please Charles, just try a little of the soup. You have eaten nothing for almost three days and we beg of you to break your fast."

After a pause I stood up and caught sight of the distraught look on Elizabeth's face which prompted me to add, "Please forgive me and believe my words when I stress that I am not being melodramatic, the truth is that I have no appetite; in fact I am tempted to believe that my appetite died when …."

Unable to complete what he was going to say he choked back a sob and rushed to the sitting room to await Moneysa's return.

At the appointed time the coffin arrived and was escorted into the house by Brother John wearing his black silk stole and reciting the prayer book words of office, as I led the family and other mourners in the wake of what was a procession of tears.

We stood as sentinels of grief as the coffin was lifted on to its bier after which the bearers stood to one side. The coffin was jet black in colour and decorated with raised engravings along each outer edge. Fixed upon the lid was a gold plated plaque inscribed with the following epitaph:

MONEYSA GANTON

1761 – 1781

Slowly the senior undertaker approached the coffin, paused and bowed before it, then almost indiscernibly removed the holding screws and lifted the lid and placed it against the wall.

I walked to the foot of the coffin and gazed upon my wife who seemingly lay sleeping. Her black hair was arranged in ringlets upon her shoulders and her head rested on a silk cushion. She wore a light blue linen shroud with long sleeves and turned up white cuffs matched with similar trimmings around the neckline. On her feet were light blue stockings. Her hands were crossed at her midriff and her double heart wedding ring was clearly visible as was the beloved red pendant round her neck.

I fixed my eyes upon her face and mentally prayed over and over again, "Please Lord Jesus, just as you raised Lazarus from the dead, please give me back my darling wife," until I felt myself trembling, only for the strong voice of Ruth to restore my senses with her motherly command, "Charles, drink this now."

She had predicted what might happen and secreted a glass of laudanum in the room which she now thrust into my hand. Without argument I did as I was instructed, drained the glass, and was helped into a chair that had been placed at the head of the coffin.

A hand touched my shoulder and a voice, which I believe came from Elizabeth, whispered, "Rest here awhile Charles and be at peace with Monnie."

I awoke with a start to the sound of a distant clock chiming eight low pitched notes and immediately remembered Moneysa lying asleep just a few feet away.

Bending over the coffin side I gently kissed her forehead, and held her ice cold hand in mine, as I gazed longingly at her face and thought of all we had enjoyed together. "Why we have been robbed of a life time of bliss can only be answered by God but, my darling wife, please know that it is better that we had those brief years together, during which we fell in love and married, rather than never to have met at all."

A discreet cough cut short further words as I looked up and saw Brother John standing in the orangery with Elizabeth at his side.

"May we keep vigil with you Charles in memory of our pledge that the 'Valiant Four' will always look after each other."

Looking down at Monnie, in the fading light, it seemed that she smiled at the quip made by her brother through law as if to urge me to act upon their compassion towards us.

I turned, walked and then ran over to them, and we held onto each other as a trio in grief yet sustained in love. We spent the entire night oscillating between Moneysa based conversations and dozing in our chairs; yet each one of us was so very grateful for the presence of the other two as we awaited the new day when we would commit Moneysa to her final place of rest.

From time to time I would wander over just to hold Monnie's hand or run my fingers through her hair whilst telling her over and over again how much I loved her and that I was relying on her, in spirit, to journey with me to our home in India.

I felt so confident that even death's grip could not withstand the strength of our love and that Moneysa would hold the light, as symbolised in the candle ceremony she led on our wedding day, which would guide me back to her presence.

Suddenly there was a gentle tap on the door and it slowly opened to admit Ruth, bearing a tray of warm drinks, as the eastern sky responded to the first light of the approaching dawn.

......

A muffled stillness filled the house as its inhabitants moved in silent homage to Moneysa who, in a short time would take her last journey in this life. The family and staff had tearfully filed past her open coffin as I stood, with bowed head, creating an ineffaceable image of Moneysa in my mind; lest time should dare to blur the memory of my greatest treasure.

As the undertaker slowly lowered the coffin lid into place my eyes dwelt on Moneysa's face until she was hidden from me.

My reverie was broken by the gentle touch of my father's hand on my shoulder, followed with, "Come on Charles, Moneysa would want each of us to be strong in her memory, and not only the family but all the mourners depend upon us." Nodding my agreement I walked immediately behind the coffin as Brother John, wearing his funereal robes, slowly led the procession out of the house.

It was at this stage that I noticed, for the first time, that Mr and Mrs Salter, and Matthew, had been joined by other faces that under happier circumstances I may have recognised. We stood with lowered heads as the coffin was carefully placed within a glass sided black hearse, drawn by two black horses complete with funeral plumes. The cortege, included five coaches filled with mourners, proceeded slowly out of the grounds of Ganton Hall and along the road to the village.

Villagers stood reverently, with heads bowed, at the church gates and in two lines on either side of the path, as the bearers carried Moneysa into the church. Brother John led the coffin, and father and I walked immediately behind followed by Elizabeth and Ruth. I was aware that many people were present but, not surprisingly, I have no mental record of who they were; yet they were not slow to pass on their condolences to family members.

As the coffin was placed before the altar I became overwhelmed with the fact that less than two weeks ago Moneysa and I, on that same spot, became man and wife.

Nevertheless the funeral service progressed with the touching tenderness of love wearing its coat of tears; which is what I would have expected from Brother John who always preached from his heart. Yet my attention frequently wandered to the coffin upon its bier and the focal point of my love that rested within its dark embrace awaiting.......... here I paused because there was more I wanted to add but, as a rising sob threatened to burst out aloud, I tried to regain control of myself.

"Be strong for the others Charles," I muttered; yet the shake of my body was noticed by my father who gently supported my arm in a bond of silent compassion.

Although it was a bright sunny day the procession to the grave side radiated a dark shadow of finality, from which many of us knew that life, for us, would never be the same again. We had lost an attractive young woman from India who had revitalised our local English culture and, for good measure, had honoured me by becoming my wife; a gentle nudge from father reminded me that the undertaker was offering me the opportunity to sprinkle soil from his bowl onto Moneysa's coffin in her final place of rest.

In a hoarse whisper I said, "Ashes to ashes ..." then a massive lump in my throat rendered me silent and father finished off the traditional "dust to dust."

As we stood in silence at the edge of the open grave I became aware of a man, wearing a black cloak, who had managed to make his way to my side. Immediately Matthew stepped forward and stood close behind me ready to pounce if this stranger offered even the remotest threat to my safety.

"Forgive my intrusion Charles," caused me to raise my head and immediately I recognised Neville proffering his hand to me. I stared at him, then at his hand, and slowly clasped it adding the words, "We are brothers in grief." Neville held up a single red rose, and looking into the open grave, asked my permission drop it onto the coffin. I nodded my head and thanked him as he let the rose fall from his hand on to the coffin lid. He momentarily paused and gazed within the grave then, struggling to control his emotions, he quickly disappeared into the crowd after which, so I was later told, he left England in order to study in Italy.

I too was in a prime position and was able to detect both a written note attached to the stem of the flower together with the wording, and style of writing, which I have copied below:

AMERE SHEBA
VALEO
N

There can be no doubt that Sheba is Neville's name for Moneysa and 'N' is Neville. However the words 'amere' and valeo' are presumable from a language that is literally foreign to me.

CHAPTER THIRTY TWO

Inquest at Ganton Hall

The following day my solitude was broken with the arrival of some good news which was a scarce commodity in my life of late. Unheard by me a mounted courier had arrived with a message addressed to my father which was meant for me since it related to our return journey to India. The heart of the message was that the original convoy scheduled to take us to India, prior to the death of my wife, had not yet sailed due to inadequate fleet presence covering the trade route to India.

This breaking news encouraged me to briefly research the reasons why the most powerful fleet of its time was unable to protect the nation's trade interests. It emerged that following the Franco-American alliance in 1778 and the entry of Spain into the war as an ally of France fundamentally changed the war at sea. Thereafter, England was unable to maintain overall maritime supremacy, due to a massive deployment of naval warships needed to blockade America at the height of their War of Independence. In parallel a substantial presence was maintained in the English Channel to guard against invasion. This left French and Spanish warships the freedom to take the offensive elsewhere which had caused the India convoy to be postponed.

However reports from fast sailing naval sloops confirmed that enemy warships were now in port being refitted after many months at sea during the height of winter. This good news was the signal for the Indiamen, and naval escort vessels, to take on board all necessary provisions and set sail five days hence.

Magistrate Derbie Salter had hastily arrived, together with his court clerk cum scribe, in order to establish what would be done with Cymol; whilst Ganton Hall worked at full capacity to ensure that father and I were ready to travel to London docks in the morning.

The meeting began with prayers led by Brother John followed by a summary of the circumstances surrounding the murder of my wife. It would tax the hardest of hearts not to appreciate how agonizing this meeting was for me but, in turn, I am aware that you need to know all that transpired. Nevertheless I would ask for your understanding in that I do not want to draw out these proceedings, and have sought to summarise my reporting style in a way designed to reflect accuracy whilst minimizing personal pain. Thus:

1. Cymol admitted that he had murdered both his mother and sister.

2. His reasons were that Moneysa's return to India, as my wife and bearing our child, would be an affront to Islam. After he had killed his mother and sister his intent was to shoot himself, but the gun had malfunctioned after he had hurriedly re-primed it. He remained adamant

that it was better that all three should die rather than face the wrath of the mosque on their return to India.

At this stage the clerk read a statement voluntarily made by Cymol in which he described the state of his mind that caused him to murder both his mother and sister:

"After the family meeting my mind was filled with horror at the fact that Moneysa had left Islam and was to marry a Christian and, to add further to my grief, she was already carrying his child. I could not face the disgrace ahead of us when we returned to India so I decided to kill my mother and sister after which I would kill myself and become a martyr to my faith.

When the time came for us to board the coach for London docks my sister asked me to collect mother from the cottage and join them as quickly as possible. Walking to the cottage I realised that if I did not act now then all would be lost, so I literally ran the remaining distance to where my mother was. I found her lying asleep on the bed fully dressed and prepared for someone to collect her; which made it easy for me. I gently yet firmly pressed a chair cushion upon her face and held it in place as her hands feebly clutched the air around her until all movement ceased.

I removed the cushion and gently kissed her forehead after which I took the gun from a bag in her bedside drawer. Quickly I primed the gun then placed a ball in the barrel after which I put the powder bag and a spare ball in my pocket, because my final act would be to turn the gun upon myself. After that I left the house and hid alongside a large rhododendron bush that overhung the path in the hope that Moneysa would come to investigate my delay.

I did not have to wait long to hear her approaching footsteps and when almost level with me I stepped out and pointed my gun at where I thought her baby would be. My words of judgement were, "You have repeatedly insulted our faith so you and your baby must die together."

She stared at me in total amazement and with outstretched hands said, "I am your sister. Why are you doing this Cymol, why ……"

My reply was to press the trigger and the crack of the explosion was matched by a short scream as my Moneysa fell upon her side and lay still as blood began to form a pool upon the path.

Immediately I heard men shouting and coming towards me from all directions.

In panic I ran away from the scene and hid in a bush where I tried to prime the gun but, in my haste, most of the powder was lost upon the ground. I had not realised that guards had been posted around the woods so, with fast beating heart, I raised the powder deficient gun to my head and pulled the trigger. The sound of hammer click upon metal told me that all was lost as two men punched me to the ground and tied my arms behind me. Then one of them hit me again and I screamed at them, "Must I must die at the hands of infidels?"

The clerk held the written account up for all to see Cymol's signature witnessed and dated by a further two signatories.

3.   My father identified the gun as one issued, by the East India Company, to all employees for their personal safety. He further confirmed that, as part of his staff induction, Drebar had been given such a gun for the protection of his family.

This type of gun had its origin in England during the 16th to 18th century when occasions of robbery and violence were high, meaning that affluent members of the public walked around with guns on their person for self defence.

They were small pistols that were easily concealed and bore the nickname 'Saturday night special.' They were favoured among the gentry who would carry them in a waistcoat pocket and women hid them in their muffs.

They were muzzle loading pistols which meant they would have had to be primed before setting out on a journey. Also they were notoriously inaccurate meaning that the murder weapon was fired at Moneysa, from a very close range, in order to achieve what it did.

4. At this stage Derbie Salter read out the doctor's report which, in general terms, confirmed that Moneysa had been shot and judging from powder marks on her clothing the gun was almost touching her when it was fired. She had died from internal injuries that had promoted a massive loss of blood. Her mother showed all the symptoms of having been forcibly suffocated.

Struggling hard to control the pain of his emotions Charles begged the meeting's pardon and walked over to the window where, with hands behind his back, he stared across the lawn at what he and Moneysa lovingly called 'our secret little forest.'

I do know that he had not set foot within that woodland or indeed ventured into the village since the death of his wife; preferring the solitude of his room and the company of his memories so tragically curtailed.

For the sake of completion Derbie Salter informed us that he had consulted a university colleague, who was an expert in eastern religions, and had placed before him Cymol's reasons for committing the double murder to thus deflect full retribution from Islamic law.

Without hesitation the expert confirmed that Cymol's reasoning was questionable, since it did not appear in the

Koran, and was only practised by extremists who were present within, and in turn distorted, many of the world's leading religions.

Appearing composed Charles returned to his seat, drank a glass of water, and gave his full attention to the next stage of the proceedings.

5. Derbie Salter announced that the meeting had reached its final stage wherein we must decide what must be done with Cymol. For the benefit of our non-legal minds he summarised the requirements in which cases of murder, or indeed a wide range of other crimes, could be placed before the Assize court.

Under 18th century law an Englishman could prosecute any crime and, in practice, the prosecutor was usually the victim or someone close to the injured party if deceased. It was up to him to file charges with the local magistrate, present evidence to the grand jury and, if the grand jury found a true bill, provide evidence to present to the judge.

Those convicted for murder were hanged or, in certain circumstances, were transported for life or pardoned on condition that they enlist in the army or navy.

According to pre court reports the fact that Cymol had admitted murdering his mother, followed by the wife of a man of the 'gentry' class, would be more than sufficient to seal his fate. Additionally the 'gentlemen of the jury' were, essentially, men who loved their wives and mothers and would quickly align themselves with the pain of the victim and his family. Thus, if the case was proceeded with, Cymol would certainly die upon the gallows.

The final decision rested with me as the aggrieved husband and, to some extent, with my father who was Moneysa's guardian.

Looking straight at me Derbie Salter apologised for adding further strain to my already ponderous burden of grief, and asked if I would like a brief adjournment in order to consider what my response would be.

I thanked Derbie for his concern but assured him, and all present, that I had already thought the matter through and that my mind was made up and I was ready to make public my decision.

Reacting to his nod of approval I rose to my feet in the knowledge that Cymol would live or die in accordance with my wishes. Momentarily I had mental flashbacks to Drebar playing with Cymol and Moneysa as children, watched by their smiling mother Lajila. But now only Cymol remained to represent that once happy family group and fate had given me god like powers of life and death over him.

"From the onset I must stress that I would willingly inflict upon Cymol the most horrendous form of death known to mankind, if at the end of it Moneysa would come back from the dead and into my arms."

Briefly Charles faltered and was close to tears. He hastily drank some water and acknowledged Brother John's hand of support upon his arm. Then fully composed he was able to continue.

"Obviously this can never be the case so, on the first assessment of the situation, nothing would be achieved in putting Cymol to death for I firmly believe that he is of sick mind.

The option would then be to take him back to India and leave him to the judgement of his peers which may not turn out in my favour. He may incite the mosque and others into believing that we were responsible for the death of his mother and sister thus causing ill-feeling and acts of aggression against our presence in this rich commercial area of India.

I know, from my trade dealing experience with local leaders, that if their traditional ways are upheld and respected then favourable commercial agreements are guaranteed. If perchance Cymol could, and I believe that he would, incite ill feeling against East India Company employees then His Majesty's government would not applaud me for adding an Indian uprising, in a prime mercantile area, to their already overstretched military and naval resources.

Thus in National interests I do not believe that Cymol should be allowed to return to India meaning that father and I would return according to the original plan. In all honesty I could tell everyone there my wife had died and that Drebar's widow and family would remain in England albeit that, in certain parts, my late wife would be thought of as Elizabeth Salter.

Since Elizabeth will never again set foot in India I would ask for your forbearance and understanding of the reasons behind this undeclared charade; which are entirely in defence of English trade interests that are vital to National wellbeing."

Looking around the room I was aware of nods of approval from Edward and Derbie whereas Brother John, with his chin in his hand, appeared to be striving to form a decision based upon his convictions.

"In the absence of institutions for the effective care of the insane I am left with only one option which is to prosecute Cymol for the wilful murder of my wife and my mother through law. From his signed confession, in which he showed not the slightest degree of remorse, I have to conclude that the state of his mind may lead Cymol to kill again, and create even more sadness in lives as yet untouched. Gentlemen, I thank you for hearing me ….."

With that Charles's voice trailed away as he slumped back into his chair and fixed his gaze on the carpet at his feet.

"Thank you Charles for your logical summing up of the situation and I would like it recorded that I am in full agreement with you." This was followed by a nod of approval from Brother John and, "I too agree" from father who continued, "I blame myself for what Cymol did. As you will remember Charles, we had a meeting back in 1775 when the mosque officials asked if Cymol could accompany his sister to England in the role of spiritual advisor. **If only I had refused their application then we would not have been having this meeting today.**"

"Father, it is all in the realms of hindsight that was not remotely obvious at the time. You must not blame yourself,"

"I agree with you Charles that my mind should not dwell within the realms of 'what if' but it does little to lessen my pain, which grows incessantly, such that I now dread returning to India and perhaps sitting again in the chair from which I made that disastrous decision."

"Edward, you are my dearest friend," added Derbie as he walked over and sat beside his comrade of old. "You and your family have suffered grief in abundance and all you need is the opportunity to rest and take full stock of your age, health and situation and then decide how you will spend your autumn years.

You are welcome to reside in my house and I feel certain that Elizabeth would welcome your presence here, because we all love and respect you and seek only to enhance your welfare."

Immediately, I went over to my father and, kneeling alongside him, I concurred with all that Derbie had said and offered. I reassured him that I was well able to manage my life in India, and were he to accompany me he would spend long periods alone because of the fanatical application I gave to my work.

With a half smile he acknowledged my reasoning and, holding Derbies hand, asked if he could remain awhile in England until the black clouds had moved away. With that Elizabeth and Brother John joined Derbie and added their joyful support to his decision.

In no time it was unanimously agreed that Edward Ganton would initially remain at Ganton Hall, then move in with the Salter family to help with estate and judicial matters, but only on the understanding that Charles wrote regularly from India giving an account of his progress. With a wry smile Charles agreed to this.

Derbie Salter then stood up and asked if there was any further business to be discussed, and solemnly noted the shake of all heads.

Following this he asked his clerk to arrange for Cymol to be formerly charged with double murder and for all the evidence to be lodged, via a barrister, with the Assize Court in time for him to appear at the next sitting.

The final act was prayers led by Brother John that brought some peace and much hope into the grief stricken minds in that room.

CHAPTER THIRTY THREE

Charles returns to India

As my last act before leaving Ganton Hall Elizabeth and Brother John accompanied me to the village in order that I may first take leave of Matthew, and then view the headstone that had been placed on Moneysa's grave.

"May I make a request?" asked Matthew as we turned to leave his forge.

In response to my nod of the head he continued with, "Please Mr. Charles let me come to India with you as your man servant….."

Swiftly I interrupted, thanked him for all the love and service he had already given us, then I reminded him that he was urgently needed to assist the Reverend John and all the villagers, more so because he had ploughed his reward wealth into looking after their needs. Reluctantly agreeing with the logic of my advice he went on to engulf me in a farewell hug as he whispered, "God bless Mrs. Moneysa and yourself."

With measured tread and heavy hearts we walked up the steep path to the grave of my wife, which was just to the left of the church door. Standing in silence our eyes focused on the small monument, which had been designed and urgently commissioned by Elizabeth and Ruth, and I thought of....thought of ...but my mind was becoming confused and all I wanted to do was throw myself upon the grave; until the gentle voice of Elizabeth reminded me that I was not alone because their love and support was ever with me.

In my jumbled state of mind I looked down at the silent ground, so very lonely, yet my love of all loves was within its cold embrace. Very soon I would be several thousand miles away and then who would look after my wife.........

........John sensed my building emotions as he gripped my arm and whispered, "We walk with you through your valley of the shadow of death ...."

Nodding my head I thanked them both for their support, as I lapsed into restrained silence and gazed at the headstone.

It was similar to many headstones I have seen with a curved top and, within the arch was what appeared to be an inlaid pattern of the letter 'W.' Compared with other headstones of this era it was rather small and its message was brief, as indeed was their marriage'

**Here beneath lies the body of my wife
Moneysa Ganton
Who left this life on the 17th March 1781 aged 20 years
'Brief was our marriage yet eternal is our love'
Charles**

I looked, and even tried to smile at those around me as I again thanked them for their love and support, freely given to my wife and myself........ then my voice again faded as inner remorse washed away my words.

However, and in memory of the one I love, I did rally with the words, "As Monnie would have said – thank you my ever best friends."

Soon we were back at Ganton Hall with the coach waiting to take me on the first section of my journey ending at Greta Bridge, where I would meet the London bound stage coach. As I reached the main door of Ganton Hall I turned and gazed longingly at the portrait of Moneysa. There was no need for even mental words because the eternal bond between us was enough, yet without warning my mind was filled with that often mentioned yet haunting tune I would ever remember her by.

Once outside I walked down the row of staff shaking their hands and consoling those in tears and, perhaps, Ruth wept more than most as she threw her arms around me. She smiled and agreed when I asked her to take good care of Elizabeth and she sobbed profusely when I thanked her for all she had done for Monnie and me. Suddenly the now familiar face of the little kitchen maid nervously appeared before me and, after a curtsy, she handed me a small bag. Thanking her I peered into the bag and found that she had made me some mince pies. "For your journey sir," she added before bursting into tears and rushing into Ruth's arms.

Briefly Elizabeth held on to me with her head on my shoulder then, through tear filled eyes whispered, "Remember what I said Charles," then she slipped away to console Ruth and the young maid.

Brother John hugged me and promised he would keep me up to date with developments whilst, with a wry smile, urged me to do the same. Then father threw his arms around me and blessed me with his paternal love; then as if rehearsed we said together ...."Just as Moneysa will forever bless and love us ...."

Soon I was waving from the coach window to those I left behind, perhaps never to see some of them again. As the scene faded my eyes focussed upon the waving quartet of love and friendship known as father, John, Elizabeth and Ruth until I could see them no more.

Slumping back into my seat I muttered out loud, "Is this the end or just the beginning?" After I closed the coach window I drew the carriage rug round my knees, thought awhile, then muttered, "Who knows, who really knows?"

Charles, for reasons known only to himself, said very little about his journey from England to India and he resumed the following dictation, in earnest, only when the sea journey was drawing to its close.

I suppose I have been fortunate in that all my sea journeys, to and from India, have been undertaken in times of war or uneasy periods of peace without mishap to myself or the ships around me. However on this occasion I really felt alone amidst several families making the same journey on behalf of the East India Company, except for a young husband and wife who were answering their call to become Baptist missionaries in the far north of India.

Each group was friendly towards me and tried to draw me into their socialising and, in response to their appeals, I once joined them at dinner with the captain. I must have been a complete bore to all present due to my lack of appetite, both for food and conversation.

Eventually they left me alone to pace the lee side of the quarter deck or seek the solitude of my cabin, books and memories.

Quite suddenly, or so it appeared to me, we had arrived in India and our small fleet of merchantmen slowly kedged into position taking advantage of the inflowing turn of the tide. Then with a mighty roar the metal cables ran out as the two enormous bow anchors thundered into the water.

Standing at the rail I noted that we were a considerable distance from the docking area and already a flotilla of smaller craft were approaching with, what I later found, was the objective of first landing passengers and their belongings before the ship, in similar manner, was relieved of its cargo.

Quite independently long boats from the escorting warships, with an officer in full uniform and naval cocked hat in the stern, seemingly raced one another in their quest to reach the dock side.

Clearly there had been a change in docking procedures that had puzzled Charles so much so that I briefly researched the period for possible clues as to why this had happened.

It soon became obvious that voluntary recruitment of sailors on to naval warships, in the late 18th century, had ceased and the Admiralty relied almost entirely upon those pressed into service via the notoriously violent attentions of the press gang, particularly along waterfronts and in dockland taverns and brothels.

Although Admiralty instructions were that the crews of ships plying the vital trade routes with India and the East would be exempt from the attentions of the press gang, there was no one to police this directive when the ships were several thousands of miles away from London.

Additionally experienced merchant seamen would be prime acquisitions for crew starved naval vessels. Thus it was no surprise that merchant vessel captains strictly forbade any crew member from setting foot ashore and, in turn, pretended not to notice boatloads of dockland wenches who came aboard to meet the needs of lonely and loved starved sailors.

In due course I was ashore and reunited with my luggage in a Company coach as I began my journey home, and the challenge of my new appointment, tinged with life directing memories that I would soon have to face and somehow live with.

The heat was intense; which is not surprising since it was late May and the hottest part of the year and little relief was noted when I opened both carriage windows to admit dust and noise from the busy streets.

Progress was restricted due to many market bound hand carts piled high with a wide range of sale items with barefooted men, bent almost double between the shafts and a male family member pushing at the rear of the cart. Alongside every cart were women, some in colourful saris and others in rags, walking with excess sale items including vegetables, cotton ware and even furniture in their arms or balanced upon their heads.

In one busy street my coach was forced to stop in order to allow a group of drivers to round up a number of escaped and thoroughly terrified bullocks, that had demolished some of the street stalls, to the anger of vociferous stall holders who were demanding immediate compensation albeit in vain.

At one stage a 'liberated' chicken alighted on the open window sill of the coach and peered in, only to think better of it and duly flutter away.

As an aside I must add that the sight and actions of the described chicken had its origin with other earlier 'random memories' which I discussed in my opening section of this narrative.

As my coach resumed its progress I closed my ears to the turmoil outside and sank back in my seat staring at the empty place before me. My mind drifted aimlessly between the present and its challenges, and the past with its joyful and tragic memories when, without warning, I had cause to hold my breath as a vision of Moneysa slowly appeared on the seat before me.

She smiled at me and said something that I could not hear.

Then she proudly looked down at the advanced state of her pregnancy and gently placed her hand upon the child within. Instantly I was on my knees before her and my hand joined hers upon the beneficiary of our emotions; only for my vision to fade away......... leaving my head and hand upon a hot fabric seat.

In a daze I slowly stood up merely to fall backwards into the opposite seat as the coach responded to a series of deep ruts in the road.

Looking at where Monnie had been sitting I pleaded for her to come back only to realise that I must have experienced an hallucination unless .... "Unless what?" I asked the turmoil of a mind that had no answers.

In desperation I rummaged in my pocket for my hip flask and quickly drained its contents of warm yet effective spirits of brandy. Feeling tired, and without food for several days, meant that my speech was already slurred as I asked myself the question, "Charles Ganton has your hip flask taken over as your ever best friend?"

"Who knows," I muttered to myself, "who the hell knows ......and who the hell cares," as I sank into the stupor of brandy induced sleep.

—

Charles spent the next 29 years (1781 – 1810) of his life immersed in his work for the East India Company from which he gained a varied experience of commercial dealings ranging from palace based negotiations to less formal transactions in primitive, and sometimes hostile, areas of India. At all times he had to be aware of competition from other nations, who also viewed India as a lucrative source of income, yet through original and basically honourable techniques he was able to gain the advantage.

If my intentions had been to write a novel then much could have been derived from his commercial activities, in particular with rich area Mughals (also known as Moguls) with whom he did good business in terms of Company profit and his own esteem. From snippets of conversation I have a strong feeling that he was once abducted by Portuguese competitors but managed to escape, and went on to use the incident to his own advantage.

Needless to add if I were to include all his company sponsored business adventures, that occurred during the next 29 years, then I would at least double the size of the narrative before you without advancing, by one iota, the purpose of this work, which is the story of Charles and Moneysa Ganton.

Without doubt his life remained a 'parallel reality' between daily work and the living memory of his beloved Moneysa who, in his mind, was always by his side. **Only thrice in this period did those 'parallel' life styles converge, which will be fully related to you in Charles's own words.**

But before then I will give you a schematic outline of his life, in India, during this final period of his life so that it may serve as a background to those three events that he considered to be so important to this, his narrative.

Charles was welcomed as a potential boost to Company activities more so in the face of competition from other parties who represented commercial and war related pressures. As indicated above Charles both met and exceeded Company expectations in these and many other areas that eventually led to him being appointed to the board of directors around the year 1807.

On arrival he received many reserved condolences over the untimely death of his wife who, as predicted, was thought to be Elizabeth Salter. Naturally Charles left the matter in that context so as not to complicate Muslim relationships which, as it turned out, were conspicuous by their absence because the Muslim fraternity made no attempt to contact him.

Charles was never attracted to other females, including those who were 'orchestrated' to gain his favour, through the efforts of families looking for a good marriage for their daughters. He managed to remain, in their estimation, a thoroughly eligible widower with excellent prospects whilst, in his own convictions, he lived only for the day when he would be reunited with Moneysa.

He thoroughly enjoyed his work which, as he admitted only to himself, helped free his mind from the ever present pain of losing his wife. Often he would remain at work in the Company Office, and sleep in an apartment provided for senior managers, until the lack of suitable food drove him home, not out of hunger, but through the knowledge that he must eat or suffer the consequences.

He did occupy the former Ganton residence but had no need for a large domestic staff.

His housekeeper and cook was a widow named Jarita, who knew the late Drebar and his family and the rest of the staff consisted of two housemaids, a kitchen skivvy and two stable hands. Jarita's late husband was also an Englishman employed as a warehouse manager for the East India Company and, in the fifth year of his service, he and several others were killed when a store building collapsed on them. Subsidence following a heavy monsoon season was blamed for the tragedy. The Company had however awarded a little compensation to Jarita together with her present role of housekeeper and cook to successive senior managers.

Jarita was about five years older than Charles. She was very efficient and caring, and worked hard to prepare meals designed to attract his reluctant appetite which she personally served to him. It is fair to report that Jarita was the only female who made any impact upon him in that he trusted her and, in turn, she gave him a 'willing ear' when he wanted to free his mind from problems.

Jarita never allowed familiarity to intervene and remained in the capacity of a loyal servant and friend throughout their time together. When at home Charles mainly worked at his desk or sat reading on the veranda, as he did with his family seemingly a life time ago.

In frequent moments of melancholy Charles would sit and stare at a hillside crater from which a water dislodged bush almost drowned Moneysa during monsoon floods, and then he individually recalled happier times when they played together as a family group; whilst never forgetting a five year old Moneysa who, on this same veranda, first came into his life when she gave him her beloved toy called Ergar.

Thus ends my brief account of events that are not directly related to the main theme but have been compiled to hopefully give to you a small insight, into the life exclusively lived by Charles, during this period of his career in India.

However I now want to lead into the first of three occasions when his past life came to the fore such that they formed part of his original dictation from 'Monnie's rock.'

CHAPTER THIRTY FOUR

Brother John visits India

I frequently received letters from England which literally forced my hand, and conscience, into replying far more often than had been my custom. The majority of the letters came from the hand of Brother John and centred on life within his parish and the exploits of Matthew in his role of Sexton and carer of what he called his 'village flock.'

Two or three letters a year were the norm from my father as he counselled me to work at a pace that would not injure my health; after which he would launch upon some historical aspect of the East India Company drawn from his long experience as a senior official. He also updated me with county affairs and his involvement in work on behalf of Squire Derbie Salter whose wife Elizabeth died suddenly in the year 1790. This sad news had been the subject of an earlier letter from Brother John.

Perhaps the most memorable letter, to date, was one received from Brother John in 1784 to inform me that Elizabeth had accepted his proposal of marriage which was solemnised, by the area Bishop, during autumn of the same year. On receipt of this excellent news I had the urge to rush off and tell Monnie, only to remember that I was truly alone. I could but hope she already knew about it for, in truth, she did predict they would become man and wife.

However upon this day in Advent 1799 I had before me a letter from Brother John which was different both in its tone and brevity. Using a minimum of words John explained there had been developments he felt he must enlighten me about in person, rather than leave them to the mercy of written words travelling thousands of miles. Consequently he requested that I immediately reserve a berth for him on the next Company vessel out of London.

I did so without further delay and wrote a letter of confirmation to be delivered by special courier, courtesy of a high speed naval sloop of war carrying despatches to London.

Naturally Charles realised that the message his brother would carry from England would not, by any stretch of imagination, be good news; but rather than speculate he, true to his nature, buried himself in his work.

Eventually the time came for him to collect his brother from the dockside and convey him back to the sight, and memories, of his former home in India. I did gather that, by agreement, the reason behind his visit would not be announced on the coach but would wait until a time, such as now, when they had privacy and comfort to talk at length.

Thus on a warm evening, in late March 1800, the brothers again relaxed together on the veranda of their childhood listening to the familiar 'music of India' performed by a multitude of creatures in the surrounding forest.

"It is so good to see you again John and I note that you have gained a little weight. Married life is obviously to your advantage but increasing responsibilities appear to have encouraged the presence of no small amount of grey hair which, I must admit, does make you look even more distinguished."

"Thank you Charles," he replied whilst studying me in the light of the many hanging oil lamps. "I am certain that you have lost weight and your face is thinner than I remember which does raise concern within me. Are you overworking and under eating Charles?"

As if on cue Jarita appeared with a tray bearing a decanter and two glasses which led me to confirm that I would never starve, whilst in her care.

Jarita smiled shyly and was about to take her leave when John rose and thanked her for looking after his brother and went on to urge her to keep a watchful eye upon me. Somewhat embarrassed Jarita gave a little bob and promised John that she would do as he asked.

Despite frequent references to the ongoing eventide bird songs, which John was happy to hear again, we ran out of general conversation and lapsed into a somewhat portentous yet significant silence, which John knew he must break, by making the first move to explain the reasons behind this overdue reunion between brothers.

Looking me full in the face, with a rare measure of tragic seriousness, John uttered the following words that alarmed me when first heard, and still do as I relate them to you. "Charles, were I not a man of God I would be convinced there was a curse upon the Ganton family."

For once I was without appropriate words and could only stare at John who was too emotionally filled to continue until, with great inner effort, he rose and walked to the veranda rail in order to recover his composure. After a few moments he turned, faced me, and slowly began his narrative with, "Charles, it grieves me to tell you that our beloved father is no longer in this life."

He wore a look bordering on desperation as I, in a trance-like state, went over to him.

We tried to speak but words fled from us; yet brotherly love won the day when we threw our arms around each other and wept bitterly, not unlike two little boys who could not find their much loved Papa.

By and by I led him back to his chair and poured out two generous glasses of whatever was in the decanter, which we slowly drank as we got our thoughts back into order.

"Are you up to giving me more detail John?" I gently asked of my brother.

"Yes Charles and thank you for your patience. After you left it was father's cherished habit to spend his evenings sitting before the fire, in the entrance hall, reminiscing over events of his past life. If he had an audience he liked it even better, but if alone he quietly spoke to himself with frequent references to Moneysa, as he smiled lovingly at her portrait on the wall above him. On many occasions he would fall asleep and even spend the night in front of the fire claiming that he slept well in the process.

However early one morning I awoke to a strong smell of smoke and the sound of dogs barking and horses neighing.

I quickly roused Elizabeth and raced out on to the landing to be met by a blanket of smoke and the sight of the hall and staircase well alight, with sparks flying upwards setting the first floor curtains and wall hangings ablaze. I could see no signs of father and he did not respond to my frenzied shouts. The inferno below was rapidly gathering momentum and there was not a moment to be lost. Furiously I beat the alarm gong on the landing and was relieved to see Ruth and the four resident maids appear. They responded immediately to my order to make their escape from the rear window overlooking the flat roof of the stables.

By now it was obvious that the old house with its dry timbers and abundance of combustible contents was doomed, and that if father was in the hall then he could not have survived the flames rapidly advancing towards us, which left me with no option other than to hurriedly sweep Elizabeth along as we made our escape with the household staff.

The two ostlers hastily turned the terrified horses out into the paddock and without delay ran after us to shelter beneath trees away from the danger area. Elizabeth was shivering in my arms as Ruth added her body heat to mine as we sought to keep her warm and reassured.

Looking back at the conflagration it was evident that we had escaped not a moment too soon. Flames, which were already licking out of all windows, had even broken through several parts of the roof and, to add to our misery, the first flakes of an early snowfall were obvious around us.

Then above the loud crackle of burning wood, the sound of collapsing roof timbers and hiss of countless sparks as they jostled their way up to the heavens we heard a familiar voice calling to us – yes, it was Matthew who had seen the glow, feared the worse and had thrown blankets and anything warm he could find into his wagon, and in record time was galloping to our aid.

Soon we had Elizabeth wrapped up warmly in Matthew's cart but matters were not looking good because Elizabeth was six months pregnant, and the shock of losing father, the house and almost our lives brought on her delivery but it was too early.

Ruth and two experienced maids worked hard and saved Elizabeth but my child ….my darling little child …" Here John broke down as he muttered, "Was stillborn."

We sat in shared grief, unable to speak, and even the night sounds faded as if in respect for our loss. After a while

John looked at me as he struggled to arrange words from the depths of his grief until, with his hands clenched on the table, he continued with, "Charles, there is one more distressing happening that Elizabeth implored me not to tell you but I feel, as my brother, you need to know all that happened; as if, God bless you, you have not already had more than enough to bear.

Although we never heard of Elliott or his cohorts again there was at least one enemy who thought it necessary to badly damage the memorial grave stone that we set up for Moneysa. The stone was damaged beyond repair so, rather than attract further attacks, we planted a rhododendron bush over the spot where your wife is buried, in the hope that you would agree with our actions."

I no longer had words to cope with all that I had heard so I just reached out and gripped my brother's hand as we, silently, shared our grief together.

John remained with Charles for a week in which they gave each other brotherly support, and Charles wrote a letter of condolence and friendship to Elizabeth, for John to deliver by hand.

During their many conversations I must record Charles's personal regret that he never returned to the spot where Moneysa died.

John, too, confirmed that neither he, nor any other family member or friend, had set foot in that woodland since the tragedy, and the former cottage had been left with doors and windows open as a mark of surrender to the encroaching forest. Apparently Elizabeth had ordered that the entrance to and from the woodland must be securely fenced off and so it still remains, overgrown and alone. This statement of fact will have bearing upon later facets of my narrative.

Further discussions were of no direct consequence, and rather than spend time on peripheral events, I will move on to the second occasion that Charles judged sufficiently important to include in his dictation from 'Monnie's Rock'

CHAPTER THIRTY FIVE

Conversation with a Spiritualist

I had remained faithful to father's tradition in that Christmas was an occasion when the term 'family' was meant to include household staff, who sat interspaced with family, around the seasonal dinner table, and the 25th December 1804 was no exception to this custom of delight.

Even by my sparse eating habits we enjoyed an excellent meal, after which we retired to spend the evening in social camaraderie around a Yule log fire, which was at odds with the ambient temperature. Even by Indian standards it was unduly warm but in deference to the season, as celebrated in England, it was agreed that this Christmas we would have a fire in the grate.

The absence of musicians made little difference to the joviality of the occasion as the punch bowl lubricated nervous tongues, thus opening up conversation and story telling to the delight of everyone present. It was the younger of the two maids who enjoyed telling eerie Jinn stories, of dubious credibility, which were given background effects in the form of groans and moans, together with an incredible impersonation of a creaking door, from one of the ostlers.

Jarita fully participated in the party spirit but drew their full attention when, in a low and mysterious voice, she cautioned us to be aware that restless Jinn were a fact; and that she had the ability to contact both bad spirits and those of good will.

I later discovered that the name Jinn, which was a new expression to me, is an Islamic title for a restless spirit. Although Charles kept up the requirements of being the party host I could sense that inwardly he was dwelling upon something that had its origin in Jarita's claim to be, in English terms, a practising spiritualist.

The tradition of servants returning to their parent's home on the feast of Saint Stephen is, obviously, not an Indian custom. Nevertheless I gave permission for the newly married older maid, and her ostler husband, to spend the day together in the smaller of the two staff houses which I had allocated to them, whilst the younger maid spent the day with her parents in her home village.

Without doubt Jarita, who lives in the house once occupied by Drebar and his family, is an excellent cook cum housekeeper and is totally indispensible to me, despite the oddities of my behaviour, which never cause her to waver from her quiet yet positive style of house management. On the first Saint Stephen's day following my return to India I invited Jarita to dine with me, in the evening, by way of thanking her for a year of loyal service. Happily this tradition has continued and tonight will be our 23rd dinner engagement.

In her quiet and reserved way I know that she looks forward to this highlight of her year, because it is a rare opportunity for her to put on her best clothes; and to be served rather than serve. Yet during the day she was about her many duties in her inimitable way and gave no indication that her mind could possibly be anywhere other than on her immediate work.

For my part I spent the day between my desk and pacing up and down the veranda thinking about Moneysa, who was particularly close to me this day, and what Jarita had said the previous evening about contacting those who had left this life. During my veranda pacing I briefly met up with Jarita and reminded her about our dinner appointment and that I wanted to discuss something very important with her.

On hearing this, her smile changed to worried concern which may be expected from one whose entire existence depended on being employed by the East India Company. However I was quick to assure her that the subject for discussion was not related to her house duties as her work and service record was, as ever, truly impeccable.

"What I need is your skill to help me with an emotional problem that I have carried these last 23 years. The matter is very confidential but I know it to be safe with your proven honesty. Please Jarita, will you help me?"

Although taken aback and a little unsure, she stammered out the words, "Of course I will sir, if I am able."

"Good," I replied, "I will look forward to joining you at the table come 8pm." As she turned to leave I called her name, she paused and faced me wondering what was to come next. I just smiled at her and said, "Thank you Jarita ...thank you." She returned the smile and swiftly disappeared into the house.

The dinner arrangements went well and the young kitchen girl, as cook and waitress, excelled herself both in the eyes of her supervisor Jarita, and the master of the house.

In her role of invited guest Jarita wore her best sari in two shades of green, enhanced by a pattern of small flowers embroidered in gold thread that reflected light from the table candles. Around her neck was a beautiful gold necklace set with dark green stones, she wore matching earrings and a bangle around her left wrist. Each year Jarita expressed her regret at having to refuse the offer of wine with her meal because she was of the Hindu religion, but Charles with a grin, admitted to being a 'spirit gulping Christian' and asked her permission to drink on regardless.

"I just do not know how you do it," I said to Jarita as we discussed the ageing process. "I know that we are about the same age, yet my hair is showing silver threads whereas you do not have a grey hair in your head. Added to this I have developed a stupid cough that cannot be blamed on tobacco because I gave up smoking years ago……but enough of this lest I become bad company for you."

With that Charles rose and held out his hand by way of inviting Jarita to join him on the veranda. By now she felt comfortable at being the annual dinner guest, of a senior area manager, so she happily accepted his hand as he led her to a well upholstered chair.

As if awaiting her cue the young kitchen girl, cum hostess in the making, approached and set down a tray complete with glasses and two decanters holding, respectively, coconut milk and brandy. Before leaving she responded to Charles's gratitude with a curtsy and glancing towards Jarita, she gave her an 'impish' grin which Charles pretended not to notice; whilst mentally recalling the loyal maid, who loved making him mince pies, all those years ago at Ganton Hall.

Jarita looked with appreciation at the coloured veranda lights from the comfort of her chair and then, almost shyly beneath lowered eyes she murmured, "Thank you Mr Ganton for treating me as a guest at your table also for your constant kindness to all your staff. We are grateful to you, sir."

"I, too, appreciate your work for me, Jarita, and that of the team you manage so efficiently, so, in anticipation, I will be eternally in your debt if you can help me with a problem I am about to place before you. I urge you to accept that what is to follow is a serious topic, calling for serious answers; hence you must be freed from the restraint of convention. Please remember Jarita that 23 years ago we agreed that this would be our special night, during which you would not refer to me as sir or mister; but as Charles."

Clearly she still felt uneasy at having to bridge this massive gulf of etiquette and she clutched at her bracelet, in a moment of severe agitation, at the thought of equality within a society that constantly taught the contrary.

I gently put my hand on hers as I repeated my request. Slowly she raised her eyes and looked me full in the face as she clearly said, "Charles, thank you for allowing me to use your name." For a moment a massive pressure built up inside me on hearing the almost forgotten musical quality of my name, when spoken with an Indian accent. Although mentally disturbed I loved every moment of it, for it was as if Moneysa herself had spoken to me from her grave.

Jarita sensed my emotion, and placing her hand upon mine she calmly asked if my request was for her to contact my late wife. "Yes please," I murmured and stared down at the table.

"Very well Charles, but I must first change and prepare incense and candles over in my house, do you mind waiting for a few minutes?" "Not at all," I replied standing up as she left. "Wave to me from the door when you are ready and I will come over." With that I promptly sat down only to immediately stand up and begin pacing nervously along the veranda as I dared to hope that, on this very night, I would both see and speak to my wife again.

Mentally I pleaded with the powers of my destiny to briefly unite me with Moneysa, as an overture to the time when we would be together eternally. My mind was in turmoil as I paused in my stride and drank a glass of brandy, hastily followed by a second one when I saw Jarita waving me over from her house door.

A distinctly 'heady' aroma of musk-type incense attacked my senses as I entered a room that Cymol once used as the family prayer centre. Jarita, wearing a long silk like black dress and matching veil, waved me over to join her at a small round table in the centre of the room which was dimly lit by a number of candles. Although the curtains were drawn I could hear the faint sound of evening birds in chorus with crickets chirping in the grass and the chatter of monkeys gathering in nearby trees.

"I never met your wife but I once saw her, at a distance, many Christmas seasons ago so with your help I will call her to our presence. Please place your hands palm down upon the table and allow me to place my hands on the top of yours as we both clear our minds of everything other than the image of your wife."

Prior to the death of Moneysa I was very sceptical about conversing with the dead although it was very fashionable in England. However, considering that Jarita thought of Elizabeth as my late wife, it would be an excellent opportunity to test the genuineness of what, in some areas, was practised both as a religion and way of life.

"Charles, permit me to stress that it is essential you look directly at my face, fix your eyes upon mine and never lose concentration." I nodded my understanding whilst wondering if she was about to hypnotise me into thinking that the face soon before me would be that of Elizabeth?

"Your hands are still tense Charles. Please relax your entire body and allow your mind to be filled only with the memory of your wife as you stare deeply into my eyes. Do not keep your wife waiting ....I can already feel her presence in this room."

Under the circumstances I was, for the first time, able to study Jarita's face without causing her alarm or discomfort. Advancing age had been very lenient with her for other than faint lines around her eyes, and the corners of her mouth, there was little to suggest what her true age was. She had a thin face wearing a permanent look of sadness, as shown by the set of her mouth, and a melancholy look deep within her eyes.

Suddenly, I realised that I was losing concentration again when Jarita quietly prompted me with, "Charles, free your mind from distractions and picture your wife within my face."

Those who know me better are aware that I have not the disposition to sit for too long in a state of inactive silence and the onset of restlessness was nigh, when my 'heart missed a beat' as the once familiar voice came back to me with, "Charles, at last I can see you again."

Before me was not the face of Jarita but that of Moneysa just as she was before that dreadful happening. A very faint scar on her forehead, which was a legacy of the Foxton road accident, ruled out the possibility of deception. I was totally at a loss what to say or do as an avalanche of words built up, but tarried at the door of my vocal chords. In my confusion I begged of the vision to hear her voice again, in words telling me who she was, as our eyes basked in our long lost reunion. I felt that Moneysa shared my uncertainty when she replied, "I am known by many titles beginning with Monnie, who is your ever best friend, then I am your wife and above all I love you Charles and I will never leave the place where I ceased to breathe until I can leave with you."

I desperately tried to reach forward and hold my wife, run my fingers through her hair and tell her again of the depth of my love for her; but my hands were firmly held upon the table by nothing other than supernatural strength from one so small. All I could do was cry out, "Moneysa, I love you and always will." I noted her smile of understanding when, in the blink of an eye she was gone, and I found myself repeating my words of love to the face of Jarita.

Slowly my head sank on to her hands as I whispered over and over again, "Please Lord, take me now that I may eternally walk with the one I love." Suddenly, an inner energy drove me to my feet and over to the door.

Looking back at Jarita in the dim light I told her that I had pressing questions to ask of her, and that I would be grateful if she would join me on the veranda at her earliest convenience.

Sitting at the veranda table I was confused and felt bitterly cold so I gratefully acknowledged the warmth radiating from a generous intake of brandy, as it favoured my inner channels. There can be no doubt that I had briefly spoken to Moneysa and the sight of her glorious face was still to the fore of my mind, but…but…but confusion and reason were tearing me apart as they battled for control of my senses.

All of a sudden I became aware that Jarita had quietly joined me and was sitting staring at her clasped hands upon the table.

"I am sorry that I failed to acknowledge your presence, and I dare to think that you may be as perplexed as I?"

Still looking down at her hands she gently shook her head as her reply reminded me of her self held status. "It is my position to serve and not ask questions sir."

"Jarita without your input I will never come to terms with what happened this evening. Please first ask of me then be prepared for my questions that will be answered, even if we spend the entire night on this veranda."

Appearing more at ease Jarita looked at me and asked the question that must have been at the forefront of her mind, "Who was your wife? Clearly it was not Elizabeth because the girl I saw and the voice I heard was that of Moneysa, the daughter of Drebar and Lajila Akbar."

Forgive me for intruding but I must stress that this was the first and only time that I heard reference to the family name held by Moneysa.

"You are correct with your observations. It was a fact that Elizabeth and I were engaged to be married but the whole venture came apart shortly before the planned marriage in England. The latent bond between Monesya and I then burst into fruition and we married; only for my wife to die a sudden and violent death on the very day we were due to begin our journey back to India. Also to add to my anguish Moneysa was carrying our child, which would have been born soon after our return to this house.

The East India Company, as well you know, encourage marriage between English staff and Indian nationals but the Muslim fraternity, of which Moneysa was a lapsed member, may well have reacted differently. Hence the assumption that Elizabeth was my late wife was never corrected. I know, even without asking, that you will carefully guard what you have just heard."

Jarita rarely showed facial emotions but she was clearly moved by my statement, and my trust in her, as she replied with, "You have my word of honour that I will never betray your confidence for I respect you as if you were…….." She never finished defining the 'as if you were' addendum and, out of courtesy, I did not press her for an answer.

The ensuing hours were spent discussing spiritual matters relevant to life and death and, in particular, how the soul of Moneysa had responded to the almost instant death of her body. Charles was desperate to know where his wife was as, in turn, Jarita was keen to help him come to an understanding.

I spent considerable time collating all that was relevant from this lengthy discussion between Charles and Jarita as the latter sought to explain the mysteries of life and death, in terms that were acceptable to Charles who, it has to be admitted, was more inclined towards worldly than spiritual matters. Jarita spoke with great knowledge of her topic in a way that was both instructive to Charles and soothing to his disturbed mind.

*In the interests of brevity, and also to keep in focus the main items from this lengthy discussion, it may be of benefit if I summarise **the two areas** which were central to their conversation using, for ease of reading, my understanding and presentation order of the original words spoken:*

Area One: Expected death
When a person is aware for whatever reasons, that death is imminent, they are often unknowingly prepared for the moment that their heart will cease to beat.

It is like a continuing journey during which they step out of their earthly remains and become a soul awaiting transformation to the state of an eternal spirit. Often the wandering soul seeks to retain social ties with their earthly homes and loved ones and occupies a 'limbo' state between the world and afterlife. During this period the soul must learn how to 'be dead' and, within this transitional state, contact with their earthly associates does happen; while those whose hearts still beat attempt to reconcile themselves to the bodily death and new spiritual life of the person departed.

Area Two: Unexpected death

Jarita effectively explained the state of mind that Moneysa was in when, literally in a flash, a gun shot entered her body and her heart ceased to beat.

Moneysa was newly married, and shared an eternal love bond with her husband. She eagerly anticipated their future in India, a journey they were due to embark on that very day. Also she was carrying his child which added further joy to her life; in fact she loved every moment until evil stepped in and immediately deprived her of the life she so dearly loved.

Imminent death would be the very last thing upon Moneysa's mind that fateful morning and her soul would cling on to her last known place of happiness, which was the path where she fell. Stunned she would watch her lifeless body being carried away; then witness the many onlookers and mourners sadly walk away from her until she was totally alone.

Prior to that gun shot Moneysa was the centre of attention and loved by everyone, but now she felt alone and deserted. She would see those dearest to her weeping around her coffin and grave where she was not, yet that woodland spot, **where she still resides**, was left deserted; and even her *husband Charles never came to look for her. Effectively yet innocently the soul of Moneysa was shunned, and totally starved of familiar contact, and so remains to this very day; trapped within that woodland awaiting liberation by the one she loves.*

In essence that account contains all the pertinent points that were raised and stressed by Jarita and challenged by Charles, for several hours, until he finally accepted what she had said.

"Unless I am mistaken those are the first rays of dawn breaking. Forgive my selfishness by keeping you awake all night and, at the same time do accept my eternal gratitude for putting my mind at rest by showing me the way forward.

Please Jarita permit me to pose my final questions," I asked without awaiting a reply. "Should I immediately return to England and visit the place where my wife died?"

"In due course," she replied. "Please remember that time is meaningless in the spirit world whereas we mortals are slaves to its presence."

"Then hear my final plea Jarita. When I do return to the place where my wife died then how can I make contact with her and release her from captivity?"

Gently she placed her hand upon mine as she almost whispered, "You cannot liberate Moneysa from the place wherein she is held."

In shock I made as if to stand, but made no move when I realised Jarita had more to say.

"Charles, you must first die and return to the spirit world and, when divinely commissioned, your soul will return to this life within someone else. That person, be it he or she, will enable your soul to release Moneysa from this plane of life. Within the Hindu faith this process is called 'reincarnation' but I know not if it forms part of your beliefs."

For a few moments we sat in silence. I was soon to learn what Jarita had to the fore of her mind but, as for me, I felt at peace and as close to Moneysa as I ever could be in this life.

"Thank you Jarita, for all you have told me. You have given me hope but I must first use my remaining human time to digest your words of advice." Jarita did not answer immediately but gazed beyond me, as if mesmerised by the green of the bushes and trees responding to the fledgling light of the new day. "You must be very tired Jarita."

"Please sir, may I say something?"

"Of course, say what you wish and I will learn by it…. and do not hesitate because words said reflect the person who said them."

"No sir, I cannot because I must not take advantage of your kindness towards me."

"Nonsense," I cried in my best 'stern voice.' "As master of this house I require to know what my housekeeper, councillor and friend wishes to ask of me."

"Very well sir. I want you to know that when you do decide to leave India then I will miss you very much and…." Here she paused until I gently took her hand by way of encouragement, "I remember Moneysa as a lovely young woman and I am so pleased that she was blessed with you as her husband."

"Thank you, Jarita, thank you so much for saying that which, from you, I know to be the truth." She must have noticed that I was close to tears, as with her hands holding mine, she whispered, "Do not grieve because truth is the hand maiden of love."

Christmas of 1804 remained with Charles as the time when he had that all too brief reunion with Moneysa which was never again repeated. Charles had the message of his heart confirmed that Moneysa still loved him and that somehow they would one day be together for ever.

The loyal, faithful Jarita and he still had their annual dinner together and they often discussed matters connected with the after life.

In recent times they somehow developed a system whereby they would sit together on the veranda and discuss their respective work for the day, or sometimes they would sit in silence watching the sun set to background sounds from various tropical creatures.

Despite promptings to the contrary Jarita found it difficult to stray from the servant to master relationship, but she had the ability to use titles such as 'Sir' or 'Mr Ganton' with a measure of warmth in her voice that largely compensated for the formal nature of her address.

However there was a time early in 1811 when Jarita threw all caution aside when Charles joined her on the veranda.

"Good evening Jarita, has the day gone well for you?" As I sat down, Jarita, who had obviously prepared herself for this moment, stood up and addressed me with, "Charles, I must speak frankly with you."

I gazed in astonishment at her for the easy way in which, without coercion, she had used my Christian name.

"For many months, nay years, you have suffered from that dreadful cough which you insist is a routine Indian malady, but I know differently. When your bedding was changed this morning the maid showed me your pillow which was bloodstained and, apparently, this is not the first time it has happened. Please Charles; I implore you to speak to your doctor."

Pausing for a while, I mentally digested what she had said and the urgency with which she had delivered it. In silence I stared at her and noted a look of alarm, tinged with fear, which was evident in her eyes as if imploring me to take urgent action.

"She is right," I muttered to myself as I looked up at her still anxious face.

"Thank you Jarita for your concern and I am grateful that you have woken me up to my stupidity. Through my stubbornness I have ignored symptoms that unerringly match those suffered by my late mother, who died from consumption, in this very house 40 years ago. All the evidence I needed was there yet I was stupid enough to think that a regular dose of brandy and laudanum would banish my chest pains."

Then without warning, and as if to prove my misgivings, I fell into a bout of severe coughing which was the cue for Jarita to hastily pour me a glass of water. "Upon my word I will visit my good friend the doctor tomorrow," I wheezed, as I ignored the water and reached out for the brandy decanter.

Sufficient to say the following is the third and final occasion that Charles selected for special mention in his narration from Monnie's rock.

CHAPTER THIRTY SIX

Charles leaves India for the last time

Facing my doctor across his desk I paused awhile in order to absorb what he had said; then slowly asked of him, "Should you not be wearing a black head covering when passing such a sentence upon me?"

"Truly it grieves me Mr Ganton that I should be the one to give you this news, more so since I have known you and your family through many years. Such was the gravity of the situation that I obtained the opinion of two of my colleagues, one of whom is a specialist in tropical chest and respiratory infections, and they came to the same conclusion as me."

Momentarily, I gazed out of his window at the bustle of life outside as bullock carts rumbled over the uneven roads, and Indian life jostled to coexist in the crowded street, all unaware that I was under sentence of death.

"Thank you for being forthright doctor and I ask you to be equally candid when giving your opinion on the length of time I have left in this life?"

He hesitated awhile as he studied his notes, then with a look of resignation he shook his head and said, "If you remain in India I doubt if you will survive the next season of intense heat and high humidity, which is only a few weeks away. If however, which I believe is in accordance with your plans, you return to the clear and cooler air of England you may well live to the end of this current year. You have a very strong stamina Charles but, sadly, consumption is fast destroying both your lungs. I am truly sorry to give you this news; please believe the sadness I feel as I seemingly draw a curtain upon the honoured memory of the service your family has given to India."

In silence we stood and shook hands as I departed for a meeting with the chairman of the Honourable East India Company.

During the next two weeks I literally stood back and watched Company led activity, which accelerated on my behalf, following their reluctant acceptance of my resignation. They began by despatching an urgent communication to Brother John and Elizabeth advising them of the serious condition of my health, and that I was due to arrive in London in August 1811.

Then I was honoured with a sumptuous farewell dinner and showered with numerous gifts. In quick succession I had a private dinner with the Chairman and my brother directors, after which I was presented with a banker's order for a large sum of money that had been paid into my London account.

As the coach rumbled home through the bustling and noisy streets I recalled wondering what good money was to me now, other than to pass on to my brother who was my sole legatee. Then I had a brilliant flash of inspiration that I must act quickly upon, because I only had six days left before my departure for England.

"So help me, I will do something to assist Jarita with her finances, so that she will not have to work on deep into old age," I said to the passing street scene.

Feeling much more relaxed after that decision I stretched back in my coach seat, and moved in unison, as it responded to the uneven road surface. After all I was a seasoned traveller on Indian roads.

Two days later I summoned a rather bemused Jarita into my study, introduced her to a financial manager from the East India Company, and was delighted to see her puzzlement turn into joy when I told her of the substantial cash payment I had deposited in her name. Additionally, she had not to worry about managing her finances because the Company would do it for her, thus ensuring her money was well invested to yield an attractive and regular income.

"It is my way of thanking you Jarita for looking after me and encouraging me to eat during the last 30 years." As for Jarita she was literally in a state of shock and, between drying her tears, all she could manage to say was a repeated, "Thank you, sir."

In the afternoon I showed my successor and his wife around the house and grounds which again involved Jarita, who had a second bout of joy, when the new owner invited her to continue as housekeeper and cook for his family that included two lively young children.

Then, as if by hidden direction, the hustle and bustle of the last few days gradually subsided, as if to give me my last opportunity to gaze at the house and grounds from which I had derived so much happiness.

This was my last day in India.

My coach had arrived and between me, and its open door, stood the household staff in a line of silent grief awaiting my next move. For the last time I stood on the much loved veranda, and briefly recalled faces and events that had shaped my life, as I gave a little wave to the scene I was about to leave.

Would anyone be too harsh in their judgement of me if I claimed that, in my imagination, many shades from the past waved back at me? With my hand on the rail I murmured, "Goodbye India and God bless you for giving me Moneysa," and my eyes filled with tears as I walked towards my coach.

In turn I shook hands with the household staff until finally I stood before Jarita as tears ran down our cheeks.

My "Goodbye Jarita and thank you" had hardly left my lips before she threw herself into my arms and whispered, "I will never forget you, Charles." We held on to each other as my hand ran through her black hair and I gently kissed her forehead.

Suddenly I was looking down at Moneysa and then she was gone as I, with a sob, rushed over to my coach and, as if in slow motion, waved goodbye to my land of love and happiness.

Charles had an uneventful passage back to England but he found the cool sea air and falling temperatures, as England drew nearer, to be advantageous both to his health and optimism. "Perhaps the doctors got it wrong and, bye the bye, I may soon be fit to return to India," he frequently said to himself.

Four East Indiamen sailed together mainly to give support should one of them be damaged or dismasted in a storm because enemy ships were, for the moment, a feature of the past. The war with America ended in 1783 when they achieved independence and, in 1805, Vice Admiral Lord Nelson totally destroyed the combined fleets of France and Spain at Cape Trafalgar; although during the battle he sadly lost his life.

Emperor Napoleon of France was now aware that his power ended when the sea reached the flanks of his horses so he had turned his attention to a land campaign against Russia and, according to a recent report, he had occupied Moscow.

The fact that the ships were able to moor at the East and West India docks in London, without fear of crew loss to the press gang, again confirmed that England was living in a 'corridor of peace;' with an abundance of discharged seamen on the quayside rushing to volunteer their services to the first merchant ship officer who appeared on the scene.

As promised John was waiting for his brother on the quayside and soon they were being driven through the crowded London streets as they headed for the coaching station and the final stage of the journey to Greta Bridge.

CHAPTER THIRTY SEVEN

Reunion at Greta Bridge

"You have lost a little weight, but for someone in a reported terminal condition you look fit enough to me," exclaimed Brother John as our stage coach made good progress in its northerly direction. "Thank you John, and despite a little extra around the waist you look in prime condition yourself; perhaps you are the 'comfortable friar' that Shakespeare had in mind?"

After awhile our general banter subsided a little and I asked, "How is your parish ministry?" Much to my surprise he, rather than answer, turned his head away and studied the fast moving scenery as if preparing himself for the reply he owed.

"Are you alright John? I sincerely hope that all is well with your work."

"Charles, last time we met I burdened you with a catalogue of disasters that, sadly, continued when I returned home from India. We considered that you had been given enough bad news hence I decided to wait until now to add to your grief.

Yes, my parish work was going very well despite declining numbers in favour of migration to nearby towns, where work in the newly opened cotton mills and iron smelting factories was plentiful; with the added attraction of a regular weekly wage.

Action on our part was required. So together with the ever faithful and hard working Matthew we decided to try and make the village a better place for them to live, rather than languishing in a forest of smoking factory chimneys and gloomy tenement buildings. In due course the three of us decided upon our programme, and it was in the late spring of 1801 when the first of our many plans was put into action.

Elizabeth and I were on the village green for a ceremony to mark the erection of a maypole, having decided to restore this community attraction that was stamped out during Cromwell's rule. Following the restoration many maypoles had reappeared in English villages although we, in our part of the country, were lagging behind.

Matthew had enthusiastically applied his full energy and ability to the project. A hole had been dug and Matthew, from the edge of the green, was bellowing instructions to a group of villagers who were hoisting the pole into a vertical plane so that it would slide into the prepared hole.

Obviously matters were not as they should have been so Matthew ordered them to stop hauling and he began to run over to the working party when, only a short distance away, he suddenly fell forward and lay still *(as mentioned in the description of my earliest recollections)*.

Thinking that he had slipped and was merely fooling around Elizabeth and I went over to him and found that he was no longer breathing. We shook him and shouted his name to no avail.

By now the villagers had let the pole fall to the ground, where it still lies to this day, as they gathered around in a circle pleading to know what had happened to their beloved leader. I sent two men in our chaise for the doctor who confirmed our fears that Matthew had died instantly from a sudden and massive heart attack. It would appear that his heart had suddenly given up trying to support his huge frame and his life came to an abrupt end.

We, and all the local people, were distraught; the place literally died with him as the remaining inhabitants, convinced there was a curse upon the entire district, left for a new life in whichever local town took their fancy. The village has been deserted for around eight years and many of the cottages have collapsed and the area is fast returning to nature.

My parish church, without a congregation, closed its doors and rapidly fell into decay. Within a short passage of time the already weakened tower succumbed to a severe winter storm, and is now a mound of rubble protruding through the overgrown churchyard."

I waited in vain for John to continue but grief had silenced his tongue as I, in vain, searched for words to ease his anguish, whilst suffering greatly over the news of the death of my dear friend and life saver Matthew. Lulled by the rumble of the coach wheels I slipped into a reverie as the pictures of grief, so vividly described by my brother, replayed within my mind until I became aware that he was staring at me.

"I once shared my fears with you and I do so again," he murmured almost to himself. "I do believe that the villagers are correct in their fears that there is a curse upon us all. I often wonder if Elliott's hatred is behind all that has happened."

Realising that I must, despite my grief, try to raise my brother's spirits I fell back upon family unity as our defence shield against the forces of ill which, surprisingly, appeared to have some impact upon him but, by contrast, they left me totally unmoved. I heard them as purely dead words that had been dredged from the sea of darkness that, to my mind, would soon engulf us all.

Nevertheless he did rally a little and I was able to thank him for breaking the news to me, and commiserate with him over the demise of our treasured friend Matthew, coupled with the loss of his village parish and church. After that we both drifted into silence and, as it turned out, I fell into such a deep sleep that I missed two sets of horse changes and finally awoke to the cry, "Greta Bridge."

As I made to get off the coach John's hand held onto my arm causing me to turn to him in alarm.

"What is it John?"

"There is more Charles and forgive me for leaving it until the last moment to tell you. It is about Elizabeth......" With that he burst into tears as a coachman opened the carriage door.

"Close that bloody door and leave us alone," I bellowed as the intruder quickly complied.

"What is the matter with Elizabeth?" I gently asked of my brother.

"Her mind has been damaged beyond repair by all that has happened. It was a relentless deterioration that worsened as progressive catastrophes entered her life beginning with ......"

Here John stopped, then observing the look of expectation upon my face he added, "Well, there really is no more to say."

"No John there is more," I added. "You are forgetting our brotherly bond, meaning you can unburden your mind to me of all people. What were you going to say?"

Staring at me in desperation, as if trying to anticipate how I would respond, he almost blurted out, "It began when Elizabeth realised that she would never be your wife. I spent many months seeking to console her and, possibly, succeeded just a little in my quest. However, in the process I fell in love with her and, much to my surprise she accepted my marriage proposal but, as I later found, it was just pretence. She could not bear to be alone. Nevertheless we worked well together despite the many times she inadvertently referred to me as Charles. Then her father added to her grief when he announced that the tragic death of our father in the Ganton Hall fire, together with being denied his dream of becoming a grandfather, and the death of his wife was all too much for him to bear. Hence he went ahead and sold the Salter estate and retired to his birthplace in Somerset.

Charles, prepare yourself for what is ahead because the Elizabeth you are about to meet is not the one you last saw thirty years ago. She is but a shade of her former self despite the attentions of several specialists who have failed to control her frequent bouts of character change. At times she acts like nervous child who is totally dependent upon Ruth and me then, without warning, she will suddenly explode into raging bouts of near insanity until the laudanum we force into her takes effect. Following these attacks she will revert to her normal self and is totally oblivious to the slow collapse of her mental state."

John paused as if too weary to continue then, with effort, his concluding words were, "And she is a living tribute to my claim that our families are truly cursed."

I searched in vain for the correct words of reply but they fled from me. Sensing that there was nothing further to be said John got out of the coach and I quickly followed him, wondering what the next shock would be.

"There are matters I must attend to Charles not least arranging the transfer of your belongings into the family coach and organising a meal for the three of us. It is no secret that you still occupy a special place in Elizabeth's life and, with that in mind, she asked to meet and talk with you privately because, bless her, the news of your terminal condition has almost destroyed her."

With desperation upon his face John fell silent and just stared at me, almost as if words had fled from him. Then, gripping my arm, he implored me to bring happiness back into Elizabeth's life because his faith was failing him and he no longer knew what to do.

Filled with despair he hurriedly turned away leaving me to walk slowly into the inn, and pause before the parlour door which was slightly ajar. I tapped on the door and edged it open to see Elizabeth facing me ……….. wearing a sari donated by Moneysa.

Trying to disguise my amazement, and to accept the situation as it was, I moved towards her and our hands joined together, in a tight grip of reunion, which was sufficient to silently yet effectively bridge the thirty years we had been apart. Her sunken cheeks and the wild almost manic stare in her blue eyes mirrored but part of her suffering, which turned into joy as she threw her thin arms around me. Suddenly her words and emotions were released when, with a hint of hysteria in her voice, she cried, "My darling Charles, my darling, darling Charles thank you for coming home to me. Seasons have come and gone but my love for you is as strong as ever. Come and sit with me in the window that I may see you better in the light of God's day."

Still holding hands we sat and looked at one another as memories spoke words long stored within our hearts. " Do you remember that lovely day in the Indian forest when the four of us sat fully dressed, in a mountain stream, and splashed water at whoever was the nearest?" I smiled and was about to add to the account when Elizabeth leant forward and kissed me once, twice and then yet again as she added, "The last time I did that was to the accompaniment of haunting metallic chimes on the lakeside all those Christmas evenings ago."

She paused before asking, "Do you share my memories Charles?" I nodded and was about to speak when her hand went over my mouth as she declared that she still loved me with the same intensity as she did all those years ago.

"John knows where my heart really belongs, yet out of his love and care for me, he asked for my hand in marriage. I agreed because he is a good and kind man although he too has wilted beneath the strain of all that has happened, beginning with the terrible death of Moneysa. Since the demise of his parish he no longer has an active ministry and his bishop has given him time to rest a while then begin again; but I do not believe that he ever will for his life is between his books and writing desk. Please tell me if I am boring you, Charles."

"It is essential that we talk Elizabeth because we both need to diffuse the hurt within."

"Thirty years ago I predicted that one day you would come back to me alone and sad and that I would look after you. That remains true but I did not realise at the time that I too would equally need you; so do not think ill of me because of what I must ask of you.

I love my husband as a good friend, companion and supporter of my soul but every time we become close then, in my mind, I am in your arms as we share emotions that life took away from us. Please Charles, as perhaps the last act of our lives, can you bring yourself to pretend that I am Moneysa and for a few moments hold, love and kiss me as my heart desires? I am wearing her clothes and I have something else that will help you accept me as Monnie ………"

With that Elizabeth reached beneath the window bench and produced a small cloth doll which she proudly held up and said; "Now another Ergar has come to my ever best friend."

In panic, I looked away unable to tell Elizabeth that no one, even in pretence, could displace Moneysa who will always be at the centre of all I love and wish for.

Her eyes pleaded with mine as her lips came closer until I could feel her warm breath upon my face and her body pressing ever closer to mine. Mentally I began to panic because I did not want to add to her pain by rejecting her advances, but I would not betray my bond with Moneysa ……… then my anxiety was dispelled by a gentle tap on the door as Brother John entered and, joining us in the window recess, he totally ignored all that he had seen upon entering.

Almost as if by divine intervention Elizabeth became more at ease and an atmosphere of family normality slowly returned.

After a reunion meal, with conversation embracing memories interwoven with laughter, sighs and tears, the trio left Greta Bridge and set off for home via what was Matthew's village.

They alighted briefly to view a scene of overgrown desolation composed of collapsed cottages and a derelict 'smithy' with its rusty anvil open to the elements. It was not possible to gain access to the unkempt churchyard but it was obvious that the entire north end of the old building had fallen to the ground. I was aware of several feral dogs which, no doubt, were the descendants of the long since abandoned village dogs. They kept their distance until the coach pulled away which was the signal for them to launch an attack upon the heels of the moving horses. Fortunately the two coachmen were experienced in such matters and, with unerring accuracy, their whips repeatedly cut into the pack causing them to scatter. Several, in their haste to avoid the whips, fell victim to the coach wheels and became instant food for their ravenous colleagues.

In sadness they drove on and turned into the drive of a smaller square shaped house that stood a little further back than the original Ganton Hall. It had been constructed out of stones salvaged from the former building, and some still bore signs of having been exposed to heat and smoke. Charles did comment that the fenced off entrance to his 'woodland of dreams' was no longer within the house grounds, which received no comment other than the fact that it was still owned by Elizabeth, and may soon be donated to the parish council.

The house door was opened by a young maid and the trio entered a much smaller entrance hall from which they turned right, into a medium sized yet comfortable reception room. The maid closed the door behind them as Elizabeth pulled a bell cord near the fireplace.

I had moved over to the window to study the garden when the door opened and silence descended which, bye the bye, I became aware of and duly turned to discover the reason.

A voice from the past greeted my ears with, "Hello Mr Charles, you look even more dashing than ever." There, before me, was Ruth looking older and plumper but no less friendly as we rushed into each other's arms.

"It is impossible to think of the Ganton family without the inspiration of Ruth within its midst. It is good to be back with you my friend," I exclaimed between hugs and kisses. "I have prepared a special dinner for tonight so I expect a good appetite from you Mr Charles, and I will be at the table to see that you eat your fill."

In truth it was a good dinner party and afterwards it was remarked that a little of the former family spirit had returned, as the four of us drank coffee and brandy together, in post prandial conversation. In fact Brother John proposed a special toast that began with the words:

"We may now struggle to smile having been robbed of all those joys which once made a secure raft for the Valiant Four, as we happily drifted through this life. Now we are reduced to three who share equally the pain of death, illness and separation but are not totally lost because, at all times, our dear friend Ruth has been our strength. She never wavered from her role of supporter and source of help and inspiration, regardless of the storm clouds around us. So on this special occasion Ruth I want to give meaning to our gratitude by making you an honorary member of the Valiant Four. Please tell me that you will join our exclusive group."

Immediately she joyfully accepted the offer and her infectious laughter brought momentary joy into each of our lives, which literally shone upon faces so long denied even a passing smile.

"So let us each be upstanding and drink to the health of Ruth and long may she bless us with her presence," concluded John as we toasted Ruth who, for once, was without words.

The following day I was given a detailed examination by an eminent doctor who had travelled a considerable distance in order to offer his opinion which, as I expected, confirmed that my condition was terminal and that death could be a matter of a few days away.

This devastated Elizabeth who collapsed in a flood of tears and was comforted by John and Ruth as they struggled to control their own emotions.

In stunned silence I studied awhile the autumn scene through the window then, turning, I announced, "If that is indeed the verdict then tomorrow I will, for the last time, return to the woodland that Monnie and I loved so very much."

I was trying to remain strong but the sight of those sad faces caused me to turn again to the woodland scene as, in the strengthening wind, the trees appeared to bow their heads as if adding their respect to our grief. I would dearly have loved to turn and face my friends, and speak words of comfort to them, but the close proximity of my own tears would have added yet further to their burden of sorrow.

Thus with my eyes fixed upon 'our secret little forest' I murmured for all to hear, "Please remember that when I do leave this life then it is my dearest wish to be buried at the foot of one of those trees."

CHAPTER THIRTY EIGHT

Death of Charles Ganton

"Keep well wrapped up and do not over-stress yourself," were the words of well meant concern from my dear loyal friend Elizabeth who, despite all that she had suffered, firmly believed that my return from India would restore peace and happiness to the three of us.

As we left Ganton Hall together she made light of the fact that only yesterday a specialist doctor had confirmed that my illness was terminal, and there was nothing that he or the medical profession could do to extend my life beyond the next few days. With rising optimism Elizabeth continued with, "I did not believe all that the consultant said because, for once, I know more than he does. It is a truth, unknown to him, that fresh northern air is your best medicine," she declared, "It is a fact that your cough has steadily eased since you came home."

Her words of hope, so frequently contradicted by fact, meant little to me as we approached the entrance to a wooded paradise that Moneysa and I called 'our secret little forest.' It looked overgrown but, in character and retained memory, nothing had changed and without effort I could picture my wife waiting to welcome me. My unexpected greeting of, "Hello Monnie, your aging husband has come home," was accepted by Elizabeth, who knew what this reunion meant to me.

She also knew that for Moneysa and me this woodland had, for a while, been our only sanctuary against a rising tide of acrimony that, although isolated, was intent upon our destruction. It was impossible for this developing force of evil to ever forgive us for brushing aside the demands of convention as our cherished love blossomed into marriage, which lasted for only seven wonderful days, before this malefic force of ill will found and murdered my beloved wife within this leafy domain.

"Tormentor of my soul know that I will ever hate you for what you did," was my muttered curse upon my antagonist only to be followed in louder terms with, "You may laugh at a dying man grieving for his lost wife but, be assured, the power of our love will soon crush your serpent skull."

"Are you alright, Charles?" cried a startled Elizabeth as she gripped my arm, both alarmed at my outburst and the bout of coughing that had developed in its wake.

"Yes thanks," I eventually replied as we continued our slow walk aware that no one had set foot in this woodland place for thirty years; which was a fact that filled Elizabeth's mind as much as it did mine.

"See Charles, I have had men remove fencing from what was the entrance path at the foot of the slope; but do be very careful for it looks like a wilderness, the branches have spread so far they have almost obliterated the old path. It worries me Charles, please let John and myself come with you."

"No thank you Elizabeth because this is a journey that I must make on my own albeit I am thirty years too late."

"I do not know what you mean but I will wait, hope and pray that you will come back to me very soon, then we can start our lives all over again ….just you and I, Charles ….." were words that faded in my ears as, now alone, I began my slow ascent through the rich undergrowth.

The sudden re-appearance of a long absent human being went by unnoticed as, with great intent, nature entered the restless stage of its annual cycle. Oblivious to my presence gusts of cold wind reminded the trees and bushes that it was autumn as it sought and stirred, within its eddying embrace, nomad leaves until they became golden mounds of refuge for creatures fearing the chill to come. I paused to admire the architectural ability of the wind at work whilst giving my own life force, cum breathing power, time to recover.

Soon the terrain levelled off and from the positioning of well remembered trees and rhododendron bushes I began to trace what was our original path, despite a new crop of fallen autumn leaves. As I trod that familiar woodland footpath my mind resounded with recollections of those far off days with such questions like "Do you remember this Charles? Or do you remember that?……" as evergreen memories became words that fell from my lips while I walked and talked alone in my world of distant dreams.

Suddenly inspired I called out aloud, "Yes, I do remember the time when Moneysa and I walked hand in hand through the ancestors of these fallen leaves. We were very happy and the conversation was of no consequence until suddenly I sensed 'mischief in the air.'

Monnie had slipped her hand out of mine, and tarried to study the bark of a nearby tree whilst I walked slowly ahead.

Without warning I was engulfed in an avalanche of fallen leaves as repeated armfuls were thrown upon me from behind." Quickly I retaliated until, with arms around each other, we fell happily into a large pile of leaves, out of breath, and agreed a truce from hostilities.

We lay there in peace as I carefully removed fragmented leaves from her hair whilst making plans about how we would spend the day. Moneysa agreed with my suggestion that we went to the village and talked to those involved with the parish end of year party; but on condition that we rest awhile after our battle with the fallen leaves.

For some time we lay side by side with our hands locked together in restful silence as we watched the leaves falling and squirrels racing through the trees, with birds urgently flying around for no reason other than their love of flying.

Raising herself up on to her elbow Moneysa looked down on me, smiled and declared how happy she was, "In truth Charles, my idea of heaven is to spend eternity here with you," she whispered, as her slim forefinger gently smoothed my eyebrows causing my eyes to close in appreciation.

Through my bliss I opened one eye in acknowledgment on hearing my name and, "After our marriage in India can we live in the same house that you were born in and where I first met you and your family?"

When I lifted my hand to caress her shoulder length tresses I found myself, momentarily, without words as the vision of her dark brown eyes held mine in a deep yet unspoken bond of love.

Overcoming an initial stammer I replied, "Of course we can," and a wide smile lit up her face when I added, "Then there will be many years of total happiness with lots of little Chamon's running around the house."

Her eyes filled with tears as she ran her hand through my hair and whispered, "Thank you Charles and please let us always love each other like this and never allow anything to keep us apart."

"Nothing will ever separate us, Monnie ...that I promise
...."

Then words were no more and became mere spectators to the depth of our emotion as slowly our lips met and we gradually submerged into our bed of leaves and the comfort of our oneness.

Without warning, reality intervened and dismissed this treasured memory as a bout of painful coughing racked my body. I felt tears running down my face induced perhaps as the product of consumptive pain, or the memory of happiness now lost ... I know not and it is too hurtful for me to dwell upon the difference.

"Keep going Charles, you must never give in," was the self induced battle cry that I shared with the trees around me followed by, "If only ..... If only real life was like a traditional romantic novel."

I picked up a handful of leaves and let them slip slowly through my fingers as I visualised, in story book fashion, a sudden gentle glow lighting up the way ahead and then, as my imagination gained momentum, I saw Moneysa walking towards me in her blue wedding gown inviting me to come home.

Instantly I was young again and with our hands clasped together, we walked happily away into the beckoning glow of eternity as the ethereal music faded away.

Watching the last leaf fall from my hand I murmured, "No Charles, those are silly dreams that can never be. Remember what Cymol said about the fate awaiting his sister both in this life and the next. Have you forgotten the enemies you made, and all the deep disappointment that your actions and attitudes brought into the lives of others, not least those of your good friend Elizabeth and her parents?"

Through pain I am able to smile that an out of place word as 'forgotten' should form part of any indictment against me because such an attitude is totally absurd. How could I ever forget the hurt of separation that dominates me or deliberately close my eyes to the daily presence of Moneysa in my fading life.

Despite Elizabeth's optimism I know that the doctor was correct and, for the first time, I have been forced to accept that my life is fast drawing to its close; yet what a fool I have been to keep to myself the outcome of the séance, held shortly before I left India, when I learned about the fate that had befallen my wife.

I now know that the suddenness of Moneysa's death, which occurred at the peak of her happiness and long before her appointed time, has left her trapped in this woodland of memories; and I am the sole legatee of the whereabouts of the one I love above all others. Whilst I am alive she is able to reach out and walk with me, wherever I am, but when I leave this life Moneysa will be a lost soul within this leafy prison.

So much is clear, from my Indian sessions with Jarita, that only I, in spirit form, can liberate the soul of Moneysa and thus enable her to return to the spirit world. I accept that my soul will return in another's body but how do I draw that person, whoever he or she is, to this very place where Moneysa died?

Momentarily, I was distracted as a withered leaf fluttered down upon my shoulder and rested awhile, before sliding down my coat to its forest floor grave.

Was this a sign to me?

Suddenly I seized on to the thought that the very trees, rocks and natural fabric of this woodland may well retain and care for the spirit of Moneysa and my dying words as both await rebirth?

Whereas falling leaves symbolise death reborn as buds in the warmth of spring, could not words spoken from the depth of my heart rest in this place until reborn, in the life of one who has been drawn to this place, because of the presence of my reincarnated soul in his or her earthly body?

I could feel my heart rapidly beating with excitement, perhaps to the detriment of my failing health, but it was of no consequence. It was suddenly very clear to me that, without fail, I must commit my story to this woodland scene that it may, in the fullness of time, be transmitted into the life of that future stranger who will be host to my restless soul.

I know that I am doing the right thing for appearing before me is a now moss covered mound which I know to be 'Monnie's rock', where she sat to remove her tight shoes and duly forgot them, when latent feelings became living emotions as I carried her to the house......and then ....." I paused, wiped my eyes, **and realised that I must tell of all that happened in a constructive and time related manner, for ease of future narration.**

Hence sitting upon 'Monnie's rock' and in the fullness of faith I began my verbal account, in this woodland of recollections, in trust that my spirit endowed words will linger like falling leaves until reborn within another's care.........."

.... Much later I heard voices that little by little filtered into my mind as I slowly became aware of where I was and that a considerable period of time had past and it was almost dark. I felt cold yet I was free from coughing and chest pains which was relief indeed, but fatigue was my master and a pillow to rest upon would be a mistress without question.

I have no concept of the duration of my narrative which matters little to one who measures eternity to be one minute without Moneysa in his arms. Nevertheless I well remember what I set out to do is now finished and the time has arrived for me to leave words, from my very soul, to await rebirth in the life of another.

"Charles where are you?" came the familiar voice of Brother John, followed by the echo of Elizabeth's voice carrying the same question, prompting me to steadily rise to my feet with the help of a tree branch for support. They both saw me and, with cries of concern, ran over and assisted me as, with my arms around their shoulders, I began my final exit from where Moneysa was held captive.

"Goodbye for a brief moment, Monnie," I muttered to the fallen leaves and with head down we slowly picked our way through the undergrowth. In order to lift their spirits I commented that the last time I left this woodland I was carried out by Matthew and would that he were here now, only to realise, on reflection, that it was not the best thing to say under the circumstances.

As we left our 'secret little forest' a curious owl in the trees above hooted what sounded like 'goodbye.' Immediately I began to chuckle to myself as I remembered how well Moneysa could impersonate an owl.

"Like to share your joke with us Charles?" asked Brother John.

"Well now," I began, only to sink to my hands and knees as a severe coughing bout overcame me.

In due course they were able to get me back on my feet and we finally arrived at the house and, with Ruth's help, I was carefully lowered into an armchair before the fire.

"Perhaps you were correct Elizabeth when you praised the curative powers of northern air because my chest pains have gone; and when I am free from this fatigue I may be able to return to India as a Company advisor. But for the present time I am very much in need of a powerful elixir and there is none better than my favourite tune. Please play it for me Elizabeth; you must remember the one you first played in India."

"Of course I will Charles and I will play it on my new instrument called a piano in which every string has its own hammer."

My mind wandered to the beauty of that melody as I tried to fit the tune to the words 'my ever best friend' until I was distracted by a flake of soot waving at me from a burning log ......then I felt myself beginning to drift.... as if into a long tunnel feeling ....very...very...tired....

John indicated to Elizabeth and Ruth that Charles was slipping away from them. With a cry Elizabeth stopped playing, ran over to him, and sank to her knees holding and kissing his hand whilst praying that God would restore him. Ruth's arms were around her shoulders as, between her tears, she tried to console Elizabeth. In solemn silence John placed his hand upon Charles's shoulder in an attitude of prayer.

For my part I had to make a sudden yet urgent decision. Should I remain within Charles Ganton, and risk slipping into the abyss of death with him, or must I immediately leave in the manner described by my mentor?

I chose to remain with him for one reason only, and that was to satisfy my curiosity whether or not Moneysa came to lead him away from this life.

.......I no longer have any bodily feeling ....mist is surrounding me .... that flake of soot is still waving ......why has Elizabeth stopped playing ....and why is she crying?

Suddenly, as if expelled from my other self I, Charles Cane, briefly stood alongside three grieving figures, then I was back in the woodland, facing the familiar rhododendron bushes, but without Charles Ganton who I now knew to be dead.

For the first time I was self supporting but the woodland was different and so was the time in which I found myself.

There were fewer trees and bushes and, through many gaps in the greenery, I could see distant mountains and hear the sound of a motor car on a nearby road. The path was wider and firmer and bore imprints of walking boots and, coming towards me, was a man with a rucksack on his back, accompanied by a woman and two children who were oblivious to my presence; in fact they appeared to walk through me.

Before I had time to digest this scenario I found myself back on the mid terrace plateau and sitting on the bench well known to my mentor. I knew that I had completed my journey and had returned to the year 2009; but my real and urgent task had just begun.

Quite suddenly I realised there was an urgent commission, central to my narrative, which had been confirmed through all the guidance I had received, and all that I had seen and heard on my remarkable journey through the life of Charles Ganton.

My commission was to find and liberate Moneysa from her prison upon earth.

CHAPTER THIRTY NINE

Over to Charles Cane

In some ways I am sad that, after almost 65 years, my parallel lives have finally converged and my days of discovery are almost over. I have enjoyed the learning experience through which my knowledge was enhanced both by my mentor and, much later, by the Indian mystic Jarita.

As a result the young Indian lady who began walking with me when I was 14 is no longer a stranger and I feel a bond of strong friendship both with her and many I met within the pages of my narrative. This situation did not 'just happen' and, before I move to my final act, I would like to share with you all that I know about the forces that placed Moneysa Ganton at the centre of the work I have presented to you.

When Moneysa was about to embark upon her new life, in the company of the husband she loved, she was at the pinnacle of her happiness. This all ended abruptly, when a major traumatic event tore her life away and left her dead on the woodland path. At that moment the thought of death was far from her mind because life in India with Charles, and their expected child, was the light that illuminated her hopes and guided her dreams for the years ahead. In an instant that light was extinguished and her grieving husband was left to embrace her blood stained body, surrounded by devastated friends, on that dreadful morning long ago.

We know how grief affected the lives of her friends but what happened to Moneysa?

Death had struck her down in a murderous act that was sudden and completely unexpected, yet the urge to live her dreams was stronger than the call of the spirit world. Because she could not return to her mortal body her soul, or part of it, was left to wander alone absolutely lost and confused.

This phenomenon is known as soul fragmentation which resulted in the soul of Moneysa, in modern terms, becoming 'grounded' yet able to move about the earthly plane and become momentarily detectable by spirit sensitive people. Many of us can bring to mind a fleeting sensation of being touched by someone unseen, or in moments of grief sense that a hand, rather than the wind, had gently moved our hair.

But let us move on and spend a few moments thinking about Charles Ganton, particularly at the moment when his wife died in his arms. You will recall that he lost consciousness and went into a state of deep shock lasting several days. It is reported that a grief fuelled state, such as this, can also cause soul fragmentation meaning that part of Charles Ganton could have remained, with Moneysa, as an amalgam of their respective souls.

No one would deny that the earthly bodies of Charles and Moneysa Ganton rest in two lost graves, and that their remains will now be almost indistinguishable from the soil around them. However, their souls are very much alive and, accepting my comments above, they are in a state of spirit attachment; albeit Charles is in the spirit world and his wife cannot escape from the site of her earthly demise. They are soul mates faced with eternal separation unless their plight can be corrected which, in essence, is what my entire narrative was all about.

I began writing this account with the same depth of interest I gave to laboratory research programmes that led to my name appearing on several patents. I abhor guess work and I refused to allow this sworn enemy of research to cloud both my earlier career, and my dedicated intention to write, as accurately as possible, all that you have read in 'My Ever Best Friend.' However, I must admit that, mentally, I am not the same person who began this work because I now know my true identity; together with the fact that only I can liberate Moneysa and direct her to the spirit world where she truly belongs.

But how can this be? Moneysa never knew Charles Cane and would only trust the words of her soul mate, and husband, Charles Ganton, who died almost two hundred years ago.

This is a ponderous dilemma that can, nevertheless, be immediately resolved by those who will accept that I was Charles Ganton in that previous life time. That same person who was specifically reincarnated, and given the name Charles Cane, in order to rescue his beloved Monnie from the woodland glade only he knew about.

Without doubt reincarnation is a contentious topic that I will not brush aside in the hope you did not notice it.

It is an ancient belief that the human soul passes through a succession of lives, and the idea had its origin in northern India (circa 1000 – 800 BC). The concept of reincarnation first appeared in early Hindu scriptures (Upanishads) and it has always been an integral part of classical Buddhism. The same topic greatly influenced Greek philosophers, including Pythagoras and Plato, through whom the theory of reincarnation became firmly established in Eastern and Western doctrines. From the early Christian church (100 – 250AD) there exists documents related to the three scholars Justin Martyr, Clement of Alexandria and Origen that taught of the pre-existence of souls through such words as, "Is it not rational that souls should be introduced into bodies, in accordance with their merits and previous deeds?" (Origen. *Contra Celsum 1,xxxii).*

Conversely, there are several learned books that attack the doctrine of reincarnation thus alerting us to a minefield of entrenched opinions, for and against the subject, from which we must make up our own minds.

I admit to once being a devout *doubting Thomas* when faced with accounts of previous lives, and was quick to change the subject less offence may be caused.

However, the advent of all that led me to write 'My Ever Best Friend' reversed my previous scepticism towards the topic because, to my mind, **there was no other logical explanation to cover all that I have reported to you**. Elements of reincarnation are consistent not only with my narrative, which undoubtedly came from the mind of Charles Ganton, but my experiences which began 65 years ago.

The spirit attachment between Moneysa and Charles would readily explain her presence, by my side, which I became aware of in the 14th year of my life. That same spirit attachment led me to Silver Hill in 1948 and my first awareness that a certain 'something' happened there, which I have shared with you through the pages of my account. Permit me to stress again my belief that the soul of Charles Ganton was reincarnated for one reason only; and that was to rescue his beloved Monnie who, for the reasons I have explained, is held prisoner on this earthly plane.

Thus my work is almost over and, as Charles Ganton, I have one glorious task yet to do; and that is to liberate my wife, Moneysa, from the forces that hold her in this present age.

CHAPTER FORTY

Silver Hill 2009. The final act

Thank you for remaining with me throughout our walk which began in the summer of 1766 and has now reached its end on the 26th December 2009.

Before we part I must leave with you my final chapter that, in terms of its origin, is opposite to all I have written. My previous words were those dictated by Charles Ganton, and were reflective of all that had happened. Today we are faced with the future which neither Charles Ganton, nor indeed any of us, have any control over.

Consequently my mental pen now waits in anticipation of what may, or may not happen, in this woodland of memories.

My wife (Sandra) and I spent the Christmas period close to Silver Hill and, on the morning of the 26th December, entered what Charles and Moneysa called 'our secret little forest.' The spiritual draw of these woods again burst upon me with the same impact I first experienced in 1948; but now matters were very different. In recent times I have learned much, meaning that I returned to Silver Hill as a 'man with a mission,' rather than a wanderer searching for something I could not understand.

It struck me just how much the geography had changed since the 1780's. The entire area is now a national park and the trees and bushes, covering Silver Hill, are the subject of professional cultivation; thus providing access for the many walkers who enjoy this and adjacent areas of beauty. It is still gorgeous woodland but a far cry from the wild and uncultivated little forest, much loved by Charles and Moneysa Ganton whose prevailing presence I found, at times, to be overwhelming.

Still present was a predominance of large rhododendron bushes, much loved by Monnie, which I am told are of vigorous growth, and need to be controlled lest they overwhelm other woodland specimens. Thankfully there was still a rhododendron bush on the site which, to me, was the very epicentre of my memories; for I know it to be the same spot where Moneysa died from gunshot wounds, inflicted by her brother Cymol.

Many would claim that it was pure coincidence, and perhaps it was, but as we reached the place where Moneysa died both Sandra and I were startled by the sudden 'crack' of a gun being fired. It turned out to be the first of several shots to be heard as the Boxing Day shoot began.

Although the present bush had been trimmed back, and the surrounding area was much more open, the soul of Moneysa was undoubtedly there waiting and longing to greet me, although I could not see her. After a few moments of mental relaxation, through a technique taught by my mentor, I was fully Charles Ganton holding both her hands, talking and laughing as if we had never been apart. One big difference was the fact that the density of woodland growth around me had returned to as it was in 1781, meaning that although Sandra could still see me, the attached souls of

Charles and Moneysa Ganton had returned to the age so dear to them.

Because I was lost in this timeless conversation I could not see Sandra who, fortunately for record purposes, took the following photograph in which I am mentally talking to Moneysa on the spot where she died.

It was obvious that Moneysa had no knowledge of what had happened to her, and she even reminded me that the coaches were waiting to take us to India. Finally, I was able to contain her exuberance and slowly explain what had happened to cause her, unknowingly, to be a prisoner within this wood. It must be remembered that time is of no consequence in the spirit world and the fact that I had died 200 years ago meant nothing to her because 'now' was still her yesterday.

Eventually, and with trepidation, she accepted the situation when assured that her 'ever best friend' had returned, within another body that she could not see, just to release her to the spirit world until the time came for us to meet again.

Momentarily she panicked and, through her tears, repeatedly told me that she loved me and did not want to go anywhere without me. Her concerns gained momentum as she pleaded with me not to send her away. I shared her grief and longed for the emotionally correct answer which, suddenly, came to me through the words, "Monnie you are a prisoner on this spot and only I know where you are. My mortal body is old and it may not last much longer. If it were to die now then my soul will return to the spirit plane leaving you alone in this wood, perhaps lost for eternity, because I am the only person who can liberate you. Please Moneysa; please hold on to our love. It must be a very precious love we have because time itself has intervened and given us these few brief moments together in trust that we will use them well."

Wrapped in each other's arms, I whispered, "Moneysa, I release you from this place. Return dear soul to your land of rest and hold aloft your light to guide me home."

Although my words were few, they were enough. Perhaps for the last time my fingers ran through her hair, and I gently kissed her forehead. Through her tears Moneysa's eyes met mine as, with a smile, she tenderly touched the side of my face; and then she was gone. Her earthbound imprisonment was over and I, alone, returned to the year 2009 upon this hallowed spot known as Silver Hill.

What I felt was a tingling sensation and I temporarily felt light headed. I went over to Sandra and we shed a few tears; then, with a cry of surprise, I grabbed my camera and took a photograph of the scene I had just left. I must add that the weather was cold and dull, with frequent snow showers, which unexpectedly gave way to a burst of sunlight illuminating the rhododendron bush, as if to guide Moneysa home to the world of spirits. Here is what we saw:

The photograph has not done justice to the full brilliance of the sunlight, but it lit up both the immediate area and our trust that all was now well. In sincerity I add that if this incident was yet another coincidence, then the timing was truly impeccable.

I cannot leave this historic Boxing Day visit to Silver Hill without a few words about 'Monnies Rock,' which I first became aware of following revelations revealed through the help of my mentor. As this was my first post-mentor visit I was keen to find this landmark and, as it turned out, I was far from being disappointed. Please observe the rock in the foreground of the above photograph which can be nothing other than 'Monnie's Rock' that was frequently referred to and, in the following extract from page 284 of my narrative, Charles Ganton, who was sitting on the same rock, fixed its actual position through this statement ......

"As I turn my head to my left I can clearly see the spot where Moneysa died in my arms….."

EPITAPH

How do I feel after this experience?

I recall that I have walked for 65 years with Moneysa at my side, but now she has gone.

Her departure has left me with a range of feelings that are almost like characters entering and leaving my stage of life. Suddenly spiritual loneliness will stand aside for widower's grief which, in turn, will fade in the spotlight of hope for the future wherein our destiny lies.

So often we become our worst enemy when we think of life and death as a pair of opposites.

This is not the case because, in reality, life is a continuum with birth and death the two doorways into and out of our earthly phase. Birth, death and rebirth is a cycle that turns and completes itself over and over until, through divine trust and love for one another, we refine our soul into the pure gold of an eternal spirit.

Thank you for giving me this opportunity to share with you the memory of 'my ever best friend.' Through your good will, and the specialised help from those I named, Moneysa has finally reached her place of rest.

Shalom.

Charles